UPDATED EDITION

A School Leader's Guide to Excellence

COLLABORATING OUR WAY TO BETTER SCHOOLS

Carmen Fariña and Laura Kotch

Foreword by Lucy Calkins

HEINEMANN
Portsmouth, NH

Heinemann
361 Hanover Street
Portsmouth, NH 03801-3912
www.heinemann.com

Offices and agents throughout the world

The authors and publisher wish to thank those who have generously given permission to reprint borrowed material:

Figure 1.11: "Creating a Climate for Change: A Building Principal Uses Her Philosophy and Experiences to Show How to Create Change" by Carmen Fariña was originally published in *IMPACT II/Teachers Network Star* (Volume 15, Number 2, Spring 1995). Reprinted with permission of Teachers Network, www.teachersnetwork.org.

Library of Congress Cataloging-in-Publication Data
Fariña, Carmen.
    A school leader's guide to excellence : collaborating our way to better schools / Carmen Fariña and Laura Kotch.
        p. cm.
    Includes bibliographical references and index.
    ISBN-13: 978-0-325-06092-7
    1. School management and organization. 2. Educational leadership. 3. School improvement programs. I. Kotch, Laura. II. Title.
LB2805.F25 2008
371.2—dc22   2007045379

Editors: Kate Montgomery and Zoë Ryder White
Production: Elizabeth Valway and Patty Adams
Cover design: Suzanne Heiser
Front cover photos: Principal with kids: Getty Images/Comstock/Stockbyte; Children in line: Getty Images/ Erik Isakson; Apple in hand: Getty Images/Gary Roebuck; Large group of kids outside: Getty Images/Lonely Planet/Juliet Coombe
Back cover photo: Getty Images/Comstock/HIP
Typesetter: Kirby Mountain Composition
Manufacturing: Valerie Cooper and Veronica Bennett

Printed in the United States of America on acid-free paper
18 17 16 15 14   ML   1 2 3 4 5

This book was previously published under ISBN-13 978-0-325-01138-7 and ISBN-10 0-325-00138-9.

We dedicate this book to the hardworking, passionate, and committed educators who strive every day to create places of excellence.

In the face of often conflicting messages and increasingly challenging demands, you stay focused on what matters most—the children you serve, the classroom instruction you provide, and the collaborative community you nurture. We are particularly grateful for the support of the educators in New York City who have invited us into their lives, trusted us with their stories, and reaffirmed the power of relationships to transform schools.

May this book provide sustenance and support.

Contents

Foreword

In January 2014 when Carmen Fariña was appointed Chancellor of the largest school district in the world, it was not only the teachers and principals of New York City who rose to our feet, shouting with glad hoots and hollers, wiping tears from our eyes, hugging each other with relief and with hope. Educators across the land joined us. At last, at last. At last we can put the focus on spreadsheets behind us, we can turn away from efforts to turn schools into businesses, student learning into profit and loss statements. At last we can resume the work that drew us to this profession in the first place.

When Carmen Fariña and Laura Kotch wrote this book, Carmen was Deputy Chancellor and Laura was the Executive Director of Professional Development and Curriculum for New York City schools. For a time, these two marvelous educators gave the largest city in the world a taste of what is possible when schools are well led. Principals forged support groups, as did teachers. Educators began criss-crossing the city, learning by visiting each other's schools. Good work was showcased and studied.

But that was almost a decade ago, and since then, New York City teachers and principals have lived through the kind of change that other districts have experienced as well: a Copernican shift toward data, data, data. The entire system has become consumed with testing, measuring, counting losses and gains—and with competition, instead of collaboration.

There aren't words enough to express how glad we are that Carmen has been appointed as Chancellor. Educators across the nation are hoping that this appointment will be emblematic of a sea change—a nation-wide movement toward the kind of humane and effective education system that Carmen and Laura have worked to build for years. That sea change will only take place if Carmen is not the only one leading with love and justice—but if all of you who are reading this book lead that way as well. As Martin Luther King said, "Change does not roll in on the wheels of inevitability, but comes through continuous struggle." This book offers both the strength and the clarity of vision necessary for each of us to join in and make this sea change a reality, not just for New York City, but for all of our towns and cities.

The good news is that choosing collaboration over competition, choosing a focus on children over a focus on data, does not mean a dilution of rigor. In fact, Carmen and Laura have helped us to realize that sky-high standards will *only* be achievable when school leaders', teachers', parents' and children's voices are at the table. What will be required is that every one of us must find new reserves of energy in order to rise to the challenge of today. That will be possible when we hold on to hope, optimism, and each other.

For Carmen and Laura, the goals of the Common Core—high levels of comprehension, strong writing skills, critical literacy, reading and writing across the day, the school, and kids' lives—have always been a driving force. They have always kept a laser focus on dramatically lifting the level of student learning. The title of this book—*A School Leader's Guide to Excellence*—says it all. Yes, this is a book about leading with respect, about creating richly literate cultures in schools, and about locating and celebrating strengths in a school. But it is also a book about keeping one's moral compass aligned to the North Pole of student growth. The way to reach these ambitious goals is through leadership that rallies rather than shames, leadership that is more about influence than about compliance.

In every endeavor, Carmen and Laura have led with vision and with a gritty resolve to make schools into places where everyone learns as much, as fast, as deeply as can be. This book can bring that vision and resolve into your own life, your own school, district, or city. Here, Carmen and Laura set out, in knowing detail, the steps you can take to turn your school or district into a place that brims with excellence. You'll find a score of ways to lure parents into a committed relationship with the school community, ways to create a more cohesive, excited, effective staff, ways to ignite teachers' enthusiasm for professional improvement, ways to turn supervision into the richest possible mentorship opportunity, ways to create a school-wide leadership network that rallies everyone to outgrow him or herself.

When Mayor Bill de Blasio introduced Carmen Fariña as the Chancellor of New York City's schools, he signaled to children, parents, and teachers that he is ready to begin a new chapter in the history of public education. He signaled that he recognizes that schools can only rise to the challenge of today if educators, parents, and children are enabled to be decision makers, if our voices are at the table, if our knowledge is valued and tapped. He signaled that excellence and collaboration go hand in hand, and that the best school leaders are first and foremost teachers. How grateful we are to him—and to Laura and Carmen.

—Lucy Calkins
April, 2014

Acknowledgments

We are privileged to have been immersed in work we love, supported by families and colleagues who believe in our power to make a difference.

From our earliest years, our families encouraged reading and talking about books, and our dinner conversations centered on what was worth fighting for to make the world a better place. A career in public service, teaching in particular, was considered a worthy and noble profession and rising through the ranks and breaking existing barriers was an expected course of action. Our parents and one very special aunt were powerful role models for us and helped us become who we are today.

The students who passed through the classrooms and schools we served are the real reason for the work we do each day. The light in their eyes and the people they have become inspire us and remind us daily of the pleasure and purpose of teaching. We acknowledge the parents who send their children to schools each day, trusting that the educators will personally connect with them and lead them into joyful learning.

We were fortunate to be teachers during a time when collaboration and bottom-up change were flourishing, and we are grateful to the principals who connected us to the best and brightest thinkers. The networks we formed with these colleagues gave us the support we needed to become risk takers and decision makers. Many of the ideas in this book are rooted in stimulating conversations with our colleagues at PS 29 and PS 321. The communities we formed with them gave us the vision and the confidence to reach out to a larger audience.

In our various roles within the educational system, we worked with many dedicated teachers, staff developers, and administrators who embraced new ideas and taught us so much about the realities of practical applications. They reminded us that the ideas most likely to take root are organic and work best when they are adapted to fit the needs of each community. We are eternally grateful for the learning that blossomed from our work with Lucy Calkins and the Reading and Writing Project at Teachers College and the communities of PS 6, District 15, District 2, District 10, Region 8, and ultimately the entire city of New York. In each of these communities, we have been blessed with the support of an amazing team of educators who embraced the vision and made it a reality.

The constant encouragement of our colleagues and friends helped us stay focused on and committed to writing this book. Our critical friends reviewed each chapter and gave us their honest feedback to ensure that the book would be practical and user-friendly. To Anna, Denise, Eileen, Esther, Medea, Edna, Steve, Leslie, Anna Marie, Dorothy, Rosanne, Danielle, Anthony, and Sarala, thank you so much for providing a continuing intellectual discourse and a network that is always supportive and nurturing.

Writing this book together during a transitional year has been invigorating and enlightening. It has allowed us chunks of time in which to talk and listen, write and revise. In the hours we have spent together, we have reminisced about our lives as educators, shared personal stories about our families, thought deeply about the work that has been and is yet to be accomplished, discussed the people who have influenced us most, laughed about our embarrassments, and shared our passion for the work. This precious time has reinforced our belief in the importance of quality talk to clarify thinking and the power of collaboration to shape action.

This book could not have been written without the loving support of Kate Montgomery, executive editor at Heinemann, whose gentle touch and wise council kept us focused, encouraged, and productive. We looked forward to her emails filled with concrete suggestions and just the right amount of celebration. Alan Huisman took our words and worked his magic, making them sound so much better. It was a pleasure to have a developmental editor whom we could trust to understand our intentions and whose edits always amazed us for their clarity, polish, and integrity of message. We are grateful to Elizabeth Valway, our production editor, and Elizabeth Tripp, our copyeditor, for making us feel like real writers and for making our work look professional.

Our husbands, Tony and Paul, gave us the gift of time and allowed us to spend weekend after weekend writing while they perfected their golf games and suntans. We are grateful for their love, encouragement, and support and for their belief that we had something to offer our readers. Their willingness to support our collaboration stemmed in part from their amazement at the harmony of our work and the way we could read each other's thoughts and finish each other's sentences—almost like a good marriage. We thank our children, Marisa and Tony, Mia and Dave, Micah and Marivi, and Nicole and Kevin, for making us so proud and for reminding us that public education does matter. We are grateful that you have chosen to continue the challenge of striving to make the world a better place. We also thank you for your willingness to become our teachers in matters technological and in so many other ways. Charlie, Ben, Ford and Isabella (and the other grandchildren yet to be), you have made our quest for excellence in public education both personal and compelling. We hope the readers of this book will be your teachers and principals, committed to helping you succeed in this increasingly complex world.

Introduction

Carmen's appointment as the Chancellor of Schools in January of 2014 was an amazing New Year's gift for the educators in New York City from a new mayor who understands the importance of choosing a leader who has a deep understanding of teaching and learning to support our schools. As a classroom teacher, staff developer, principal, superintendent, and Deputy Chancellor, Carmen experienced both the challenges and the joys of making schools work. She formed lasting bonds with students, parents, teachers and principals. Colleagues talk about Carmen's generosity in sharing her talent and time. She brings her energy, her belief, and her total commitment to the mission of educating children. The cheering ovations the principals gave her at their first meeting were a testament to the kind of humane, caring person she is, to her wisdom and humility, and her willingness to serve.

In this new year, we are hopeful that this appointment represents a new chapter in public education—a signal that the tide has begun shifting, that it's time for educators to take back their schools. In choosing Carmen for this position, we see the mayor's recognition that years of experience and accumulating wisdom are currency that can earn a place at the forefront of decision making. It is a validation of what those of us inside schools know to be fundamentally true—that meaningful and lasting change requires the voice, input, and buy-in from those who do the work every day. As you can imagine, Carmen has been working day and night to communicate the mission, restore morale, and support educators across New York City. Therefore, she could not participate in the writing of this new introduction. The words you are reading are mine, but the beliefs that guide the words are shared.

As I think about all that's happened since the first printing of this book, it's clear that these past six years have been hard times for teachers and school leaders. The focus on using test scores to evaluate the effectiveness of teachers and schools, the mounting pressure of accountability, the disrespect for the profession and the public shaming of teachers, the culture of competition and the lack of governmental support for the public schools have sapped the joy from our classrooms and demoralized the community. We witnessed the balance of what matters most shifting from nurturing people to analyzing spreadsheets, from sharing what works to competing against one another, from supporting schools to closing them. Surely, the time has come to join together to reframe the conversation.

The big ideas in this book are even more relevant and compelling today in light of the need to restore joy, renew energy, and provide a sense of shared purpose. In an environment that has too often focused on blame, educators are hungry for meaningful feedback and recognition of hard work. Thoughtful compliments are gifts that go a long way toward connecting us and restoring morale in our schools. We recognize that the classroom is and will always be where the most important work happens. The relationship between teacher and student is the fundamental transformative bond. We remember the teachers in our lives who believed in us, who understood who we were and who we could become, who gave us inspiration, a new way to make sense of the world, and the skills and knowledge that insured a successful path in life.

Throughout my career, one of my favorite parts of visiting schools is watching wonderful teachers in action. It is easy to recognize these talented teachers because in their classrooms, students are engaged and articulate, environments are overflowing with meaningful work, teaching moves are purposeful and strategic, and the room is alive with the voices of students and a palpable sense of energy. I always take a moment to give an acknowledgment by walking over and shaking teachers' hands to tell them how much I admire their work. It's amazing that such a simple affirmation has such lasting power—teachers I encounter years later always remind me of the handshake and tell me how much it meant to them.

We all want to be noticed and appreciated for the good work we do. We want our words to be heard and our actions recognized. One of the most painful outcomes of the push for accountability and the competitive culture has been the feeling of powerlessness and the sense of isolation that so many leaders and teachers describe. When educators daily face overwhelming challenges along with competing mandates that don't make sense and lack coherence, too often they lose faith in the belief that the system can work and that their voice can make a difference. Yet, talking with educators from around the country, it is clear that we share the same mission and the same struggle. Raising our voices together, we will be heard. The decision of the New York State Board of Regents to extend the evaluation period of graduates based on Common Core to 2022 was a direct result of teachers, parents, and school leaders speaking up. It is our hope that the larger community of educators will find courage in our book—courage to join with like-minded leaders, to take action, to refuse to be silenced and alone.

We believe that excellence can be shared and replicated. The building blocks of what works well in one classroom or school can be exported to build consistency and community across classrooms and schools. We believe that conversations and collaboration work better than competition and isolation. Teachers and leaders learn best from watching each other in action, reflecting on the impact of their teaching moves on the work that students produce, and revising their craft. In schools where doors are open and teachers are given both time and opportunity to learn from each other, everybody gets smarter.

In this book, we've outlined specific strategies that we've used to build learning communities, including one-to-one conversations, book of the month, nurturing teacher leaders, and celebrations. This step-by-step guide will support you in implementing rituals of connecting, healing, and affirming people—all of which will help you to retain talent, nurture leadership, and build sustaining collaborative communities.

One powerful structure for extending conversations and exporting best practices is to invite teachers within or across a grade to form buddy classes. These might focus on any content area with students matched to learn with buddy and teachers planning their lessons, studying student work, and sharing strategies. We have seen the power of creating buddy schools as well. One way to match schools is to link schools with the common concerns (for example, how can we support our English Language Learners) so that they can work together to find solutions. Another is to support struggling schools with a partner school with expertise and the capacity to share their strengths. The buddy schools structure rewards successful schools by recognizing their achievements and enlisting their expertise to extend the success of the community. We know that authentic and lasting change occurs when we create structures that provide educators with ongoing conversations that build on successful practices by sharing expertise to confront challenges. Taking back the schools means giving educators the opportunity and power to work collaboratively to address the struggles and invent shared solutions.

As we all are aware, the Common Core Standards raise the expectations for our students in dramatic ways that demand more rigorous teaching and learning. Reaching these standards can only happen in schools where adults are immersed in an intellectual community. It can happen in schools where teachers have the time and opportunity to form study groups, read challenging texts, talk with peers about meaning-making strategies, to write and reflect on their new understandings and the resulting shifts in thinking. In schools where teachers analyze the standards in the context of their authentic reading and writing, they are better able to move students to higher levels of achievement. We recognize that there are no short cuts on the path but the journey will be worth the struggle if teachers join together to think more deeply about their own reading and writing process, and use that reflection to teach in ways that move all students to excellence.

An article in the New York Times recently by Thomas Friedman quoted Laszio Bock, the senior vice president of people operations for Google, about what he looks for in hiring for one of the world's most successful companies. He says, "For every job, though, the No. 1 thing we look for is general cognitive ability, and it's not IQ. It's learning ability. It's the ability to process on the fly. It's the ability to pull together disparate bits of information. The second is leadership—in particular emergent leadership. What we care about is, when faced with a problem and you're a member of a team, do you, at the appropriate time, step in and lead. And just as critically, do you step back and stop leading, do you let someone else? Because what's critical to be an effective leader in this environment is you have to be willing to relinquish power."

Thomas Friedman gives this summary, "In an age where innovation is increasingly a group endeavor, it also cares about soft skills-leadership, humility, collaboration, adaptability and loving to learn and re-learn. This will be true no matter where you go to work."

The path to reach this ambitious and worthy goal will ask the best of each of us and will take the united effort of us all. But just imagine the kind of promising future we could have if our schools succeeded in graduating students who demonstrate their ability to mobilize their curiosity to discover new understandings, employ their intelligence to question what is and what could be, and focus their leadership and collaborative skills to solve problems and invent solutions. May our book serve as a blueprint to follow in creating places of excellence.

An Invitation to Join Our Collaborative Community

This book invites you to join the community of leaders who are dedicated to bringing about academic excellence, who understand the power of the individual, and who work hard each day to form a collaborative community. In our developing roles as teacher, staff developer, principal, and district leader, we have become convinced that people need to be moved in personal ways and that leaders who strive to become effective communicators, proactive listeners, and inspirational models use their personal stories to convince the community to take risks and embrace change. We are fortunate to have been part of the New York City Department of Education's talented community of learners, who have taught us so much about transforming our schools and the power of stories to personalize our mission and call our communities to action.

Education is first and foremost a people business, and the relationships we foster are crucial. Listeners are hungry for the personal anecdote that provides insight into change and encourages a willingness to explore new approaches. Our experiences define us as vulnerable human beings who invite others to see who we are and connect their lives to ours. We are social beings, and the stories we tell about what happens to us help us make sense of our lives. Stories invite people to continue the conversation, which promotes the sense of community and tears down the sense of isolation. The uniqueness of the experience, as well as the individuality of the voice that shares it, unites people into a community.

Choosing which stories to tell and how best to tell them to get the desired results is an acquired and then well-practiced skill that all visionary leaders possess. There are always connections between the speaker's story and the listener's experiences that reinforce the message and make it meaningful. Strong leaders know how to relate their anecdotes to the audience and to current issues in education. Leaders use what they've experienced along with their beliefs to create their vision and inspire others.

In the stories that follow, we tell you who we are, what we have experienced, and how we have grown into the educators we are today.

Laura's Story

In elementary school, I was part of a class of "rapid learners" who covered three years of curriculum in two years, growing very close during that period. My fourth-grade teacher, Mr. Lowenthal, was the kind of up-close-and-personal teacher I dreamed of becoming; he made learning an interactive and joyful adventure and treated each of us as adults who could voice our thinking in the safe and supportive community he created. I remember the committee work and the project-based learning, which made social studies come to life, connected the real world to our life in the classroom, and integrated reading and writing with content studies. Mr. Lowenthal taught me the power of listening intently and connecting with each student; he also showed me the excitement of collaborative learning. The teacher I became was inspired by the benchmark he established.

As a classroom teacher, my goal for my students was for them to fall in love with books, read and write with energy and passion, and develop habits of mind that would allow them to make their voices heard in the classroom and beyond. The classroom library was the center of our world, the place students found their "just-right" books and engaged in lively conversations. I learned who my students were through the books they read and the ones I read to them; shared texts guided our conversations and defined our community. Wanting other teachers to embrace literacy, I made my own learning public and invited my colleagues to join me. We formed a network—only four teachers at first, but it grew until the majority of the staff were encouraging one another, visiting one another's classrooms, and studying professional books together. I became a part-time staff developer, which allowed me to present demonstration lessons in many classrooms, including those with special needs students and English language learners. The enthusiasm of the students and the amazing things they said and did convinced many reluctant teachers that this way of teaching could work for them. The school became a model site, hosting visitors from near and far; the more we shared our story, the stronger we became.

I realized the experience of uniting one school community around literacy learning could be replicated in many schools if the same conditions were in place: leaders who actively promoted the mission; a credible, knowledgeable, and nurturing agent for change; many wonderful new books and time to learn about them; and respect for each member of the community. As a literacy staff developer working with Tony Alvarado in District 2, I was able to test this theory. An outsider, I had to prove myself, gain the trust of the staff, and find the delicate balance between listening and telling. I had to learn how to see through to people's intentions and listen to their hopes and fears. I needed to understand how each person is influenced by his past experiences with change, his relationships within the school culture, and his readiness for and comfort with risk taking. There were teachers who immediately invited me into their classrooms and eagerly embraced new ways of teaching and learning and those who refused to acknowledge my presence.

I learned how to put my ego aside in order to nurture and support others. I developed numerous ways to celebrate all visible signs of progress, from being willing to let students sit on a rug in the meeting area instead of in regimented rows of desks to deciding to participate in a workshop or visit a colleague's classroom. I discovered the importance of bringing books to teachers, catering wonderful lunches, removing obstacles, and following up quickly on the promises I made. Connecting with the movers and shakers in each school whose influence could open doors for me helped foster buy-in; the nucleus of a collaborative community grew. It was humbling work and required a positive attitude, thick skin, and a good sense of humor. I suspended disbelief, took a leap of faith, and believed in people, and they rewarded and amazed me. Over time, as teachers opened their doors to share their practices and engage in rich conversations focused on teaching and learning, their classrooms evolved from silent, worksheet-driven, barren environments to interactive, exciting learning communities.

When I was recruited to head the literacy initiative in the Bronx, I decided to take the job because of the energy, vision, and commitment of the school principals and the superintendent and her deputy, Irma Zardoya and Ray Rosemberg. We recognized the enormous need for professional development that would engage all stakeholders in interactive learning and provide the link between theory and practice. We began by drafting a framework that communicated the literacy mission and described the structure, components, and practices in a reading-and-writing workshop. We blitzed the staff with a series of meetings in which we shared evidence of the current low level of student learning, stressed the urgent need for change, and invited them to talk with us about their underlying beliefs. We recruited and trained an army of staff developers, who gave demonstration lessons and workshops and visited classroom after classroom. We trained school teams, offering choices about when and how to participate and helping them obtain text sets. We created many opportunities for teachers and administrators to visit other schools within the district as well as schools in District 2 to see what lay at the end of the path they were being invited to follow. We affirmed what they were already doing well and encouraged them to imagine possibilities. We looked for principals who would open their schools as models, and we celebrated forward momentum. The challenges of the five years I spent in the Bronx were enormous, but the unity of purpose and the shared belief that our students deserved the gift of a thoughtful curriculum and the power of literacy sustained us.

It took more than five years for the test scores to reflect the progress evident in classrooms and schools, but the numbers began to rise, slowly yet steadily, and they continue to do so today. Equally important is the evidence in the classrooms, which shifted from being tightly controlled and teacher driven, with students sitting in their desks in rows and silently filling in the blanks on worksheets, to being excitingly interactive, with students reading a variety of authentic books and talking with partners about the meaning they were making. Writing began to flourish; students were immersed in writing across all curriculum areas, telling the stories of their lives, eagerly sharing them with one another, their parents, and the entire community. Consistency in student-centered interactive learning grew as teachers were supported and encouraged to try new ways of empowering students and encouraging their growth. As we celebrated the small successes, teachers grew more comfortable at sharing their practices with one another and more confident in listening to their students and following their lead. The intellectually vital community we created attracted the best and brightest teachers, who were eager to be part of the exciting professional development we offered. The community we built was sustained as the teacher leaders we nurtured grew into the next generation of school leaders.

Carmen's Story

My life in elementary school was a totally different experience from Laura's. A first-generation American born to immigrant parents, I started school as a non-English-speaking student. My kindergarten teacher consistently marked me absent when I didn't respond to the name she consistently mispronounced during roll call. In a very real sense, my father was my first teacher. He accompanied me to school and insisted in his own quiet way that my kindergarten teacher repeat the correct pronunciation of my name after him so that she would honor his daughter's presence in her classroom. The marginalization I felt because of my teacher's inability or unwillingness to pronounce my foreign last name has remained with me and has created my deep commitment to welcoming, nurturing, and personalizing every student, teacher, and principal from the first time we meet through the entire time we work together.

In this same elementary school, I was faced with teachers who believed that rote memorization and spouting back facts made you an excellent student. Thankfully, my father worked with me at home, encouraged me to question my teachers, and found newspapers and books to support our family's history and cultural perspective. I vividly remember him reading me fairy tales at night in Spanish from a book he had ordered from Spain for just this purpose.

As a high school student, I was suspended for questioning the teacher's opinion on the Spanish Civil War. When my father came to school to pick me up, he took me directly to the library and helped me find a book that supported my (and my family's) point of view and suggested that my letter of apology stress my family's authentic experience during the Spanish Civil War, which was more realistic than the teacher's textbook-based interpretation.

As a young teacher, I took these experiences with me and tried to create a classroom that encouraged student talk and student ownership. In my second year of teaching, the curriculum unit on community was enriched by my father's working with my students to design, research, and build a house with running water, lights, and landscaping. The students invented a family who lived there and wrote books describing their everyday life. The unit culminated with a housewarming. A parent who was in real estate helped us advertise the house as the prize in a raffle to fund a class trip. This experience convinced me that students' collaboration and imagination are more powerful tools for teaching writing and reading than basal readers.

I was extremely fortunate to have Mr. Melov as my principal; he saw me not as a maverick but as someone who could play a role in changing the school culture. He asked me to take a leadership role with my colleagues and continued to support my innovative literacy practices. Later in my career, another principal, Ms. Zagami, created a special arrangement in which I worked four days a week with my class and on the fifth day became both an in-school and a districtwide staff developer. At this time I also set up a teacher resource center for books and other teacher materials, meetings, and displays of student work. Both this room and my classroom became laboratories for demonstration lessons; visitors were constant. This experience convinced me that honoring the strength of teachers and providing a means by which to share best practices are essential strategies for school improvement. Hosting visitors and responding to their questions makes teachers more reflective, more inquisitive, and more aware of and articulate about the craft of teaching. It also stimulates them to keep learning and refining their practices.

After twenty-two years in the classroom, I became a full-time staff developer, providing interdisciplinary social studies–based demonstration lessons in classrooms and schools across the district. To help principals offer rich social studies experiences in their schools' classrooms, I set up a network of school-based liaisons in a program called Making Connections. These liaisons met monthly at my home to write curriculum units of study, discuss resource materials, and generate new strategies to improve classroom practices. They then modeled these units and strategies for interactive learning in their respective schools. The program emphasized the integration of all aspects of literacy with social studies and provided strategies for implementation and teacher professional development. It eventually became a citywide initiative, a strong model for reflective, shared professional growth.

My leadership of this initiative led to my becoming the principal of PS 6, where Laura and I began our unique collaboration dedicated to making a good school a great school that exemplified the best practices in teaching and learning. Lucy Calkins and her excellent team were major partners in this effort. Our personal stories, revealed in one-to-one conversations, prompted teachers to adopt innovative approaches to reading and writing, personalize their relationships with their students as well as with one another, and widen their professional networks. Collaboration, conversations, and celebrations became a way of life that soon included the parent community as well. In the last five years of my tenure, PS 6 consistently ranked as one of the top three schools in New York City in both reading and mathematics. We quickly became a model for teacher and principal professional development, welcoming more than five hundred visitors a year.

After PS 6, we continued our partnership as we became the superintendent and deputy superintendent of a district whose previous superintendent had been removed. We walked into a community that was bruised, angry, and fractionalized. The lessons learned in our previous life experiences helped us heal these wounds. Our first read-aloud, *I Love You Like Crazy Cakes*, by Rose Lewis, reinforced our belief in and desire for collegial relationships and also stressed that changes were forthcoming. To be successful in this mission, it was crucial that we begin with conversations with each member of the community, model our own reading and writing practices, initiate celebrations, and clearly articulate our vision for student and adult learning, emphasizing an inquiry-based, problem-solving approach. We made very clear that our high expectations were the same for all students regardless of neighborhood, parent education and experience, or language spoken at home. We understood that some schools might need extra support, especially those in communities with high concentrations of economic deprivation, English language learners, and special needs students. In order for these schools to reach their goals, the district office needed to provide much more specific, personal, hands-on support: intervention specialists, membership in the Teachers College Reading and Writing Project, specially trained experts to work with our middle schools, and better principal-to-principal communication and support. Our school visits never focused on checklists or mandates but instead consisted of many conversations with school leaders and other members of the community that affirmed pockets of excellence that already existed and recommended next steps (often intervisitations).

As part of the New York City reform effort in 2003, districts were combined into regions. We were chosen to lead the four districts combined into Region 8. This restructuring threatened established relationships and well-formed collegial networks. It was imperative that we honor the successful history of each district while instituting the educational changes crucial to raising student achievement. Once again we emphasized listening, nurturing, and supporting, and over a period of four months, we held 154 personal one-hour conversations with every school leader who was part of our new community. Leaders were able to voice their concerns and feel more comfortable about our style and purpose. We also hosted town hall meetings in every section of the region, first for all teachers and then for all parents and members of the larger community. These meetings focused on alleviating anxiety and uncertainty, so that our energy could be devoted to educating our students.

At the same time I became deputy chancellor for teaching and learning for the New York City Department of Education, I also became a grandmother, which gave me a renewed sense of urgency. As I traveled around the city, I talked about "a school for Charlie," emphasizing again the qualities of conversation, collaboration, and celebration. My story of my dreams for my grandchild connected deeply with every audience. Principals would email me invitations to come and visit their schools, which were now "ready for Charlie." Parents would write saying they too wanted a school for their own children with a strong vision and high academic standards. In a city of 1.2 million children, Charlie continues to symbolize a commitment to public education and reforming schools one child at a time.

In living our stories, we have been influenced by many educational thinkers. These are the people we travel far and wide to hear, and we are proud to learn at their feet. Reading their professional books in the study groups we lead allows us to share their ideas with a wide audience, discuss key concepts, and form a common language and purpose. One educational innovator in particular, Lucy Calkins, has become our mentor; she constantly inspires us, challenges us to create new knowledge, and reaffirms our commitment to literacy as a crucial component in exemplary leadership. Lucy's study groups of teachers and principals share leadership dilemmas, practice their own literacy skills, and constantly reflect on how leadership is developed. Lucy's pilot schools are models of the power of shared learning and the possibilities for showcasing student voice and literacy practices that lead to improved academic achievement. At her seminars, leaders in the field stimulate our thinking, challenge our beliefs, and inspire us to rush back to our schools to try new practices. Lucy tests our thinking and affirms that our structures are sound, our practices replicable, and our curriculum on the right path.

Mentors and models are crucial in an intellectual community, for they inspire us to grow into the people we hope to become and to take on the challenges and struggles of public education. They offer us their experiences, research, and deep insight into the process of change. They guide us and stimulate our thinking, affirm and reinforce our beliefs, and give us sustenance; they keep us strong and confident enough to act. Mentors remind us that we are not traveling alone; they leave footprints for us to follow. The job of the leader is to cultivate every member of the community's willingness and ability to be a mentor for others. Mentors explicitly and publicly invite others to follow their example.

In this book we share how effective leaders build collaborative communities that positively impact student performance. Each chapter begins with a "Dear Reader" letter, in which we relate to you in a more personal way, and goes on to provide commonsense, practical strategies that we have developed over time to address the sometimes overwhelming problems we have faced. In the same way that our mentors have helped us affirm and refine our thinking, we hope we can help future generations of leaders who struggle every day to ensure that the children under their care will benefit from the best education possible. We invite you to use our ideas, try out practices that appeal to you, and come up with new ones.

Don't try to do everything; instead, assess the readiness of your community and the needs of your students and then incubate one idea. Begin by talking about this new idea to raise awareness and interest, and then implement it with the most willing and eager members of the community. Finally, after learning as much as possible from this pilot test, implement it with the larger community, making sure to provide abundant support, ample time, and many opportunities for feedback and revision.

Most of all, we urge you to celebrate the steps along the way. Have fun!

Formulate and Communicate Your Vision

Dear Reader,

We became teachers because we believed we could make a difference, one child at a time. Each new school year, we wrote a letter to our students about our hopes and dreams for them and invited them to write back, sharing their successes, their passions and interests, and the things that caused them anxiety. Exchanging letters with our students helped us establish personal relationships with them, clarified our shared vision, and deepened our sense of purpose. We remember one student in particular, who struggled to compose his letter, crossing out words, abandoning false starts, trying again. When deciphered, his draft read, "I hope you will look deep inside me and see who I really am."

These words capture our goal as educators and reaffirm the importance of nurturing relationships that allow us to formulate and achieve personal and communal goals in our classrooms and school communities. We often use this anecdote to illustrate the power we have as educators and the awesome responsibilities inherent to our belief that we can make a difference. Sharing our stories anchors our vision to authentic experiences and lets our constituents know that our commitment is personal as well as professional.

As schools increasingly become politicized, their success determined solely by statistics, educators are tempted to focus narrowly on reading and math scores rather than formulate and communicate a vision based on the original purpose of public education—to increase the opportunity children have to become productive, humane, *thinking* citizens in a democratic society. School leaders who publicly state their commitment to staying true to their beliefs, even when issues are controversial, are most successful when they can relate their vision to personal experience. For example, a principal who knows that the arts can be an avenue for struggling students to succeed academically may talk about how music played an important role in her own schooling in order to convince district administrators that additional time for the arts is better than more time for test preparation. Or a principal with a growing immigrant student population can refer to his status as a first-generation American, using his own compelling immigrant experiences to communicate the value of respecting different cultures and unite the community around a common purpose.

Sharing authentic personal stories connects school leaders to their community and makes their vision concrete and compelling. People are hungry for stories that make sense of life and put mandates in a rational and human context. Most people do not want to work alone and will eagerly join leaders who can articulate their beliefs about the present and invite participation in a vision that will effect change for the future. But many leaders find that formulating and communicating their vision and calling the community to action are the most difficult parts of their job.

The one-to-one conversations we had with school leaders helped us understand the challenges they faced and what they needed in order to be able to meet them. When we prompted principals to articulate the visions they had for their teachers and students, some of them offered disconnected goals, actions, or explanations: crises, external mandates, or problems within the community, for example. Many saw their role as disciplinarian, problem solver, and compliance monitor. Others believed that they and they alone set the school goals, which created a fragmented, case-by-case, often unpredictable approach to dealing with problems.

One principal kept repeating that her students were living in poverty, did not have the support of their parents or the community, and did not come to school prepared to learn. She also stated that high staff turnover and absenteeism made professional development impossible. Her approach to leadership was to deal with each problem herself or in connection with a small group of favorite teachers instead of establishing a comprehensive and aligned vision.

Another principal lamented the fact that more than 20 percent of her students were receiving special services. She had decided that the previous district administration did not like her methods and was punishing her by giving her the students that nobody else wanted. In retaliation, she had relegated these students and their teachers to the basement, isolating them from professional development and the interactive life of the school. Her rationalization was that these students were the district's responsibility, not hers.

Yet another principal used all the appropriate ideas and buzzwords to describe his vision but when pressed for a plan of action incorporating specific practices, he was unable to name any. Visits to his school's classrooms reinforced our conclusion that his words failed to match his actions.

Clearly, formulating a vision is a real challenge. Discomfort with public speaking and writing adds to the pressure and often leads to confusing goals and unfocused initiatives. Therefore, the first priority for school leaders is to understand that problems cannot define a vision nor become its end point. Instead, they are opportunities to *include stakeholders in for-*

mulating the vision. One of the easiest ways to have everyone commit to the vision and move in new directions is to inquire jointly into compelling questions and have conversations that trigger thoughtful actions. Our job is to encourage school leaders to ask difficult questions and enlist the community in finding solutions. The work of Roland Barth and Michael Fullan, as well as that of authors from the business community like Thomas Friedman and Jim Collins, helped us launch study groups to investigate how to formulate a vision, align the vision with daily practices, and communicate this vision and its practices in such a way that they would be embraced and implemented.

The following questions are extremely powerful aids: *What skills do our students need in order to be successful in the next two decades? Would you send your own child or grandchild to this school? Why or why not? Which members of our community are not succeeding? What can we do to help them?* Leading with these big-idea, open-ended questions fosters collaborative decisions that cover every aspect of school life and form a unified framework to engender community support. As a result, leaders are able to act decisively. Finally, we have found that character matters; school leaders are models for the new generation. Leaders who are humane, collaborative, and principled and who understand the need to support and nurture others will naturally articulate a more comprehensive vision and inspire others to adopt it.

—Carmen and Laura

Why Formulate and Communicate a Vision?

Formulating a vision and communicating it clearly and understandably provides a framework for making commonsense decisions, large and small. While every member of the community may not always agree, everyone understands that there is a plan of action that is thoughtful, cohesive, and aligned with the school's needs and mission. This mission should have prioritized goals and challenges that can be met within the allocated time frame using the available resources. Because your vision is constantly being communicated in various ways and is implemented transparently and consistently, there are no apparently arbitrary decisions or secrets behind closed doors. Members of the community have confidence in and trust your decisions.

Leaders who understand that each school is unique and that the needs of the specific community must be the driving force behind their vision are more likely to succeed. These leaders research and analyze student performance, teacher retention, parental involvement, methods of teaching, classroom resources, current and prior professional development, and rituals and traditions. They also consider their predecessors' initiatives and the reasons these initiatives succeeded or failed. Smart leaders look for patterns, break down the population into subgroups, and consider the needs of individual students. They talk with key people in the community, seeking insights and assistance. If you do all this, you will have the information necessary to communicate your vision and inspire those with whom you work to accept and implement it.

Formulating and communicating your vision ensures that people clearly understand your expectations and are working toward a common purpose with specific and attainable goals that everyone is responsible for achieving. The vision gives community members a clear focus and invites their participation in continuing conversations that may lead to adapting, refining, or even rethinking the vision; this ultimately strengthens the vision and builds shared ownership.

A powerful vision compels specific actions. Rallying phrases that are too general (*All children can succeed*, for example) or that are unaccompanied by specific actions, qualifying language, or a targeted point of entry for all members of the community will fail to engage your audience. This kind of clichéd approach to school reform does not encourage leaders to challenge themselves or others to change their beliefs or practices and fails to provide opportunities to dig deeper in order to make difficult decisions. Instead, building a vision around the community's dream for their own children and promoting ways to use talk as the major vehicle for change can serve as a beginning point for specific actions and collaborations. Visionary leaders don't rely on written memos or mandates. They take advantage of every opportunity to express their beliefs using personal anecdotes and stories, and in doing so they unite the community and call its members to action. These visions are enduring and replicable and allow others to act with passion and purpose while adapting the language to that of their own unique community.

Leaders who take the time and make the effort to edit and craft their vision and demonstrate to the community the importance of this task encourage others to do likewise. When the vision is communicated effectively, community members are able to internalize the message, and see their personal roles in the vision, and can act independently to achieve the goals. Members of the community see the intrinsic value of the vision and are motivated to do their best work. Leaders who communicate "our" vision invite others to join in, to invest their talents and skills in achieving the goals.

Getting Started: Step by Step

1. Before determining your vision or setting specific goals, study data pertinent to your school and establish priorities for the year's learning. Begin with three priorities each year, then deepen and widen them as part of a focused, transparent, and systematic approach; this is more effective than reacting to the crisis du jour. As part of your overarching inquiry into how to ensure student, teacher, and parent success, identify one academic focus, another focus that will help build your staff's sense of collaboration, and one more that will develop stronger communication with parents and others in the larger community. For example, three interconnecting goals stated as inquiry questions might be:

- How can we help our students become independent readers and thinkers through a wide variety of print and questioning strategies?

- How can we ensure that all our teachers are sharing their literacy teaching strategies and studying best practices in an environment that promotes collaboration?
- How can we encourage parents and the larger community to support students outside school and use community resources to extend the school's literacy vision beyond the classroom?

Using this approach, you may need to set aside some of your preconceived notions, and instead look for interconnected goals and priorities that fit the needs of the entire community.

2. Be willing to take a public stand on unpopular issues. Principled leaders look beyond narrow demands such as raising test scores and focus their priorities on more global initiatives such as graduating students who are inventive, analytical, literate, compassionate, artistic, and creative human beings. Meaningful educational reform demands leaders who ask inquiry-based questions: *Are our schools graduating thinking and collaborative students? Would I send my own child to this school? Which members of our school community are not succeeding? How does the embracing of my vision by the community ensure that best practices will be embedded and institutionalized beyond my life as a leader?*

3. Set specific yearly goals. This is one of the most difficult decisions you need to make. Staying focused on these goals over a period of time is equally difficult. For example, if a goal is improving student writing, year one may stress the skills and practice of quality narrative writing, year two might introduce the skills and practice of quality expository writing, and year three might concentrate on writing in the content areas. When a leader selects too many academic goals simultaneously, it becomes very difficult to align resources. Teacher energy also dissipates when too much is expected at the same time, and as a result, little is actually accomplished. Leaders who don't support their goals or who change goals too often or add too many new ones lose their ability to mobilize their communities in achieving these goals. Coordinating your passion with the strengths of your staff will ensure success and allow for more difficult needs to be addressed over time.

4. Expose wider audiences to your goals and encourage them to come on board. Repetition, consistency, and support will ensure that every member of the community remains on target. For example, if your focus is writing, you can model authentic writing; offer professional development in which teachers practice their own writing and strategize methods for assessing individual students; plan student and teacher writing celebrations; offer parent workshops on how to encourage student writing at home; and make sure that the school schedule and budget emphasize writing as a priority.

5. Make sure that every member of the community, regardless of area or specialty, is focused on these goals and that ongoing feedback and progress evaluation pertain to these goals. In connection with the writing goal, for example, you might encourage the art teacher to create an art exhibit that includes students' written reflections on their processes and their evaluation of their own work, letters in which students respond to one another's work, sticky notes from visitors responding to the exhibit, programs and invitations created by students for the exhibit, curator's notes for each piece displayed, and so on.

6. Encourage your staff members to share their best practices with one another and celebrate evidence of improvement. Ways of doing this include highlighting big ideas in weekly letters, suggesting professional books and articles teachers can read, publicizing priorities and displaying student work on school bulletin boards, encouraging classroom intervisitations, and inviting the wider community to public gatherings. Professional development might include weekly demonstration lessons that teachers observe, give feedback on, and then practice and apply in their own classrooms.

7. Understand that while you are leading the charge, you are not the entire army. The ability to collaborate, to harness the energy of both teachers and parents and expect the best from them, is essential in accomplishing your school's mission. When you model engaging collaborative practices, you help form stimulating intellectual communities that attract thinking educators who want to connect with one another. Parents and teachers can connect via study groups, teacher leaders, parent coordinators, and intervisitations to promote collaborative practice. The end goal is to develop a shared language, a common vision, and the ability for students, teachers, and parents to make independent decisions that align with your vision and promote increased student achievement. The conversations bear fruit when words lead to action that results in visible change and ongoing reform.

8. Mentor future leaders, modeling how everything you say or do has a specific purpose and is consistent with your beliefs. Make your own learning public: share the books you are reading, ideas from the conferences you attend, your passions and hobbies that coincide with your vision and keep you invested in improving the school. Sharing your life in this way clearly communicates that the priorities you are setting for the school are aligned with your personal priorities. You become a multidimensional person whom others will want to emulate. Some of the professional books that we have found most helpful in generating conversations around writing are Lucy Calkins' *Art of Teaching Writing*, Ralph Fletcher and JoAnn Portalupi's *Writing Workshop*, Carl Anderson's *How's It Going?*, and Michael Fullan's *Leading in a Culture of Change*. Figure 1.1 is a letter inviting the community to read the Fullan book together and share their responses during study group time.

9. Make your vision concrete. Here are some specific things you can do:
- Arrange your office furniture to encourage conversation.
- Display books related to your vision on your bookshelves (see Figure 1.2).
- Promote your vision on school bulletin boards.

Dear Colleagues,

How timely this month's professional book by Michael Fullan arrives for our new region. <u>Leading in a Culture of Change</u> outlines a framework for effective leadership which will help us to deal with the complex issues we face each day. The key elements leaders must possess include:

- <u>Moral purpose</u> - acting with urgency and the intention of making a positive difference in the lives of the people we serve, impacting both the direction and results of our efforts.
- <u>Understanding the Change Process</u> – guidelines that give concrete and novel ways of thinking about the elusive process of change.
- <u>Relationships are Key</u> - building strong networks with diverse people and groups foster purposeful interaction and problem solving and continual improvement.
- <u>Knowledge Creation and Sharing</u> - inside and outside the organization knowledge and building is a social process which builds on relationships.
- <u>Coherence Making</u> – turning ambiguity into meaning is a perennial pursuit.
- <u>Energy – Enthusiasm – Hopefulness Constellation</u> – conveying a sense of optimism and confidence is essential.

As we unite around a shared vision for our region, we will study strategies for effective leadership together. In our study groups we will explore research-based practices for mobilizing our communities around common goals. Together we will create opportunities for learning in context – visiting each other in schools, 1-1 coaching, small group support networks, attending institutes and courses and interacting in professional reading groups. I look forward to supporting you as we embark on this new and exciting adventure.

Sincerely,

Carmen Fariña
Community Superintendent

FIGURE 1.1 *An Invitation to Professional Study*

FIGURE 1.2 *Danielle Giunta, principal, P.S. 154 Queens*

- Keep your office door open and encourage spontaneous visits.
- Make frequent classroom visits and follow up appropriately.
- Participate in professional development yourself and provide it for your staff.
- Give your teachers a prominent role in faculty conferences.
- Greet visitors, parents, and students warmly and personally.
- Make sure the school lobby and hallways are neat, clean, and inviting.

10. Articulate your vision by speaking publicly about it—conveying your passion, personally engaging each member of the audience, and sparking further conversations focused on the vision. Here are some strategies for speaking effectively:

- Compose a mantra. A catchy, alliterative mantra, oft repeated, invites conversations and is an easy way to keep your visionary message at the center of everyone's thinking. An encapsulation of your core beliefs as aligned with your school's specific needs, it becomes a rallying cry to mobilize the community and is a helpful tool when you need to react to a crisis at a moment's notice. Concise, replicable, and meaningful, a mantra reminds your diverse audience of people inside and outside the community (including the press) of what matters most and keeps everyone, whatever his role, on target. Mantras work best when they are alliterative, for example, *equity, energy, expectations, entourage/ensemble* (see Figure 1.3) or *courage, curriculum, content, capacity, celebration* (see Figure 1.4). Use these mantras in letters, speeches, conversations, and personal anecdotes; make them the cornerstone of presentations and community meetings, repeating them again and again. Invite community members to add their own words. Mantras are open-ended; all members of the community, including students, can attribute their own meaning to them and personalize them for their own purposes. (Figure 1.5 shows how one principal translated the *equity, energy, expectations, entourage* mantra into actions.) New leaders just beginning to build a community can use them to level the playing field, connecting people in positive ways: their catchy phrasings have universal appeal.
- Share personal anecdotes that let the audience know you and connect them to the vision.
- Provide compelling statistics that highlight the goals you have set and that motivate urgency and action.
- Keep speeches concise and to the point; begin and end on time.
- Deliver the most important parts of the speech without relying on notes, so you can maintain eye contact with your audience.
- Present the same messages to different audiences, in order to demonstrate the consistency of your vision and the importance you place on

Dear Colleagues:

I hope you have all enjoyed a restful summer and are excited to be on the cusp of a new school year. I want to take this opportunity to thank you for your steadfast commitment to ensuring that all children in New York City have the opportunity to have their talents nurtured, their experiences broadened, and their minds challenged. Much of the news we hear focuses only on the problems in the school system and gives but one interpretation. However, I know from my interactions with all of you that we have many successes to celebrate, and I look forward to hearing your stories of obstacles overcome in the coming months. As I traveled throughout the city this summer, I focused on the four E's that form the basis of the work we do.

As we begin the year, I would like to remind you of the four E's so that we may speak the same language and carry the same message.

• *Equity*: Are all children in our schools receiving the attention they need to grow to their full potential? How can we ensure that students are not falling behind because of unequal access to support and resources? Have we provided the staff and training to ensure that all our students achieve excellence?

• *Energy*: With all that is asked of you as principals, it is easy to let you energy flag. Yet it is essential that we find the strength to rekindle our passion for our work and use our energy to motivate and stimulate those around us. A school that hums is reflected in teacher and student ownership of their learning.

• *Expectations*: What expectations have we set for ourselves, our students, and our schools? Without setting high standards, there is little chance of ever reaching them. Have we fostered an environment that celebrates proactive behavior? Are the expectations clear and are they based on community input and participation? Can students and parents articulate the expectations?

• *Entourage (Ensemble)*: No one can create a great school on one's own. It takes a dedicated community of people whose talents and interests are being tapped in the right way. Remember that just as each individual child needs to be nurtured in order to grow and develop, so do our communities. Parents and community-based organizations are integral parts of these communities and have much to offer.

Please keep these words in the forefront of your minds as you work with your school communities to move toward the goals we have set. We certainly have challenges in front of us, but we are not going at it alone. Let's welcome our students back to school with the same energy that we hope and expect to receive back from them as the year progresses. The beauty of our profession is that we have the golden opportunity every year to reinvent and renew ourselves and our communities. Make this the best year ever and remember to document all the wonderful moments to remind yourselves and share with your colleagues. I look forward to visiting you in the new school year and celebrating many accomplishments.

Sincerely,

Carmen Fariña
Deputy Chancellor for Teaching and Learning

FIGURE 1.3 *An Open Letter to Principals from the Deputy Chancellor for Teaching and Learning*

Dear Colleagues:

While our reach should always exceed our grasp, I was overly optimistic in thinking that I could unveil this year's "C"s one at a time. As I travel throughout the city speaking to educators, I find myself referring to any or all of them. So I've decided to make the necessary mid-course correction and get all of us focused on the same themes and goals. I've already talked about Courage at length, and I've been happy to hear from many of you about how you've used this theme in your schools.

As you think about each of the themes below, keep in mind the non-negotiable "C." Common sense is the lens for viewing each of these ideas. I focus on these areas because they make sense for the work we do in schools. Common sense tells us that, although the challenges are great, we cannot make the advances our students need without keeping our feet rooted in the basics. We sometimes take the longest road somewhere. Identify the shortest route between today and where you want to be. Sometimes that includes eliminating diversions and having plans for emergencies.

Last year I spoke about Equity, Expectations, Energy and Entourage. As we embedded those ideas in our work, we were able to draw national attention for our achievements last year. With those successes as our base, we must look at:

COURAGE: Education is not a job for the weak of spirit. This week's transit strike will test every school community. I hope that our contingency plan works well and staff is able to make it to work. Your courage will light that broad smile and "can do" attitude that will model how to make the sweetest lemonade from the citrus which New York City is confronting.

Even when mass transit begins running again, we always have to admit to ourselves what we don't yet know and turn to others for help in our learning. We also have the opportunity in February to offer struggling students another opportunity to gain valuable intervention sessions in small group settings under the new extended contract provision. While it is tough to reorganize in the middle of a school year, stay focused on the benefits your students can receive. Show courage in the way you plan and set the tone for all members of your school community.

CURRICULUM and CONTENT: The best lesson plans are only powerful when they are being used across a grade or subject area and being taught by effective teachers. Content must build on your teachers' strengths and weaknesses. Look at the glass half full (your most advanced students) and half empty (struggling students attend every school as your disaggregated data will show). Build curriculum and content to support both enrichment and intervention. Every school needs to think about how technology can be infused to drive more effective instruction. Curriculum must support each student on a continuous journey from pre-K to a diploma. Take advantage of national consultants and region led study groups to increase your knowledge base. Anita Archer, Isabel Beck and Kylene Beers were excellent when they presented to our instructional staff. Find out which colleagues in your Region went to these sessions. Ask them for an update and copies of the outstanding handouts.

CAPACITY BUILDING: Everyone has something special to contribute to your school. Help people plan to be successful. Support their plans with pd that builds on the strengths and talents of your teachers and acknowledges skills not yet acquired. High expectations are critical for staff and students, but you must spend time every day building capacity--and then allow your staff to take responsibility for activities once they have demonstrated that they can handle the job. If you think you're ever going to be able to do it all yourself, I assure you from experience that this is delusional. Yet part of our job as leaders is so easy. Think out loud more. Talk about what you're doing and why so people can get smarter along with you. Also remember that laughter is the great leveler. Smile even when you're dying and people will take their cue from you.

CELEBRATION: The most important thing you can say to your staff is, "Boy have you done a good job." It's important to stop periodically and say "hooray for me and everyone around me. We're working hard and making incredible things happen in this school." Everyone in your building is counting on you to lead the way. If the students, staff, and parents don't buy into your vision and join in these celebrations, it doesn't matter how strong your plan is. Sometimes it will be tough to identify the cause for celebration, but think about where you want to be in June. Work back from there and build in moments where the whole school community comes to celebrate your joint adventure

Remind yourself everyday of what you've accomplished while you tackle the challenges that remain. Never stop dreaming the big dreams for your students for even a second. They depend on you to be their advocate as well as their leader. Most importantly, take care of yourself so you are able to take care of others. We are entering a brave new world in February with tremendous potential. During the holiday vacation, let's all seek out one totally self-indulgent activity, something you don't normally do. Keep it legal and not deleterious to your health, but check out of reality and personal commitments for a couple hours. Then bring that renewed energy back to share with family and friends. In the end, they are the most important commitment you have. Nurture them and accept nurturing from them. Here I quote Groucho Marx, "A child of five would understand this. Send someone to fetch a child of five."

I send you and your families my best wishes for the holidays and the year to come. Enjoy the break, and I look forward to seeing you again in January.

Happy New Year,

Carmen Fariña

Carmen Fariña
Deputy Chancellor for Teaching and Learning

FIGURE 1.4 *An Example of a Mantra Letter*

**Deputy Chancellor Carmen Fariña's Four E's
(as stated at Principals Meeting)**

1. Equity—equal access to teachers, administrators, education

    ◆ Same instructional program

    ◆ Equitable distribution of space

    ◆ Parents have right to information—they should have information to help their children

2. Energy "Building Hums"

    ◆ Teachers keep their doors open

    ◆ No tomblike silence—excitement about being there

    ◆ People working together

    ◆ Parents are welcomed, spoken with, and respected

    ◆ There are people who give and there are people who sap your energy

3. Expectation

    ◆ Raise the bar on whatever you expect

    ◆ Minimal—expectations you can meet

    ◆ Stretch—expectations you want to achieve (set higher goals)

    ◆ Teacher goals—what you expect for yourself and what you expect your students (i.e. you can have class goals and goals for individual students)

    ◆ How will you focus and how will you set expectations for your staff? (Every year is a new beginning for you—it can be a new way of developing yourself and your focus for the year). I.e. Principals for HS and Middle Schools can identify two students at the top of their class and work with them through the HS/College application process—mentor them to get them to the next level.

4. Entourage

    ◆ None of us do the job by ourselves

    ◆ People help get the job done

    ◆ People you entrust get the job done

    ◆ Cabinet is a place where people share ideas that are evolving

    ◆ Inter-visitations help you to visualize what you see in a book

    ◆ What you proud of that you have done this year?

FIGURE 1.5 *Mantras into Action*

communicating with and enlisting the support of a variety of stake-holders. (A vision that is predictably and well communicated excites the community; hearing the message again and again renews energy and commitment.)

- Know your audience well; referring to the roles individuals will play and the specific interests they hold will ensure their attention.
- Ask for questions in writing and address them at the end. (If you'll be answering the questions at a later time, announce when and where this will take place.)
- Keep an attendance list so that you can contact the members later if necessary.
- Make the end of your speech memorable:
  - Share an inspiring quotation.
  - Leave your audience with an engaging question that invites thinking or personal action.
  - Read aloud a selection that fits your intended purpose and demonstrates the power of literacy to move hearts and minds.

Figure 1.6 is the text of an inspirational speech that encourages principals to act with courage to make necessary changes in their community and incorporates all of the previous characteristics.

11. Use writing to communicate your vision to all members of the community, remind people of your focus, cajole and convince people to move toward your goals, and celebrate when they do. Focus on the little details necessary to accomplish the big ideas. Here are some examples:

- *A letter sharing your collaborative mission and inviting the community to respond*: Unlike a memo, the tone of a letter is collaborative and personal: the first-person plural urges participation. Writing that communicates your personal story and your intimate connection to the recipient with a sense of energy leads to more immediate results and develops a lasting bond with the reader. The enduring written message allows teachers to review, revisit, and reflect on your vision over time and is a permanent reminder of specific feedback regarding their work. It is also a model they can emulate to communicate their vision and enlist the support of others in their sphere of influence. (Figure 1.7 is a letter from a deputy chancellor, with a response from a principal.)
- *A "wow" letter*: An example is a short note to a teacher saying you have noticed her using a strategy she learned at the previous week's workshop, commending her commitment to trying new practices and taking risks, and suggesting she invite you (and perhaps some of her colleagues as well) to observe her classroom when she uses the strategy again.

As we complete the first week of classes, we all feel that potent September elixir, part exultation and part dread. The peak inspirational message you delivered to your staff on Tuesday has already been tempered by the realities of daily school life. The first week of school always requires you to be all things to all members of the school community all at the same time. Before you head home tonight for some refueling time with family and friends, I want to place our challenges in the broader framework of the third year of the Children First reforms.

We have done a tremendous amount of tough, ground breaking work in creating a new culture of high expectations for all students. If the end of this week is nudging you into the-glass-is-half-empty mode, consider how far we have come in these past two years. We have launched a core, rigorous curriculum; created more effective and targeted professional development; focused on developing the leadership potential of educators from all ranks; created more equitable formulas for school allocations and given SLTs unprecedented latitude in how that allocation can be spent; and created dozens of new schools to attract and motivate students in our neediest areas.

Those kind of seismic changes create their own energy field. Our job now is to sustain that energy, solidify our gains, and take our students to a higher level this year. We have to tackle the achievement gaps between racial and ethnic groups, as well as between boys and girls. We still have a long way to go to make the educational experience of every special ed and ELL student what we would want for our own child.

At the outset of the reforms, there were critical voices warning that the sky would fall given the scale and pace of change. Well the sun still shines and we've taken record numbers of students closer to our goal of having all students reach standards. Many things did change, but now we are all working from a set of best practices that supports all of us. We have created a common vocabulary and process for engaging all students. We demand teaching that incorporates the student voice and welcomes parents in our schools as a critical element in the learning process.

This year we have the opportunity to show New York City that last year's gains were not a one-shot deal. The era of writing off the futures of millions of children is history. It may sometime seem impossible to face another day and take on one more problem. Just remember that this is a joint venture involving everyone in your school community. Whatever talents you and your staff possess, use them. Your parents or members of your community may also be just the resource you need. Your cabinet is your vehicle to be all things to all people. Use them wisely and strategically.

No matter what challenges and surprises arose this week, consider what Mark Twain said about courage. "Courage is resistance to fear, mastery of fear - not absence of fear. It is curious that physical courage should be so common in the world and moral courage so rare." Courage is also:

- Being willing to admit that we have much to learn. Too often we talk about what we know and don't listen to what others know.
- Making changes in programming and budgeting even if it took us days to get to this point during the summer.
- Doing a State of the School address to your entire parent body.
- Your first faculty conference.
- Remembering to be kind to yourself.

I would love to hear some examples of what you know takes courage as a principal.

FIGURE 1.6

- *Weekly notes* (see the example in Figure 1.8)
- *Daily notes* (see the example in Figure 1.9)
- *A nuts-and-bolts statement* (see the example in Figure 1.10)
- *A newsletter* summarizing current educational developments (see the example in Figure 1.11)
- *A press release* (see the example in Figure 1.12)

A Note from the Deputy Chancellor of Teaching and Learning

Dear Colleagues,

A sure sign of a great school is the buzz you feel the minute you walk in the door. One of the things I loved best about being a principal was figuring out each year what I could do to create that buzz from the minute my teachers walked in the building in September. While each of us has a unique personal style, we are all committed to the same vision of a quality, rigorous education for each of our students. Your educational vision is unique to your school community, but I believe that sharing a vision requires each of us to share with staff how our personal story drives our vision of the work.

As a big believer in sharing best practices, I want to give you some of the strategies that worked well for me—and the experienced educators who shared them with me when I first became a principal. Consider which ideas might work in your building as well.

✓ Understand that, as an individual, you can only do so much. You are the building leader. It is your vision and leadership that produces good outcomes for your students. Take a moment, however, to consider if there are areas where you can better utilize the talents of your staff. A school is a living organism, and you have to place your trust in the people who work for you. Your ultimate power will come from the relationships you form and the way in which you use the power of your position and your vision.
✓ Start your back-to-school conversations with a positive question, even if the topic at hand is very contentious. Try "how can we build on our success last year" rather than "what we tried last year didn't work, let me tell you how we're going to change."
✓ Make sure that every effort is made to ensure that special needs students (Special Education and English Language Learners) begin receiving the appropriate services on the first days of school.
✓ In making sure that your building sparkles for opening day, take time for a serious conversation with your custodian. Do a walk-through together. Set clear expectations for standards and a timetable for getting even the smallest details in place. Making sure each classroom has a wastebasket seems a minor detail, but think about a teacher trying to set up a classroom without one.
✓ Place a special Parent Welcome table in the building where parents can pick up the names and phone numbers for key staff members. Outline the best way to contact you and your teachers throughout the year. Lock in first day procedures and make sure everyone in the building knows what they are. Every out-of-classroom teacher should have a role in welcoming families to school. Parent Coordinators are a natural meet-and-greet resource. Have them hand out their business cards to parents for follow-up.
✓ If your expectations for arrivals and dismissals are not in place and understood by staff and parents on the first day, it will be tough to establish those rules later. Post those procedures inside and outside the building on the first day to get everyone in the school community on board. Pay particular attention to all exterior doors where students will enter and leave the building. Be sure you have plans for inclement weather.
✓ As a principal, it's easy to get locked into being a crisis manager. Avoid the impulse as much as possible. Walk your building, even on those first days back. Make sure all teachers have what they need for the first day. The minute you see something exciting happening in one room, spread the good news throughout the building.
✓ Make sure everyone gets a personal call to ensure that your org chart is solid and everyone is returning.
✓ Serve breakfast at least once during the first weeks to all your staff. Take your newly appointed teachers out for coffee or lunch to give them a structured way to get to know you and one another as people.
✓ Before teachers report, have your prep schedule posted and ready to go. This way all will understand their assignments for the year. Staff is confident that the schedule will hold, and students experience a predictable school day.

It's always a new year in September, a new chance to give your students the rigorous education each of them deserves. This year I am going to be talking about five "C"s, but unlike my "E"s, I'm going to roll them out one at a time. The first is Courage. Not only is this probably the most important, but it's an idea suggested by several of you.

Courage of a Principal

Courage takes many different shapes and moves about in forms that sometimes are indistinguishable for school leaders. Eventually, the form has a distinct outline and the structure, style, and construction begins to take a clearer shape.

I took the initiative this school year and had heart-to-heart conversations with all of the professionals within my school building.

I believe all of us have more substance to produce a higher quality of work on behalf of our students.

Real courage is sitting with good people and complimenting them for successful efforts from the past and encouraging them to move ahead and accomplish more in the future.

Real principal courage is looking people in the eyes and telling them straightforwardly—"You can do it better! You have it within you to produce more and achieve better results in all facets of teaching. Do it not for me alone, but do it first for the students entrusted in your charge!"

FIGURE 1.7 *Defining Our Vision*

CARMEN FARIÑA, PRINCIPAL

Calendar for the Week of January 2nd - 5th.

The Criteria of Emotional Maturity — William C. Messinger, MD

- The ability to deal constructively with reality.
- The capacity to adapt change.
- A relative freedom from symptoms that are produced by tensions and anxieties.
- The capacity to find more satisfaction in giving than receiving.
- The capacity to relate to others people in a consistent manner with mutual satisfaction and helpfulness.
- The capacity to sublimate, to direct one's instinctive hostile energy into creative and constructive outlets.
- The capacity to love!!!
  WHAT A WONDERFUL PHILOSOPHY FOR THE NEW YEAR!

Tuesday, January 2nd:
•••Progress Reports distributed with labels to be affixed.

Wednesday, January 3rd:
•••**Assembly** (Auditorium) Bathroom Behavior
     Grades 1 and 2   11 a,n, – 11:15 a.m.
     Grades 3 — 5   12 Noon – 12:15 p.m.

    To discuss appropriate behavior in bathrooms, hallways and line-up.

FIGURE 1.8 *Weekly Notes*

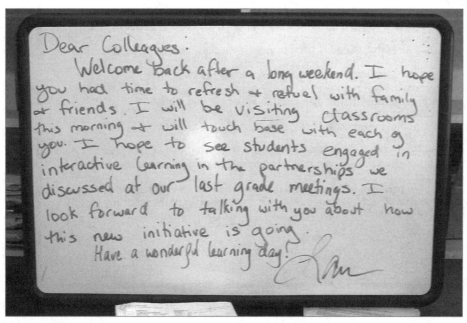

FIGURE 1.9 *A Daily Message*

Nuts & Bolts for Principals

Ideas that Get Results

Dear Colleagues:

December is an interesting month: so many celebrations and high emotions with January and testing season on the horizon. This is definitely the time to remember that you cannot meet the needs of others unless you take proper care of yourself. Be sure that your vacation plans include a large dose of time with family and friends, as well as some quiet time to reflect and refresh.

Best wishes for the new year for you and your family,

Carmen Fariña

Carmen Fariña

'Tis the season for self-evaluation. Identify how you can make your successes go deeper. If something isn't working, now's the time to consider mid-course corrections. The vacation break offers a great opportunity to change course and begin a new path. Think about:

- **10 Things My School Has Accomplished This Year that We Can Be Proud Of**: Think specifically about people who have made great progress in fulfilling their goals. Share your pride with them to both acknowledge their achievements and set the stage for next steps.
- **5 New Year's Resolutions**: Make your resolutions concrete and consider which staff would be most effective in implementing these goals.
- **3 Decisions to Be Made**: Consider your most vexing issues. Pick personnel, structures, or situations with deep-seated issues that have so far been intractable.
- **2 Things from Your Personal Life for Which You Are Thankful and Need to Be Shared:** In our busy lives, we often fail to balance and blend our personal and professional lives. Allow the people in your professional life an inside look at two things in your personal life of which you are particularly proud. There's no better way to explain your value system.
- **1 item you want to leave as Your Legacy for Your School:** Legacy can be a daunting word, but we must first dream our big dreams if we are ever going to make them a reality.

Holidays are delightful, but stressful, times. Stick to normal routines and reinforce the school's discipline code.

- Schedule parties for the end of the week to ensure student and teacher attendance.
- Be sure that all celebrations are age appropriate.
- Expand on existing school traditions, rather than trying to grow new ones instantaneously. This is especially important for new principals.
- Not all children celebrate the same holidays. Make a conscious effort to embrace and acknowledge children of all faiths.
- Consider sending a holiday message to your staff offering not only best wishes, but also reiterating your school's positive achievements. Build the message from your work on the lists above.
- Especially if you're a new principal, remember that strained child custody cases become more challenging at this time of year. Be sure that staff closely supervises dismissal on the last day of school before vacation.

FIGURE 1.10

Creating a Climate for Change: A building principal uses her philosophy and experiences to show how to create change.

by **Carmen Farina,** *Principal, P.S. 6 (New York, NY)*

"There will always be a disparity between where we are and where we want to be."

Diane Ravitch, Senior Research Scholar,
School of Education, New York University

America's schools could go a long way toward improvement if we used the above quote as a starting point for creating a school philosophy. An administrator entering a new building needs to create a climate in which change is greeted as a challenge to be met and explained within the context of a larger vision. True change can never be mandated, nor can it be arrived at only through group discussions. Change, to be lasting and totally interwoven into the school fabric, must begin with leadership and be transformed into staff development and consensus building.

Change is a facilitator, stimulator, and initiator. An administrator cannot begin to implement change unless positive human relations are established within a school building. The quality of being humane extends beyond the classroom to the entire school. Agents of change must first establish themselves as human beings responsive to other human beings. There are five "T's" that underlie the creation of a new community: Trust, Team Building, Time, Training, and Things (materials).

Trust is an essential ingredient of all successful communities. Everyone has to understand the messages being given and not feel threatened by them. Prior to organizational changes, I meet with each staff member for 30 minutes. I ask them to come prepared to answer three questions:

● What do you do best?

● What talent or skill do you have that you have never been asked to share?

● What areas of improvement do you see as a priority for P.S. 6?

Coverage is always provided to allow staff to participate in our discussions. This helps to enhance the professional nature of discussion and set a collegial tone. During my first year as principal, I covered each of the teachers' classes on their birthdays, while they took half-hour birthday breaks. I used this time to get to know students' names. Each teacher received a card with special wishes. Trust is letting people know you care, that you are responsive and consistent. Trust is letting them know your human side as well as your professional standards.

Staff members need to feel that they

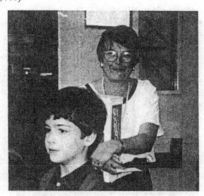

Principal Carmen Farina: "A true agent of change leads by example."

have common goals and that one person's accomplishment is shared by everyone. Extreme competitiveness destroys community spirit. To initiate *Team Building,* we begin full day planning sessions in June to work on setting goals for the following year. The sessions have a set agenda and a teacher group leader. The principal provides lunch, and the lunch break is strictly devoted to the discussion of personal topics. This day provides a framework for the following year's curriculum. Goals, expectations, and standards for each grade are set at these meetings.

Time, or lack of it, is one of the educator's greatest challenges. Everyone needs to feel that they have access to the principal. An open-door policy (with some limitations) goes a long way toward taking the time to talk with all stakeholders. My school has begun parent meetings with two representatives from each grade. These meetings have a parent-set agenda. Note taking is encouraged and minutes are distributed. This gives everyone an opportunity to feel acknowledged, while the staff is made aware of ongoing concerns. We also take the time each year to have a formal "State of the School Address" that focuses on school philosophy, successes, and areas of concern.

All principals should be required to "walk" their buildings every day. Visibility is an integral part of effectiveness. To stimulate change, you must be aware of what is happening in every classroom every day. A spoken compliment, suggestion, or comment can set the tone for further exploration. As part of the class visits, you can leave an article, note, or book in a teacher's mailbox, to let the teacher know that administrators are aware of the curriculum being covered. During classroom visits,

speak about curriculum issues first, personal matters second.

Staff development, or *Training,* is the real key to effective school change. It needs to reflect the "seminar inquiry" approach more than the "teacher as lecturer" method. All staff development must allow for debriefing and reflection. "Conversations" about spelling, writing, and math are better for true understanding than workshops.

Scheduling should reflect staff development as a priority. Administrators should attend staff development sessions with their staff, and money should be set aside to pay professionals for weekend and after-school workshops. After-school workshops should be provided to help parents understand new trends and provide foundations for communication.

Every staff development session should have readily available materials *(Things)* for immediate follow-up. Staff should make the final decisions as to what works best to implement new ideas.

To create and stimulate change, administrators must become model risk takers. They need to have a vision and give strong, unequivocal messages. They must always be willing to admit mistakes and refine successes. An administrator needs to take one step at a time and introduce initiatives in places where seeds have been carefully planted. No battle should be fought that hasn't been selectively screened for optimum success. Administrators should be aware of a school's history to understand its culture and avoid pitfalls.

Above all, a true agent of change leads by example. To convince teachers of good teaching strategies, I am first and foremost a teacher myself. I go into classrooms and demonstrate the process, as well as elicit the products. Change never ends.

School partnerships include everyone: parents, student teachers, secretaries, custodians, paraprofessionals, lunchroom staff. For effective change, everyone needs to be part of the decision-making process. Everyone needs to be consulted and ultimately thanked for making it all happen.

Finally, change has truly succeeded when it can be shared, replicated, and given away. At P.S. 6, we have initiated the next step, by becoming a professional development site for administrators. ●

FIGURE 1.11 *www.teachersnetwork.org*

DRAFT - Press Release: Collaborative Communities of Practice

The Department of Education announces the implementation of Collaborative Communities of Practice, a program designed to promote intervisitation and observation of exemplary practices. Over sixty schools have been selected as hosting schools and will offer other schools from across the city the opportunity to visit, see exemplary teaching practices, and share strategies for moving all schools towards excellence.

Research concerning the movement of schools from good to great demonstrates the power of intervisitation as a tool for continuous school improvement. As leaders, coaches, and teachers hear the story of each school's journey, they experience firsthand the conditions necessary to mobilize around shared expertise, a common vocabulary to define best practices and a shared mission.

Each region nominated some of their schools most ready to share best practices. Many excellent schools in each region were not nominated because they are already hosting intervisitations and serving as models for areas such as the arts, aspiring leaders, and intervention. Each nominated school fit the criteria for selection, which included strong leadership, collaborative professional learning communities, effective implementation of the core curriculum, student performance, interactive learning, and cultures of continued growth and sustained development. Each nominated school was visited by a cross-regional team, who spent time meeting with the school leaders, coaches, and teachers, visited classrooms, talked to students and parents, and made recommendations to a think tank representing the leadership of each region.

The first visits to some of the selected schools will take place in late February and will continue throughout the school year. We look forward to the opportunity to increase the number of selected schools as visiting schools replicate the best practices and move towards consistency of excellence.

The Department of Education in collaboration with the Wallace Foundation, Kornfeld Foundation, and Dr. Kevin McGuire from the New York State Center for School Leadership, have contributed their expertise and resources to support the implementation of this program.

FIGURE 1.12

Avoiding Common Pitfalls

When setting goals, less is more. It is much better to focus on a few necessary and attainable goals that build on the compelling needs of the community and take advantage of existing strengths than to come up with a long and varied list of objectives. Creating a laundry list of goals aimed at solving all the problems within the school community dilutes your work, creates a chaotic environment, and leads to burnout.

Setting challenging goals requires the courage to take a stand, expose inequitable or ineffective practices, and confront what matters most. It is all too easy to make surface changes or set goals that are easily met. Concentrating on making teachers happy without improving the life of the students will not transform your school's culture. Nor will focusing exclusively on goals as a reaction to external forces such as a superintendent's or school board's mandates or the No Child Left Behind Act.

Formulating and communicating your vision is an opportunity to bring many voices to the table, focus on relevant issues, and enlist community members to support your agenda. Communicating the vision in the first-person plural lets the community know that you respect them and have listened to them and that their participation is necessary for schoolwide success. Leaders who see themselves as the sole savior of the community and who try to enforce their personal vision without the buy-in of key constituents will face increased resentment and resistance. Acknowledging the input and contributions of both individuals and teams when communicating the vision promotes a deeper commitment to change and a more rapid buy-in.

Staying on message over a period of time is an indication of your commitment to the goals you have established. Personalizing mantras for a variety of audiences and repeating them constantly keeps everyone focused and working diligently. Conflicting messages or changing priorities give the impression that you are insufficiently committed to your vision, and your staff may be reluctant to buy into it. On the other hand, smart leaders know that occasionally midcourse corrections may be necessary as long as transparency and common sense prevails.

A vision tied to a radical change in culture and practice, such as moving from writing that is prompted and controlled by the teacher toward student-centered, process writing, takes time and requires that you integrate the message and align resources and support in all facets of school life. If you set goals and mandate compliance but fail to allow enough time for lasting change to occur or don't set up clear accountability aligned to the goals, you will undermine everyone's efforts, including your own.

A visionary leader welcomes feedback from the community and is willing to adapt the vision as needed. This flexibility is essential to keeping the vision alive and making it grow. If you are willing to admit your mistakes, ask for help when you need it, and give credit to others, you are more likely to accomplish your goals and embed them in the community.

Maintaining a balance between celebration and criticism when evaluating the progress toward stated goals ensures that you remain aware of what is already accomplished and what still needs to be done. It also fuels the energy and motivation of the community. Relying on either compliments or criticisms exclusively runs the risk of creating complacency or damaging morale; you will miss the opportunity to engage in serious conversations that deepen the commitment and strengthen the work.

Evaluating Success

How can you assess that your vision has been successfully embedded and is productively affecting the school community? Look for evidence like this:

• Is student achievement in your priority areas clearly visible in classroom visits, student conversations and work, teacher conversations, and a variety of teacher and student assessments? For example, in the area of student writing, are students producing more quality writing? Is more classroom time devoted to teaching writing strategies and having students apply these strategies to their own writing? Are students and teachers creating rubrics to evaluate their writing? Do students reflect on their writing goals and assess one another's writing?

• Are the teachers demonstrating their personal and professional commitment to the vision by participating in professional development, changing their classroom practices, talking with peers and parents, redefining their roles, and taking on new responsibilities? For example, are teachers observing one another's teaching as a way to identify best practices? Are they willing to become teacher leaders and extend their learning? Are they able to offer parent workshops?

• Can parents articulate the school vision in terms of their own children? Are they willing to help achieve the vision for all students? Have you established enough support and trust and demonstrated sufficient success that parents are confident that controversial and difficult decisions will be handled appropriately and successfully? For example, do parents understand how and why writing is being taught differently from the way it was taught when they were in school?

• Can the vision be adapted and replicated in other communities? Are you able to articulate your reasons for choosing your goals and your process for implementing them? Are you willing to mentor others as they replicate your practices? Are you still learning new strategies and refining your own beliefs? Have you documented and researched effective strategies for attaining your goals, thus clearly demonstrating that these practices work and convincing naysayers to emulate these practices in their own communities? Is your passion for your vision so strong that you eagerly give away your secrets for your successes?

• Has the message been so well articulated and implemented that even when you are not present (temporarily, or permanently should you be employed elsewhere), the vision is sustained? Does the community demonstrate that it has internalized the message so that it is moving independently and taking on new challenges to ensure its success?

Engage in One-to-One Conversations

Dear Reader,

From the beginning of our professional collaboration, our most satisfying moments have been the time we have set aside to talk to each other. During these conversations we share our ideas, refine our practices, and connect to each other as human beings.

Working together as principal and staff developer, we would begin and end each day by sharing our perspectives on current happenings; these conversations helped us think more deeply and strategically about the needs of the school community. After our morning conversations, we would walk through the building together and wonder how we might move the community to look beneath the surface and begin to see the need to change the status quo through urgent action. It was clear that calling a faculty conference and reciting all the things we knew needed changing or sending out a memo berating staff members and announcing directives would not engender cooperation and support.

We found that the professional stories we shared during our daily conversations reinforced our beliefs, helped us continue to challenge our thinking, and gave us the impetus to develop a collaborative action plan. Our partnership, as modeled by our conversations, demonstrated cohesive leadership, which the community wanted to emulate.

Our conversations sometimes sparked disagreements. (One was our differing approaches to the teaching of spelling: one of us believed in the value of weekly spelling tests; the other wanted to teach spelling only through authentic writing.) These differences of opinion, which reflected our individual histories and the different role each of us played in our collaboration, made our conversations richer and more stimulating and helped us anticipate problems we would face when trying to implement real change. Our conversations allowed us to share our varied experiences and viewpoints, gain insight, clarify our thinking, and set a path for approaching the staff as we moved forward.

Having experienced firsthand the power of our own conversations, we knew conversations could be the cornerstone to building community and making lasting changes in our school's culture. The conversations we subsequently undertook with each member of the school community were indeed a vital tool. We were able to introduce ourselves personally and hear the other person's perception of her strengths and needs and the role she hoped to play in the organization. One of our biggest surprises was that after giving teachers the choice of talking with one or the other of us, they all wanted conversations with each of us. This reinforced for us how hungry teachers were to have their voices heard. We each asked the same questions, but our different roles triggered different responses and opened new points of entry.

When our roles switched to that of superintendent and deputy superintendent, we also invited principals and assistant principals to join us in one-to-one conversations. We were surprised at their discomfort and hesitation, but we understood that we needed to establish trust. After the first five brave volunteers reported to their colleagues that the conversations had been engaging, reenergizing, and productive and that we truly listened and promised to follow up, other leaders quickly began to fill our calendar. We met with more than 150 principals and an army of assistant principals over a period of three months, which meant working long hours, delegating administrative responsibilities, and delaying other initiatives. However, the time invested paid enormous dividends: we learned important information that allowed us to hasten our work and lessen resistance to it.

Most professionals never have the opportunity to talk with leaders in intimate settings in which personal motivations, areas of vulnerability and need, and honest feelings and opinions are revealed. New leaders in particular often take for granted existing reputations and preconceived notions about their school community without allowing people to reinvent themselves and explain prior actions and hopeful next steps. Members of the community, on the other hand, immediately distrust any leader ready to make wholesale change without taking the time to understand existing strengths and historical perspectives. Leaders who don't make time for personal conversations often meet large-scale resentment and negative feedback because no personal connection has been established as the foundation for building relationships.

Support for new policies is possible only when leaders understand the existing expertise and readiness for change of each member of the community. Communicating a list of mandates without getting to know the individuals who are expected to follow the mandates guarantees failure.

Our conversations have humbled us and taught us that most people are hungry to contribute their knowledge and their best thinking and eager to support their leaders in the challenging and sometimes overwhelming work ahead. Leaders who believe they have all the answers themselves underestimate the expertise present within their own community and fail to engage the members of that community. Staff members will not volunteer to serve on committees until they have gotten to know you more fully during personal, productive interactions. One-to-one conversations immediately foster intimate relationships; reveal wonderful surprises about talents, interests, and passions; and help you build support networks for your vision. Mobilizing the community in this personal and powerful way transforms *I* into *we*, invites full participation, and gives each member of the community the satisfaction of knowing he has been heard and understood.

Throughout our professional lives, we have encountered leaders who set up competitive structures and star systems. This environment keeps community members from sharing their expertise, volunteering to help others, and becoming teacher leaders. Conversations are a wonderful way to ensure that you recognize and nurture budding talent and expertise. Collaboration grows as community members support one another; competition diminishes as collegiality grows. We were thrilled by how eager principals and assistant principals were to share their expertise with others, be recognized for something they did well, and talk about how they grew to understand new ideas. The community understood that our recognition and affirmation of diverse talents and strengths, which had previously been ignored, invited taking risks and sharing ideas and benefited everyone.

In our personal lives we struggle to find time for good conversations with our families and friends. This challenge extends to our professional lives—in school, too often time for conversations between adults is not a priority. Busy leaders often limit their interactions to a favored few or focus on solving immediate problems. This increases the isolation felt by teachers who do not seek attention, who do not understand your motivation or vision, who are not members of the inner circle. Engaging your constituency in one-to-one conversations demonstrates the priority you give to developing relationships, makes clear how much you value personal interaction, and models your expectation that teachers will behave the same way with their students.

We are convinced that your most powerful tool is your willingness to give people your undivided attention—to speak and listen intently, with an open mind and heart. It is only through these sorts of conversations that the community will become fully invested in reforms that yield lasting results.

—Carmen and Laura

Why Institute One-to-One Conversations?

Conversations build trusting relationships focused on teaching and learning. Conversations are a natural part of building personal relationships and can serve the same function in our school communities. They allow us to share our personal histories and our academic expertise and demonstrate our willingness to trust one another.

Even when you know your community well, one-to-one conversations each new year are a way to reconnect with, reassess, and reenergize each member. They are an opportunity to give honest feedback about past performance and raise expectations by posing essential questions and inviting each member to take on new challenges and learning opportunities. The world is constantly changing: one-to-one conversations can incorporate new educational approaches and deepen thinking without fragmenting or overloading established initiatives.

Conversations create a great incentive and urgency for change, because they are personal and targeted to the particular needs and interests of each member of the community. By listening intently, under the umbrella of privacy and confidentiality, you demonstrate your willingness to hear all kinds of information. If you then respond quickly and appropriately, you will convince your community members that you care about who they are, support their goals, and are willing to make decisions based on what they have to say. Often you may hear information that requires you to change a course of action or revise your thinking, which proves to your community that you really value their opinions. These conversations also encourage community members to take ownership of change and promote shared responsibility for specific next steps in the context of collaborative practice.

Too often professional development is viewed as having been imposed without taking into account teachers' past training and accomplishments and their present needs, interests, and goals. Staff developers who have one-to-one conversations with teachers create personal bonds and establish learning as a two-way relationship; buying into and taking responsibility for change cease to be such a struggle.

Conversations at the district level are also a wonderful way for superintendents to build trusting relationships. Understanding each principal's motivations, expertise, collegial relationships, and readiness to take on new instructional practices is an excellent foundation for making decisions about differentiated supervision. Likewise, principals who understand their superintendent's personal motivation, history, expertise, beliefs, and vision are likely to be more willing to move forward than those who don't. Each conversation adds to a multidimensional picture of what is already in place and what is necessary for districtwide student improvement. Conversations are an opportunity to validate people's accomplishments, recognize their particular context and concerns, and provide immediate assistance. They also help a superintendent understand why leaders might be reluctant to change. Open-ended dialogues change the nature of supervision by modeling the qualities of collaborative and humane leadership and encouraging honesty about educational challenges and obstacles to school success.

Identifying concerns common to a number of conversations and referring to them during public speeches is a way to assure the community that change has come about from within. In our district conversations, for example, we uncovered the common concern that special needs students were being placed inequitably; we were able to attribute the initiative for the changes we instituted in this area to the community. When teachers and principals see that the conversations they've had with you have had positive results, they are much more likely to make problems known and seek support instead of facing them alone or avoiding them and allowing them to worsen.

Conversations model interactive literacy leadership. As the classrooms in your schools become places of interactive learning filled with accountable conversations, you'll want teachers to use this conversation strategy with their colleagues as well. Make time for these conversations; allow your teachers to get to know one another personally and professionally and use this information to support one another. These talks energize the community because they honor each person's unique contribution and demonstrate your motivation and desire to include others in your decision making. Your teachers will develop trusting relationships, solidify their individual roles within the community, and undertake an ongoing dialogue about teaching and learning.

Keeping notes of each conversation so that you can remember the details will allow you to highlight the value of each individual and the importance you place on establishing relationships. Collaborative school communities whose members engage in conversations at all levels—superintendents with principals and staff developers, principals and staff developers with teachers, teachers with students—demonstrate the power of listening. Leaders who are honest and invite honest feedback from others are more likely to reflect on their own actions, question assumptions, and model being flexible. Listening intently and taking notes during conversations demonstrate that all the literacy skills—speaking, writing, and reading—can be used in authentic and meaningful ways to bring about change. The notes are tangible proof that what the person is saying is important and provide material to include in follow-up letters written immediately afterward.

Conversations impact collaborative organizational changes. Conversations signal a style of shared leadership in which members of the community take on certain responsibilities. Jobs like scheduling, filling out reports, supervising the lunchroom, beautifying the school, and leading parent tours and workshops are often more productively handled by teachers who are eager to contribute their talents in these areas.

Talking with teachers before the official start of the school year helps you address the specific needs of the community while demonstrating your belief that providing support, not issuing policy memorandums, checklists, or regulations, improves student performance. Grade assignments, specific schedules, professional development, team-teaching arrangements, electives, and extracurricular programs are some of the decisions that result from these conversations and lead to school renewal and staff buy-in. On the district level, conversations with principals reveal problems such as inequitable budgets, unfair high-risk student placement, inappropriate approaches to teaching struggling students, ineffective teacher recruitment, and an imbalance between autonomy and consistency that require solutions. When superintendents immediately make these direct-from-the-principals concerns a priority, principals' confidence and trust in the superintendents' leadership is secure.

When conversations become part of the organizational culture and are conducted frequently throughout the year, they become a powerful tool for self-assessment by and self-directed improvement for all members of the community. Conversations provide a common vocabulary and create a collaborative culture for problem solving and decision making.

Conversations are an assessment tool. When conversations have been instituted and fine-tuned into an art, they can be used as a formal assessment tool— a contract for the betterment of both teachers and students. The conversation as contract is most worthwhile when it identifies a teacher's strengths and weaknesses and recommends areas for focused professional development. It should also include the specific ways the principal will support the teacher in these areas.

After a trusting relationship has been established in an initial conversation, follow-up discussions can include a teacher's expectations, specific action plans, and evidence of learning with regard to specific students. In order for these contracts to be valid, both participants must agree at the start that the conversations will include a beginning-of-the-year evaluation and statement of conditions, a midyear review, and an end-of-the-year assessment of evidence regarding promises kept and related student achievement. This approach to accountability is highly respectful: it holds both participants equally responsible for student success and leads to ongoing reflection, an increased ability to articulate specific practices, and the willingness to modify and adapt strategies to improve student achievement. Teachers who successfully engage in these contracts with their principals will often use them successfully with their students (see Chapter 5).

Getting Started: Step by Step

1. Write a letter inviting members of your school community to talk with you one to one (see Figure 2.1 for an example). State the agenda for the conversation, the questions you will ask, and your and the other party's responsibilities before, during, and after the conversation. The anticipated results of the conversation need to be transparent; they might include organizational changes, professional development priorities, staff roles in making decisions, feedback about your style and past decisions. You must also clearly state protocols: how to sign up, your intention to take notes and your permission for the staff member to do likewise, norms for honest dialogue and confidentiality. This tone of the letter is friendly and makes clear that participation is voluntary. The questions you ask will prompt meaningful conversation and be balanced between strengths and areas that need improvement. Tailor them to specific school needs and different levels of leadership. The initial conversation can focus on areas like these: *What are you already doing well? What do you need help with? If you were in my leadership role, what would you focus on? How can you best be supported?*

2. Clear your calendar and prepare a corresponding sign-up sheet. (Make sure to give yourself time to reflect and unwind between conversations.) Possible times to meet may include before, during, and after school. If necessary, someone should be available to cover teachers' classes while they talk with you, especially

Dear Colleague,

I would like to invite you to talk about some big questions with me during a one to one conversation. Some of the ideas you might want to think about before we meet are: What are your proudest moments and biggest successes? What are you passionate about? On which of your efforts do you get the most compliments? What are the areas in which you would like to improve? How can I best support you in growing stronger: visiting another colleague? attending professional development courses? working with a coach? What advice would you give me about how to strengthen our school community? How do you see your role in supporting change? Is there anything else you feel is important to share with me?

Our time together will be private and confidential, because I want to encourage an honest exchange of ideas. I promise to listen intently, take notes on any ideas or recommendations, and follow up immediately. I hope you will want to bring your notebook as well, so that you too can record the ideas we share. There will be coffee and cookies, and I'll do everything I can to limit distractions so that we can really concentrate (I'll post a Do Not Disturb sign on my office door and hold all phone calls). Within two weeks after we talk, I'll write you a letter summarizing our discussion (which you will then have the opportunity to revise).

I hope you will take advantage of this opportunity, and I encourage you to sign up for a convenient time. I look forward to taking with you soon.

FIGURE 2.1 *An Invitation to Engage in Conversations*

if trust has not yet been established. Once meetings are scheduled, consider them a top priority and do not cancel them unless absolutely necessary.

3. Make sure each scheduled conversation is allotted enough time (we recommend a full hour), is private, is confidential, includes real give-and-take, and takes place in a setting in which the physical positions of you and your staff member are equal and encourage eye contact (come out from behind your desk!). Provide beverage options and comfort food. Allow extra time for conversations you suspect may be difficult. Make sure everyone knows you are not to be disturbed, and designate someone to handle emergencies.

4. Think about the questions and major issues in advance, and have a notebook and pen handy so that you can take notes.

5. Model active listening (practice ahead of time if necessary): maintain eye contact, make affirming vocalizations and gestures, and paraphrase and restate (*I heard you say . . . ; Did you mean . . . ? Can you tell me more about . . . ? What if I did . . . or asked you to . . . ?*). Focus on finding common ground and encouraging collaboration. Take notes in a notebook or on index cards; highlight big ideas and include enough detail to support follow-up letters and ongoing informal conversations. (Figure 2.2 is an example of a principal's notes on index cards.)

6. Keep track of the pace of the conversation without constantly looking at your watch. Be sure to discuss all the questions, leave enough time for a positive

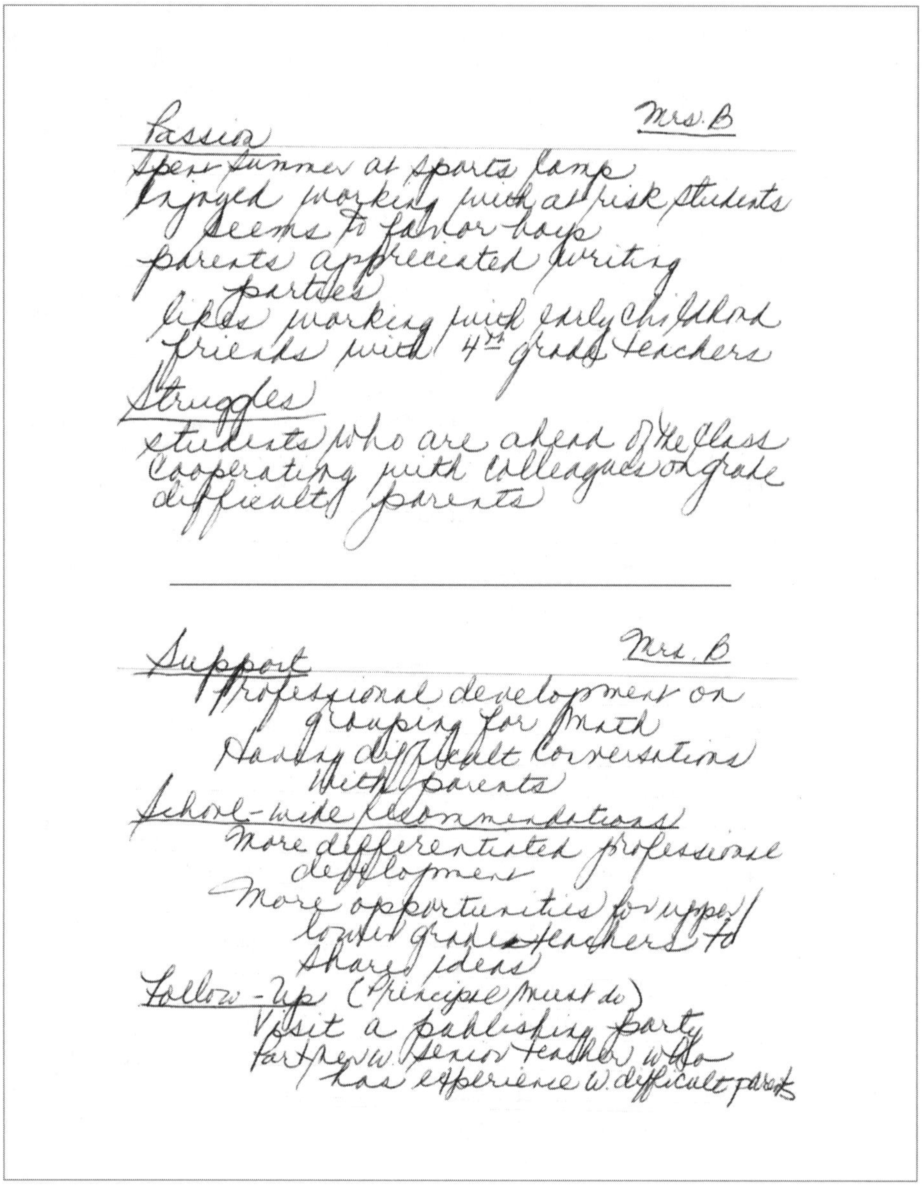

Passion — Mrs. B

Spent summer at sports camp
Enjoyed working with at risk students
Seems to favor boys
parents appreciated writing parties
likes working with early childhood
friends with 4th grade teachers

Struggles

students who are ahead of the class
Cooperating with colleagues on grade
difficult parents

Support — Mrs. B

Professional development on grouping for math
Handling difficult conversations with parents

School-wide Recommendations

More differentiated professional development
More opportunities for upper/lower grade teachers to share ideas

Follow-Up (Principal must do)

Visit a publishing party
Partner w. senior teacher who has experience w. difficult parents

FIGURE 2.2 *Principal's Notes from One-to-One Conversations*

wrap-up, and summarize next steps. If necessary, make an appointment for a follow-up conversation.

7. Provide immediate feedback in writing. Express your appreciation for the opportunity to have the conversation, summarize the points discussed, restate the agreed-on next steps (including any specific actions related to individual students), and review the staff member's professional development plan. Be sure to refer to the staff member's personal life and restate your commitment to any specific support you offered. Give the staff member a draft of this letter so she can correct any errors or misunderstandings and suggest additional comments. Asking for this kind of input reaffirms that you view the relationship as a partnership. Make the necessary revisions and distribute the letter. Figure 2.3 is a letter

I look forward to working with you and your staff this year. I know that there is untapped potential at this school. Be sure to meet at least once a week as a cabinet.

I would also ask you to explore more ways to encourage parents and corporate participation in every aspect of school life. Some partnerships might focus on after-school and career awareness and provide financial assistance.

I look forward to our next conversation and have listed some issues to focus on:

- Make sure that your new teachers receive weekly staff development to insure a successful school year. Some time should be spent discussing personal as well as, academic concerns. Your personal leadership in setting up a course of study on literacy would be an excellent way to highlight your strength and leadership. Be visible on a daily basis throughout your building.
- Create a special approach to your 8+ students that incorporates some diverse strategies (community service, career education, attendance incentives, etc.)
- Use the math staff developers to create a strong, comprehensive approach to the math program. Use them to conduct parent workshops to raise parental awareness and "demystifying" the new math.
- Continue to collaborate with the UFT to enhance the learning climate for all. The school schedule should work for students <u>first</u>. We are discussing appropriate compensation for Special Education prep coverage, but it should not require 2 teachers to cover one class. Work on instituting an <u>SBO</u> for next year.
- Use the District Team to investigate the use of grants, staff development to enhance the Delta program. These students should also be very visible conducting school tours, doing community service and perhaps entering citywide competitions (especially in math and science).
- Remembering the FISH video and encourage your staff to play with students (faculty varsity games, faculty variety show, etc.) You have many talented people and highlighting them to the community enhances the personal commitment of staff to students.
- Visit the rooms that we observed that were not student-centered and begin the write-up process. Let me know if you wish assistance in this endeavor.
- Be sure the 'deans' have a schedule of specific activities that are pro-active in nature. Certainly, working with the 8+ students as an advisory group.
- Worldly Wise would be an excellent teaching tool for your <u>Delta</u> students. Watch out for this package in the mail.
- Attendance improvement must be a priority for all Middle Schools since there is such a strong correlation between attendance and academic performance. Teacher attendance should be celebrated as well.
- Work on some air-conditioning.
- Please encourage attractive meaningful corridor bulletin boards. Also, can the lighting be improved? It leaves a strong impression when teaching is visible in every corner of the school. I am discussing this with custodians as well.

Sincerely,

Carmen Fariña
Community Superintendent

FIGURE 2.3

written by a superintendent to the principal of a struggling middle school at the beginning of the year after an initial conversation.

8. Build on this beginning conversation in subsequent miniconversations and interactions during the year. Elaborate on previously discussed matters and bring up new ones; compliment good work and progress toward stated goals; recommend readings; offer opportunities to join committees, think tanks, study groups, and networks. Take notes on these interactions on dated index cards that

you keep in the teacher's informal file. (Figures 2.4a and b are a series of these kinds of notes.)

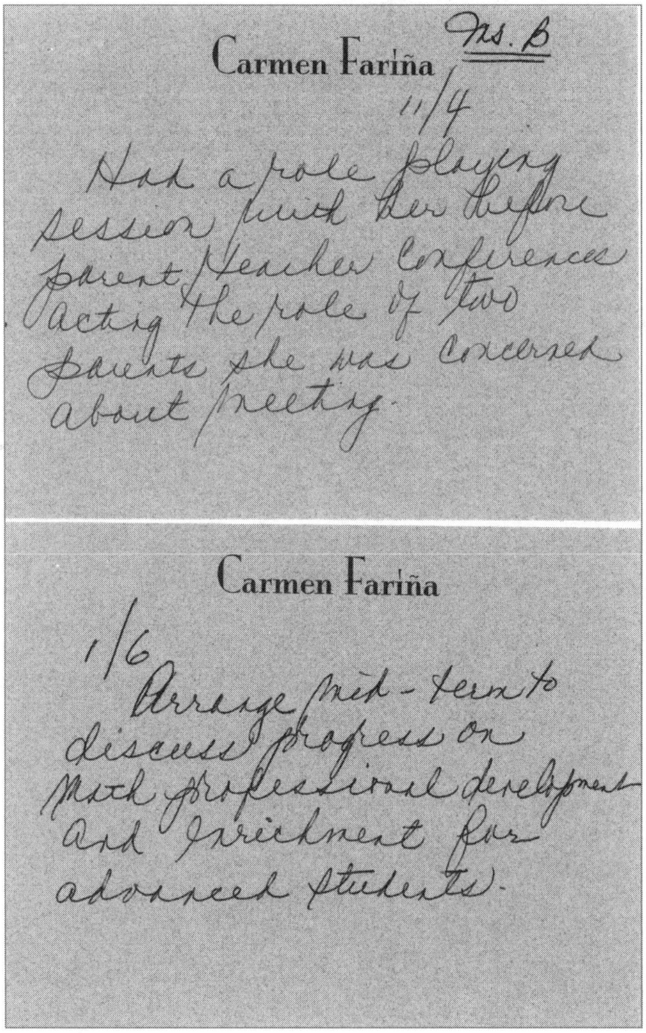
Carmen Fariña
Ms. B
11/4
Had a role playing session with her before parent teacher conferences. Acting the role of two parents she was concerned about meeting.

Carmen Fariña
1/6
Arrange mid-term to discuss progress on math professional development and enrichment for advanced students.

FIGURE 2.4a

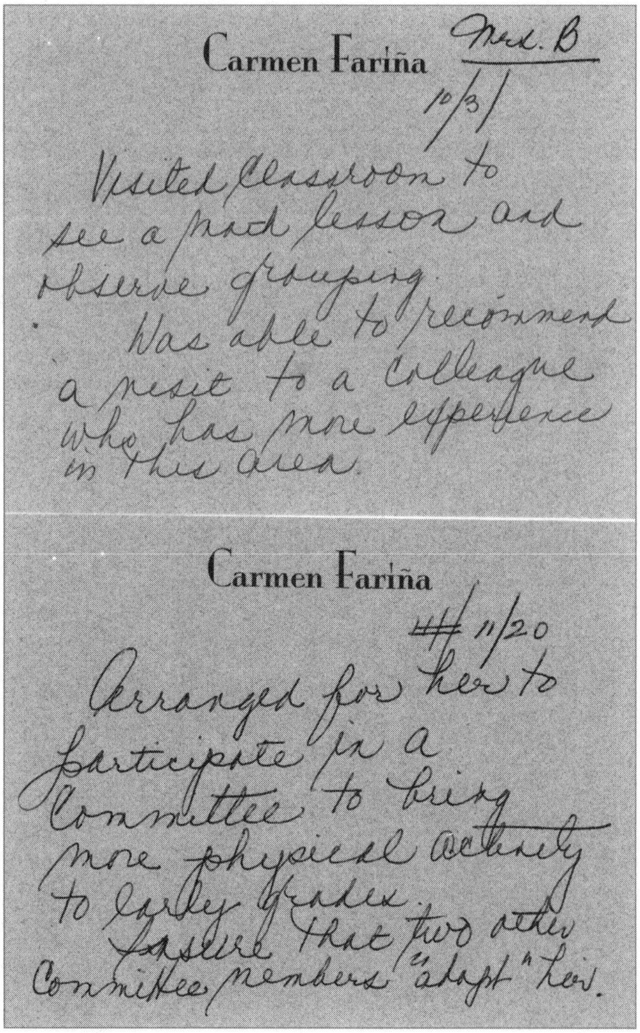
Carmen Fariña
Mrs. B
10/31
Visited classroom to see a math lesson and observe grouping.
Was able to recommend a visit to a colleague who has more experience in this area.

Carmen Fariña
11/20
Arranged for her to participate in a committee to bring more physical activity to early grades.
Ensure that two other committee members "adopt" her.

FIGURE 2.4b

9. Institute structural changes based on the conversations you have had with your staff. For example, provide common planning time for a group of teachers who have requested it, extend the existing lunch hour to give teachers more time to prepare for their afternoon classes, establish team-teaching classrooms for teachers who are feeling isolated, emphasize heterogeneous grouping, adjust the teaching schedule of a staff member who is caring for aging parents, give a teacher time off from the classroom in order to attend a professional development seminar, or ask a talented teacher to give demonstration lessons.

10. Demonstrate your willingness to change your personal demeanor. For example, if a number of staff members have commented that you look too serious, make a conscious effort to smile more.

11. Conduct another in-depth conversation (followed by another letter) at the end of the year. Make comparisons with the beginning letter to celebrate growth. Outline a plan for continued improvement. (Figure 2.5 is the end-of-year letter written to the principal who received the letter in Figure 2.3. Figure 2.6 is the principal's personal end-of-year reflection.)

I know that this year has been a challenging one in many respects. Although no leader wants to be involved in a SURR reform project, I believe that this will provide you with the leverage to continue your work in restructuring the school so that all members of your school community will be actively engaged in the process.

In reviewing your goals and objectives, as well as my visits to your school, it is clear that you have spent a considerable amount of time on creating a positive climate and an atmosphere of collegiality throughout your building. Your belief that when "human talent is nurtured, all will prosper" is a philosophy that moves us in the right direction. However, there are two qualities that are of paramount importance if schools are to work. One is the ability to communicate with all constituencies at all times. In your particular case, it means having weekly notes that let the staff know what is happening in your school for that week. It also means that cabinet meetings have an agenda with follow-up responsibilities assigned to members of the cabinet, as well as focused grade meetings with clearly defined goals and responsibilities. Communication within your own cabinet must be clear, and you must also engage them in decision-making as well as following your agendas. Communication also extends to parents in letting them know what is happening in the school, as well as how they might help in a specific way.

Another important quality that is crucial to a school's success is a strong leader that is visible at all times, and that can delegate responsibilities to a wide range of personnel. The leader must be focused and set parameters for all constituents to follow. Walking the building on a regular basis on your own, as well as with your support team, allows you to plan school-wide initiatives and to make decisions that all can follow through on.

You are now working on the school's Comprehensive Educational Plan. You have met with the entire staff to assess the school's needs and to highlight areas that will enhance the success of students. In addition, you have formed committees representing each of the academic content areas. There is a guidance committee including special education and ELL and a redesign team to work on the planning and development of "houses." This process will foster a strong community within your school so that the various facets of redesign will evolve.

The following are some areas that you should focus on:

- It is crucial that this year be spent in developing a very visible "house" structure where roles are clearly defined and the leaders of these houses are both responsible and accountable.

- I am requesting work restructuring to assist in the areas of social studies and ESL. You might want to consider an immersion class for your ESL students.

- An emphasis on enrichment practices in each of your houses would also increase community interest in your school, and I suggest that you consider accelerated academic subjects as well as art programs for talented students. These can be given as part of the A. M. or P. M. extended day periods.

- As you have indicated, curriculum and professional development are of major importance as you plan for next year and the years to come. I would suggest that you select a number of teachers to visit some schools and observe the philosophy and curriculum practices in these schools so that you can align curriculum to ensure a seamless transition between your school and the feeder schools' students you wish to attract. Your goals and objectives state clearly that you are looking for child-centered classrooms, and that you understand that appropriate materials are important. Be sure that your money is spent quickly so that teachers have everything they need to provide appropriate instruction. I also believe that your arts emphasis needs to be continued and if there is any way we can assist you, by all means let us know.

- Since administration is often a lonely job, I would encourage you to become involved in various forms of professional development with other principals. I believe your involvement with other middle school principals in study groups will be helpful. In addition, please look at the existing elementary school clusters, and if there is one you are particularly interested in joining for next year, let me know before we make assignments for next year's groups. In addition, the paraprofessionals should be encouraged to attend all district training. I will be sending a notice to this effect soon.

As you know, I have a deep affection for and believe in the mission of the school, I know that you feel the same. Now we have to create a buzz in the community that the school's determined to make improvements in the overall performance of students, especially in regard to test scores and rigorous classroom instruction. I know that your staff, cabinet, P. T. A. and leadership team are working on the redesign of the school with a clear vision for overall school improvement. I want to reassure you that the district is committed to working with the entire school community to make this the first school of choice in this district, and you have our continuous support. I look forward to working with you as you lead the school forward.

Yours truly,

Carmen Fariña
Community Superintendent

FIGURE 2.5

End of Year Visit: Reflective Questions

- **If your school has a theme, how is it evident?**

  We hope to display around the school student work that will reflect our themes.

- **Three priorities for next year?**

  1) <u>Literacy</u> – The focus will be on reading – To provide students with individual attention in reading through guided reading and reading conferences; To develop appropriate reading assessment tools; To focus intensively on reading and writing strategies (and less on genres); To teach all components of literacy concurrently (reading, writing and word and language study).

  2) <u>Math</u> – We must continue supporting our math teachers through staff development. Our new math teachers (and we have many) need to know how to implement the Math In Context program. They also need workshops on how to address the needs of the Level 1 students. We must also review texts and materials that will support our math program. Discussion between administrators and math teachers must include data.

  3) <u>Theme Houses</u> – Develop units of study for the theme houses. Curriculum must be distinct for each grade.

- **What planning will you do to effect change?**

  1) <u>Literacy</u> – Common preps for literacy teachers to meet at least once a month (i.e. looking at student work, language development); Train teachers in reading assessment ; incorporate guiding reading into the reading program; train one literacy teacher in reading recovery and modify it to meet middle school struggling readers; Study groups focusing on reading comprehension (i.e. <u>Mosaic of Thought</u>): One period a week devoted to word development; Evaluate the after school literacy program.

  2) <u>Math</u> – Meetings focusing on data analysis, teaching strategies to address Level 1 students, materials needed to support math program; Evaluate the after school math program.

  3) <u>Theme Houses</u> – Have teachers create units of study that are interdisciplinary and will support the literacy and math programs; Have teachers visit CBOs or other schools with themes to replicate best practices; Have a mid year assessment of houses.

- **What is your biggest concern(s)?**

  My biggest concern is improving our math scores. The majority of our math teachers are inexperienced and many of our students are on Level 1 in math.

- **What are you doing to address the concern(s)?**

  I will have an Assistant Principal who will be responsible for math. The A.P. and staff developer will work closely to develop the teaching practices of our math teachers in the area of planning and looking at student work. I find that teachers lack the ability of long and short term planning. They also need assistance in looking at student work to drive instruction. Data analysis is another crucial area that we need to investigate. We also need to look at our after school math program to see if it is meeting the needs of our AIS students. We will also have 7 periods of math for all our classes.

- **What help can the district provide?**

  We need a full-time math staff developer. We can make substantial progress if we have the full time support of a staff developer. We need to continue workshops in Math In Context and workshops that will introduce teachers to other programs that can support our balanced math program.

- **Who are the teachers who are in need of significant support?**

  My math teachers are in need of support for lack of experience.

- **What have you done?**

  We have done the following:
  >Held after school workshops and study groups in problem solving, computations, test preparation.
  >Attended Math In Context workshops
  >Met with contracted staff developer

- **How and what do you do to build leadership capacity?**

  I tried to involve as many staff members as possible in committee work and they are encouraged to chair the various committees. Implementation of teacher suggestions is also very crucial. When teachers observe that their ideas become reality, they are more incline to actively participate in decision making.

FIGURE 2.6

Avoiding Common Pitfalls

Successful conversations with the members of the school community who are most eager to participate create a positive buzz. Others will be more willing to talk with you after noticing this enthusiasm, and future conversations will be more meaningful. Keeping the conversations voluntary makes community members trust the process; they will be more willing to be honest. Mandating conversations negates their basic premise as a tool for accountable talk and shared responsibility.

You will get the most from these one-to-one conversations if you are willing to be vulnerable, if you take your own learning seriously, and if you make policy changes and construct new knowledge based on what you hear. Many leaders find it a challenge to spend more time listening than speaking; taking notes may help you focus on what your staff member is saying. Modeling active listening strategies conveys your willingness to seek input and thereby ensures support for your vision.

Where the conversations take place is extremely important. You need to guarantee uninterrupted privacy, and you should hold all conversations in the same place so there is no perception of favoritism.

Conversations are most productive when the purpose and structure are clearly and concisely communicated ahead of time. Distribute, in writing, the key questions that will guide the conversation, your specific expectations for the school community, and the outcomes you anticipate. This framework will anchor each conversation and, more important, foster connections between them. Directionless conversations invite distrust; staff members may feel they are being singled out or that what they say will be used against them.

Receiving continued honest feedback from your staff requires that you reflect on your own behavior and assumptions and make changes based on what they tell you. Leaders who fail to act on the information they receive in a timely fashion send the message that the conversations are a one-way street and do not lead to school reform.

Leaders should not allow members of the community to speak negatively about predecessors or other personnel or take the low road to gossip, which will undermine intellectual discourse, and subvert the establishment of trusting relationships. Never use confidential information in a negative or punitive manner.

After each conversation, you need to research and reflect on what the staff member said. Put the information into a broader context (the role of each participant in the community and the overall response of other members) before deciding on appropriate next steps. Conversations should challenge your thinking, but you shouldn't respond impulsively to a single person's comments. Becoming defensive or shutting down when you hear negative feedback or opinions that differ from your preconceived notions about what is happening in the community may be a natural response, but it will not demonstrate the emotional intelligence you need to model.

You need to give every member of the community equal time; all members have a right to have their opinions respectfully heard and their requests for support valued. You cannot meet only with a select group. However, it is important to learn how to deal with naysayers without dissipating your own energy or becoming overwhelmed by negative feedback.

Promises you and the staff member make during these conversations must be honored. If you promise timely feedback, provide it. Broken agreements destroy trust and prevent buy-in and confidence.

Evaluating Success

To determine whether one-to-one conversations are well established throughout the community, promote positive relationships, and are a vehicle for change, look for the following evidence:

- Do the adult-to-adult conversations yield important information that assists in improving student achievement?
- Do teachers recognize the power of accountable conversations in their own learning and therefore provide time and opportunity for their students to articulate their learning, define their goals, and evaluate their progress? Are teachers engaging in private conversations with students in order to discover their strengths and needs?
- Do students demonstrate an increased ability and confidence in talking accountably in all subject areas? Do their conversations enhance critical thinking? Can they engage in deep and thoughtful conversations with their peers and adults in a variety of genres and for a variety of purposes?
- Do students feel their voices are heard and that their thinking is valued in the academic and social life of the school? Do school classrooms demonstrate that student-to-student conversations are an important strategy for learning? Are students given opportunities to provide input into the way schools are run?
- Is the community focusing less on individual self-interest and more on community needs as a whole? Are organizational changes made with the community's buy-in and ownership?
- Do conversations provide sufficient information to develop a differentiated approach to professional development? Are teachers or principals empowered to design and conduct their own action plans for learning? Are conversations leading to the recognition and development of future leaders?
- Are talking and listening valued, modeled, and used consistently in the life of the school or district? Do conversations promote accountable talk and model the effectiveness of active listening? Is there more quality talk between teacher and teacher, teacher and student, teacher and parents, and student and student?
- Are conversations being expanded beyond the teacher community to include other stakeholders such as parent leaders, politicians, and the district's budgeting office? Are stakeholders more willing and able to use conversation as a tool for change and a means for resolving conflicts? Is there a predictable and consistent structure by which the community can be heard, understood, and responded to so that confrontations and controversies are minimized?

- Is there a better use of people, time, support personnel, and materials? Is the *we* voice used in dealing with difficult issues like revising school programming and policy, moving from homogeneous to heterogeneous grouping, instituting multitiered professional development, and instituting support for at-risk and high-achieving students?
- Are community members willing to share administrative responsibilities and take on the role of teacher leaders?
- Is information about interpersonal relationships and informal social networks being used to create collaborative communities and move members to independence? Do conversations endure over time, even beyond the tenure of the leader who instituted the practice?

Implement the Book-of-the-Month Structure

Dear Reader,

Books have always defined who we are as people and as educators. Even as beginning teachers, we set up libraries matched to the abilities and interests of the readers in our classrooms. We encouraged our students to choose their own books during daily independent reading, and conversations about the books took place with partners, in small groups, and as a class. Our commitment to this approach was reaffirmed by the growth we saw in our students' ability to read and converse and the strong bonds that formed over shared books.

Visitors were amazed by our students' seriousness of purpose and the deep connections the students made between the books they read and their own lives, and they were surprised by the variety of titles we offered our students at a time when paperbacks were just beginning to become popular and basal readers were the norm. Spending hours at the local bookstore exploring new titles and creating long lists of recommended books became a way of life. In short, we fell in love with books, and sharing our favorites gave us the opportunity to have enriching conversations about a book's message, its characters and ideas, and the impact it had on our own lives. Books connected us to authors, to each other, and to the community in ways that were unexpected and lasting.

This knowledge of books and our love of sharing them proved invaluable as we took on different positions in education. As staff developers, we brought cartons of our favorite books to share with teachers and leaders, often being the first to introduce the newest picture books to them. As building and district leaders, we knew that books were a vehicle for conveying important messages through rich and beautiful language, strong moral themes, and a rhythm and timbre that bonded the community. We were constantly surprised by the transformational experience of bringing picture books to an adult audience through read-alouds and conversations. Although many middle and high school principals and teachers were uncomfortable about and even resistant to being read to from children's books, as they were drawn in by the language and the messages of the authors and invited to turn and talk, they began to recognize the power of this experience for themselves and for their students. As these adults became comfortable with picture books as a leadership tool, we watched their eagerness and commitment to share these books grow.

We use picture books because although they may appear quite simple, the texts and the messages they convey are complex, and they can be read aloud to small groups (or large groups, for that matter) in a short time. This makes them extremely effective for faculty conferences and grade-level and parent meetings. Choosing which particular picture book to share is also important—and difficult—since the book has to fill a variety of needs and at the same time extend the community's conversation. The turn-and-talk conversations that follow the read-alouds invite participants to connect to the text and at the same time reflect on their own experiences. We found that giving one carefully selected picture book as a present inspired the community and emphasized the value we placed on leaders knowing books well. The books we gave them were well-crafted vehicles for beginning conversations with their communities. And thus our book-of-the-month structure was born.

The lasting impact of well-written prose and the enduring message it leaves behind, to be reread and reflected on over time, led us to create the book-of-the-month cover letter, a natural way to identify ourselves and the values we hold most dear. A personal and passionate letter inviting participation and feedback is perhaps the most important tool for beginning an honest and nonjudgmental dialogue. Distributing a book with an accompanying letter deepens the conversation, invites readers' personal responses to the experience of reading the book, and demonstrates the inherent reading-writing connection. Our book-of-the-month letters explain the reason we chose the book, share our personal connection, and model the way leaders use literacy to bond to the community in a personal as well as professional way. The letters often refer to important or controversial events happening in the community, highlight the mood, and suggest next steps. They build momentum for change; improve morale; introduce issues related to equity, higher expectations for academic performance, and improved student behavior; and remind everyone about the focus of the curriculum.

With each monthly book and personal letter principals received, we noticed an increased excitement, an eagerness to develop a library of books in their offices to share with their communities. We were delighted when many began recommending books to us for the next month!

This public practice focused our work, one issue at a time, and also built a common language that was consistent and predictable. The ongoing rereadings and conversations, presentations at parent meetings, and bulletin board displays of responses began to create a unified community. As principals visited classrooms, they were able to engage students in conversations about the books, thereby deepening their personal connections with both students and teachers.

The book of the month has become a way of life for many communities in New York City and schools across the country. Like Oprah's book club, the structure has developed a life of its own and has grown in many and varied directions. Leaders point to book of the month as one practice that has allowed them to infuse literacy into the life of their schools, to make organizational change, to motivate teachers, and to build personal and trusting relationships. Leaders who are working diligently to build their communities around reading and writing ask us to suggest appropriate titles. But we are most proud of those leaders who have made this structure their own and who continue to share their latest choices and letters with other leaders and with us.

We look forward to hearing from you, our reader, as you share with us the books that have made a difference in your community.

—Carmen and Laura

Why Implement the Book of the Month?

When we became the superintendent and deputy superintendent of a school district, it seemed natural to use the book of the month and the accompanying cover letter to introduce ourselves to our new community. We chose *I Love You Like Crazy Cakes*, by Rose Lewis, because it conveyed our appreciation for the time and commitment of our leaders to the students they served, it reinforced literacy as our top priority, and it communicated our commitment to humane and nurturing leadership. Many principals shared our letter (shown in Figure 3.1) with their teachers to highlight the values and visions of our leadership and align their mission with ours.

Dear Colleagues,

We have finally taken a deep breath and are beginning to understand the enormity of the responsibilities we have undertaken in our new roles. The past few weeks would have been overwhelming if it weren't for your support, encouragement, and informative conversations. Our conversations with you gave us tremendous insights into your particular needs. We anticipate addressing most of your priorities but ask for more time on the pressing issues of math consistency, teacher recruitment, and middle school restructuring.

We are going to share a book with you each month to underscore our commitment to literacy—and just because we love books! We have selected this first one carefully: its beautiful language and specific message are so relevant to this time and place. Several phrases from the book have special resonance:

I promise to take good care of you.

I was so excited and nervous . . .

How did someone make this perfect match a world away . . .

It was the end of one amazing journey and the beginning of another . . .

Then you smiled as if to say, "I'm home."

These phrases express some of our feelings, and we hope you will interpret this book for your community in your own way. Let's celebrate the many ways we love and value our own communities and make our own promises to one another.

—Carmen and Laura

FIGURE 3.1

In our personal lives we often read books that mirror our life experiences, introduce new ideas, let us lose ourselves in another time and place, and reaffirm our values and beliefs. The text of these books and the author's message stay with us and affect our daily lives. However, the reading experience is not complete until we discuss a book with another reader whose point of view expands our own. We derive new insights from these talks.

In every community, there are serious issues that leaders recognize and struggle to address in nonconfrontational and healing ways. The right book can help the community see its problems in a safe and nonthreatening way, neutralize delicate issues, and ignite conversations that will uncover productive solutions.

Chrysanthemum, by Kevin Henkes, is a book we have used in every professional role we have undertaken—beginning with our first faculty conference at PS 6—to demonstrate that we need to be aware of and sensitive to the diverse populations in our schools and how important it is to acknowledge the individual identities that make up our communities. The discussions that resulted allowed us to get an important message across about honoring a child's heritage in a personal and meaningful way while demonstrating how literacy can help us confront difficult challenges and unite around common solutions. Giving each teacher his own copy of the book, along with the letter shown in Figure 3.2, made our commitment to literacy very clear and indicated the priority we were giving to building a collaborative community that valued each student's unique contribution.

Dear Teachers,

As your new principal, I have searched for a book that, as we begin our relationship together, will clearly convey my educational philosophy of equity for all, especially those students from diverse backgrounds who come to us speaking another language.

Chrysanthemum is just that book! It succinctly makes the point that most students come to school ready to learn, eager to participate, and anxious about whether they will belong and succeed. Just one negative comment can convince a child that he or she is not welcomed, turning that child off to school.

By reading this book aloud during the first week of school, you will encourage children to articulate their fears about the school year ahead. Children may express these fears by talking about them with a partner, drawing a picture, or writing a letter to you. Classmates will be reminded of one another's vulnerability, especially in new situations, and be comforted by the support their peers can provide.

For you as teachers, *Chrysanthemum* speaks to the power you have over your students and how necessary it is to use that power in nurturing and supportive ways. A teacher can make all of the difference in whether or not children continue to feel positively about school, continue to feel part of the community around them.

Please read, display, and make this book and its message integral parts of your classroom work.

To all the Delphinium Twinkles of PS 6, have a successful school year!

—Carmen

FIGURE 3.2

Books are the presents teachers and parents give to establish the habit of reading and the joy of discovery. Even a very young child who practices turning the pages of a board book and interacting with the pictures is beginning to establish that habit, which we believe is essential for every literate person. A book like *Goodnight Moon*, by Margaret Wise Brown, is a favorite of new parents because it celebrates the close connection reading together affords. They remember their parents reading the book to them and want to continue the tradition.

Distributing a book a month invites the practice of reading aloud to adults in a safe and supportive setting, then inviting open-ended conversations between partners and in small groups. This lets colleagues build trusting relationships with books at the center. It also lays the foundation for deeper conversations about academic and structural goals. The letter that accompanies the book reaffirms the particular reason it was chosen and sets out the follow-up actions you intend. Often it also highlights the beauty of the language and the power of the author's message. The personal and affirming voice of the letter assures the reader that she is a valued and trusted member of the community and invites her to expand this experience within her own community.

Principals make tough decisions about how best to use the limited funds at their disposal. Leaders who choose to use these precious resources to buy a book of the month for their communities send a clear message that there is power in literacy and invite teachers to follow their lead.

Literacy leaders who know how to select just-right books to read aloud to their communities model the power and value of books as a vehicle for engaging a community in interactive conversations. When we carry books around with us and give them to the people we work with, we demonstrate our values and our priorities. The letters we write also demonstrate our belief in the power of a leader's personal voice to move the community in collaborative and unexpected directions. A leader who takes the time to find a book that meets the community where it is and invites it on a journey of possibilities values literacy as a motivating force. The letter in Figure 3.3 introduces a group of texts we put together featuring Emily Dickinson: *Poetry for Young People: Emily Dickinson*, edited by Frances Schoonmaker Bolin; "Kid's Poems," by Kevin Hill, a professional article for teachers on how to immerse students in poetry; and a wonderful biography, *Emily*, by Barbara Cooney. This collection gives an in-depth view of literacy through a variety of genres and provides the community with a wealth of resources to make the study of poetry accessible and exciting.

Book of the Month is an agent for change. *The Three Questions*, by John Muth (2002), works well in connection with organizational change. The community can reflect on the questions raised in the book: "When is the best time to do things? Who is the most important one? What is the right thing to do?" (3). The clear connection between these focused questions and the decisions about the life of a school is revealed during empowered conversations that continue over time and lead to a sense of urgency and the commitment to collaboration as a vehicle for meeting both the needs of the individual and the school's goals.

By reading aloud books that serve as agents for change, you encourage teachers to do the same with their students when facing challenging classroom behavior. Inviting audience participation, especially when discussing controversial

---

September 25

Dear Colleagues,

'There is no frigate like a Book to take us Lands away
nor any Coursers like a Page
of prancing poetry –

How well I remember hearing this poem for the first time and really connecting to Emily Dickinson. In the days when there were no paperbacks or television (yes, I'm that old!), books were the only way to travel. I also remember having Emily Dickinson as our grade poet and having to memorize many of her poems. How much more meaningful her poems would have been to me if I had known some of her personal history. Certainly, her poetry reflects her personality and her insecurities. Her personal history gives us insight into her writing and demonstrates how poetry allows even the shyest person to express themselves.

In the article Kids' Poems *Kevin Hill comments,* **"I could actually hear individual student voices. Even without the child's name on the paper, I would often know who wrote the poem."** This is also an excellent way to create student ownership over their environment and make our classrooms resonant with student voices for Parent/Teacher Conferences.

In Barbara Cooney's biography there is a wonderful phrase "so many things are MYSTERY." In each of our classrooms mysteries unfold each day and also like in this book what we do as educators are gifts we give to our students.

"Hide this away, as I will hide your gift to me. Perhaps in time they both will bloom."

How wonderful to anticipate that our labors in literacy will bloom in myriad of ways.

Sincerely,

Carmen Fariña
Community Superintendent

CF:mh

FIGURE 3.3 *Book-of-the-Month Letter—Poetry Collection*

issues, demonstrates your willingness to hear honest feedback and your commitment to engaging the community in finding solutions. Honoring differences in opinion demonstrates the importance of leading with questions and respecting individual members of the community. Issues like the use of time, the roles and responsibilities of various members of the community, and the focus on confronting difficult issues and establishing essential school priorities are all discussed in the letter presented in Figure 3.4.

Leaders who understand the challenges of student behavior look for books that address the specific behavior problems in their school and make these books part of schoolwide read-alouds, conversations, and action plans. Encouraging students to respond to these books in any number of ways—letters to the principal, sticky notes on bulletin boards, letters to other students—allows them to reflect more deeply about their own behavior and take responsibility to affect the school culture in a positive way.

Choosing books with specific moral messages conveys your expectation that the community will work on those specific issues over a period of time. Common

April 4

Dear Colleagues,

As we gather together to share our expertise and understanding about Creative Scheduling, the ritual of the Book of the Month unites us in our mission to build a collaborative learning community. The Three Questions, based on a story by Leo Tolstoy, written and illustrated by Jon J Muth, tells the story of a young boy searching for answers to 3 important questions: When is the best time to do things? Who is the most important one? What is the right thing to do? Nikolai wants to be a good person but is unsure of the best way to do that and embarks on a journey to find the answers to his essential questions. He begins by seeking the answers from his friends, the heron, the monkey and the dog but soon realizes that although he loved them, their answers didn't seem quite right for him. He finds it necessary to seek the wise counsel of the turtle, Leo, who has lived a long time and surely will know the answers he is seeking. As Nikolai and Leo begin their conversation, a storm comes up and a cry for help is heard. Without thinking, the young boy immediately runs to rescue an injured panda and her baby. The next morning the boy wakes up feeling a great sense of peace within himself and realizes that his questions have indeed been answered. Leo, the wise one, says:

"Remember then that there is only one important time, and that time is now. The most important one is always the one you are with. And the most important thing is to do good for the one who is standing at your side. For these, my dear boy, are the answers to what is most important in this world. This is why we are here."

As the Assistant Principal of your school community, you are the most important one and every day in your school you have the opportunity to support your teachers and students in learning how to use time well and make the most of every moment. Scheduling your school for maximum instructional time using flexible and creative models will insure that the talents and passions of the students and adults alike are nurtured and supported. In sharing our passion and expertise with each other, we model the spirit of generosity that we want all educators to emulate. Through our actions, we have the power to inspire, to connect members of the community with each other and to unite them around a shared mission. The more we work together to solve the problems before us, the stronger our community will grow. I want to thank you for always being the ones who take responsibility for making the system work for our students and their teachers, for your willingness to take on this essential job, and for your hard work in doing whatever is necessary to guarantee the success of our instructional essential programs this year and into the future.

Sincerely yours,

Carmen Farina
Deputy Chancellor
for Teaching & Learning

FIGURE 3.4 *Book-of-the-Month Letter—Use of Time*

problems that can be addressed include bullying, gender equity, schoolyard and lunchroom behavior, discrimination, and name calling. We have addressed the issue of bullying by pairing the read-aloud *Hooway for Wodney Wat*, by Helen Lester, with the professional book *Why Is Everybody Always Picking on Me? A Guide for Handling Bullies*, by Terence Webster-Doyle. These books help teachers generate rich conversations with their students and together develop strategies for dealing with this very common issue. Carmen sent the letter in Figure 3.5 to the teachers in District 15. The letter in Figure 3.6, from the students in class 5–301, is an example of how they took ownership for finding solutions.

Dear Staff:

Welcome to the wonderful month of March!

As we deal with test mania citywide, it is so important to keep in mind how some of our students are feeling who anticipate defeat instead of success during their test taking days and spend a little of our own time thinking of everyone's positive features (as teachers, including our own) rather than on negative aspects that still cause everyone difficulties or anxieties.

The book of the month, HOOWAY FOR WODNEY WAT, is about someone who never seems to expect a compliment, an encouraging word or to be sought out as a friend or a even a successful human being/rat.

Rodney is a wonderful rat with a slight disability, one that never really goes away, but ultimately is seen in the context of his other strengths. Wouldn't it be wonderful if all of us were able to look, not only beyond other people's disabilities but our own and focus on everyone's strengths?

Every day children come into my office who have in some way been singled out as being different. In a school of close to 900, it is to be expected that "differentness" would be celebrated, highlighted and actually integrated into our every day life. As a staff we are truly unique and I know that when I need something done, as outrageous as that task might be, there is always someone in the building who has the necessary qualification. These qualifications stretch from computer skills to calligraphy, from driving to artistic talent. Obviously, and most importantly, disability is a relevant term and one that should be reinvented.

In this book there is also Camilla who is a bully and obviously a threat to all concerned. Since this is also a very relevant topic, I am enclosing chapter I of a book that is especially written to deal with this topic. I have purchased several books and if you wish to continue this discussion, please see me. I will be sending various chapters out over the next few weeks for continued classroom discussion.

HOOWAY........ came to me as a recommendation from several classroom teachers and also carries particular weight, since class 5-301 has written it's own message to accompany this book. I love it when you recommend books to me, so please continue to keep your eyes opened for new recommendations.

In closing, I have included bit of non-fiction about the king rat:

In the spirit of our "non-fiction" initiatives!

> Okay, it's not really a rat. But the capybara (say: *ka-pee-BAR-uh*) *is the world's most massive rodent.* At four feet long, two feet tall, and up to 180 pounds, this South American creature makes a rat look like a mouse. But it's harmless to people. A vegetarian, the capybara spends most of its time swimming in marshy water and eating grass. In fact, "capybara" means "master of the grass" in a Native American language.

FIGURE 3.5 *Book-of-the-Month Letter—Addressing Social Issues*

Leaders need to balance books that give strong moral messages and call the community to action with those that express thanks and appreciation for the hard work and commitment visible in small and large ways. The more specific these letters are in naming and affirming the people and actions, the more impact they will have. Most of us are hungry for recognition and long remember the compliments we receive, and leaders who devote their time and energy noticing the contributions of individuals model the value they place on recognizing intention, effort, and achievement. Thanksgiving, New Year's Day, and Valentine's Day

Dear School Community,

    The February book of the month is <u>Hooway For Wodney Wat</u> by Helen Lester. We loved the book for it's humor and the important lessons it teaches.

    One of the lessons we learned is to not tease someone just because they are different from you. Another is to think before you speak because what you say may hurt others feelings. The situation of teasing that occurred with Wodney and his classmates has happened at many schools. Kids all over are being bullied and teased because they are different. The bully in <u>Hooway For Wodney Wat</u> is Camilla Capybara, she is big, tough and smart. The attached picture shows that the capybara is indeed the largest animal in the rodent family.

    We hope you enjoy this book and discuss what you have learned with your classmates. As Wodney would say "Happy Weading!"

Love   Our Class

FIGURE 3.6 *Response of Students to Book of the Month*

are perfect opportunities to reenergize and recommit ourselves and inspire renewed purpose and focus in the community. *Thank You, Mr. Falker,* by Patricia Polacco, is an excellent way for principals to say thank you to their teachers, and Polacco's *Mr. Lincoln's Way* is a wonderful way for superintendents to say thank you to their principals. The letters in Figures 3.7 and 3.8 illustrate the power of showing appreciation and recognizing contributions.

As leaders initiate new curriculum or emphasize the importance of an existing but neglected academic subject, the book of the month can trigger conversations and increased focus. You may decide to choose two books—one fiction, one nonfiction—that highlight varying perspectives on the curriculum area in question and that can be used to motivate students and teachers to deepen their understanding and stimulate conversations.

Sharing books related to curriculum emphasizes the priority you place on weaving literacy into all academic subjects and using quality literature, in connection with a personal point of view, to deepen understanding. These books can help launch a new curricular area by being the focus of an all-day conference or retreat that sends all the members of the community back to their schools prepared and excited to begin the study. The letter in Figure 3.9, which accompanied *Leonardo: Beautiful Dreamer,* by Robert Byrd, was written as the middle schools in our community were about to implement a new inquiry-based science curriculum.

Dear Staff,

Thanksgiving is a time to count our blessings, and undoubtedly this year you have been my greatest blessing (after my family, of course).

In a year that has been full of anxiety and some unexpected stress, you have been constant in your concern, your hard work, and your striving for excellence. Therefore I searched for a Thanksgiving book of the month that celebrated who you are as a professional staff. You are *all* Mr. Falkers.

You see each child as an individual. You love reading. You acknowledge writing as a way of projecting ourselves into the future. You understand that reading is much more than teaching isolated skills, that it is truly the "honey" of our lives. And you are models for your students as readers and as writers in your own right and as caring, nurturing human beings.

You have all created exciting learning environments in your classrooms, and I anticipate that many years from now you will meet children who will remember the gifts you gave them and thank you for the influence you have had on their lives. Keep remembering Mr. Falker's words to a struggling reader:

> You poor baby. You think you're dumb don't you? How awful to be so lonely and afraid. You've fooled many, many good teachers. That took cunning and smartness and such, such bravery. . . . You are going to read. I promise you that. (Polacco 1998, 30)

Since you are such individuals and so perfect in your own way, please consider the inscription in this book, "You will forever be my hero," as a personal message from me to each of you. But an even more personal thank-you for the special contribution you make to our school community is included on the enclosed list. I would like you to know with what ease I was able to do that this year.

Have a very happy Thanksgiving.

—Carmen

FIGURE 3.7 *Book-of-the-Month Letter—Expressing Appreciation*

Dear Colleague,

Mr. Lincoln's Way tells the story of an idealized version of a principal's life. Wouldn't it be wonderful if we could miraculously convert all the Eugenes in our lives to students who then respected authority and lived happily ever after? In reality, we do believe in transformation, and know that we have the power to make a difference in many children's lives in our own school community.

I have been impressed as I visit your schools by how many of you know individual children by name and circumstance. I'm sure that you can share stories about miracles that have occurred in the lives of children you have touched.

As the New Year approaches, and we think of the heavy duties we all carry, it is still crucial that we remember Eugene's words, "Hey, you showed me the way out, Mr. Lincoln . . . I'll make you proud of me, Mr. Lincoln. I promise."

Let us consciously dedicate ourselves to getting to know the Eugenes in our buildings, and helping to make some aspect of their lives better.

I wish all of you the joys of the season and the special pleasures of vacation that only the hard work we do truly makes us appreciate.

Cordially,

Carmen Fariña
Community Superintendent

CF:rh

Mr. Lincoln's Way
Patricia Polacco

FIGURE 3.8 *Book-of-the-Month Letter—Recognizing Contributions*

Dear Colleagues,

We chose "Leonardo: Beautiful Dreamer" by Robert Byrd for the December Book of the Month because this extraordinary nonfiction picture book, filled with richly illustrated primary source-based details and historical information which describe Leonardo's life work, speaks to the power of curiosity and imagination. As we study best practices for our middle school students and join together to reflect on our mission to engage adolescent learners in meaningful real world investigations, the story of Leonardo da Vinci reminds us of the power of intellectual curiosity, the joy of reflective planning, and the amazing possibilities of nurturing the talents and passions of our middle school learners.

Five hundred years ago during the time of the Renaissance, a great thinker and dreamer asked questions, studied the way things worked and compared nature to all things. With complex powers of observation, intense investigations, and ambitious plans, he invented, created, and transformed reality. From insects to large mammals, from storm clouds to dark caves, from sculpture to painting, from architecture to weaponry, all aspects of the world around him consumed his energy as he struggled to understand exactly how things worked. Long before the age of machines and technology, he invented movable cranes, pulleys, axles, and the bicycle. He studied the heavens, believing that the study of mathematics could provide proof of the perfect balance in all creation. His relentless wondering, inquisitive focus and constant questioning filled volumes of notebooks: over 13,000 pages all written backward, from right to left. His life work provides a legacy of discovery, filling us with awe and endless questions and inviting us to use his life as a model to which to aspire. As Robert Byrd writes:

> *"To his students, Leonardo counseled respect for beauty, goodness, and truth. All life was interconnected, he felt. He championed the potential of even the humblest among us to question and create, and so to achieve the most beautiful of our dreams."*

As Local Instructional Superintendents, you have the opportunity to inspire and influence principals, teachers and students with the model this incredible mentor provides. We can look deeply into the eyes of our middle school students and see past the masks of indifference they sometimes wear to trigger their innate curiosity, nurture and support their passions and talents, and encourage their creations and dreams. We can model our own interests and questions and help create schools where the voices of students can be heard, we can empower their ability to take charge of the world they live in each day. We can help build communities where shared interests, common goals and the quest to discover together fill volumes of notebooks. Let us dedicate ourselves to this goal as we celebrate the holiday season and begin a New Year together.

Warm wishes for the holidays,

Carmen Fariña

FIGURE 3.9 *Book-of-the-Month Letter—Introducing Curriculum Initiatives*

Books can also be chosen to highlight important accomplishments, celebrate milestones, and remind the community of the values and ideals it embraces. The letters that accompany the books have lasting power: each becomes a kind of diary entry that can be revisited and reread. When the book of the month has become an established structure, its arrival is eagerly awaited; speculation is rampant about what the leader is thinking, who is being celebrated, and—most important—how the book can be used in the recipients' own communities.

The books of the month, along with their accompanying letters, document the journey the community is taking and the role the leader plays: the history of the relationship, the established priorities, the common values and shared language, the community's increased ability to confront and overcome challenges. We display all the covers of our books and letters in chronological order on the bulletin board outside our office. Visitors and members of the community can reflect on the themes we've emphasized and the progress we've made in moving toward a shared vision. The book-of-the-month letter in Figure 3.10 celebrates a three-year-long journey.

Dear Colleagues,

Almost three years ago, we began reading a shared text during each of our monthly meetings. One of our first books, *I Am Amazed*, by Jodi Hill, set us on the path of reflecting on, affirming, and celebrating the amazing gifts we knew each member of the community was eager to bring to our teaching and learning mission.

Looking back on our time together, we celebrate each of you for contributing to the amazing journey of transformation, shared purpose, and collaborative learning. We feel it fitting, as we end our relationship with you, to close the year with another book by Jodi Hill, *I Believe*, which captures the essence of the leap of faith we take each day as we believe in ourselves, in one another, and in our community and the exciting possibilities of the undiscovered gifts of the days ahead. The book begins with these lines:

> *It isn't that something comes along and gives*
> *You a reason to get out*
> *Of bed . . .*
> *I believe you have to get out of bed and*
> *Go find*
> *That reason—every day.*

We find reason in the crucial work we do every day to support our schools in moving from good to great, to support our colleagues in solving problems and overcoming challenges, and to find the promise in the eyes of our students. Our work is sometimes frustrating, sometimes overwhelming, but always compelling and essential. The children of the city of New York are our reason to renew our dedication and commitment and to reaffirm our belief in the gift of public education—its ability to provide a better tomorrow for the next generation.

Our time with you has convinced us that working together, we can ensure that our dreams for our children become a reality. You have taught us that collaboration can transform an organization into a community that brings joy and fulfillment to every member. We want you to always remember Jodi's final lines:

> *And just so you know*
> *That some magic is real . . .*
> *Thank you for believing in us . . .*
> *And please believe us*
> *When we tell you that*
> *We believe in you.*

—Carmen and Laura

FIGURE 3.10

Getting Started: Step by Step

1. Gather background information:

   ◦ Have one-to-one conversations to become familiar with the academic, social, and emotional needs of the community and get a perspective on the history of the organization.

   ◦ Become knowledgeable about picture books by ordering subscriptions to the American Language Association's *Book Links*, *Horn Book*, the National Council of Teachers of English's *Language Arts*, *New Advocate*, and *The New York Times Book Review* and visit bookstores to browse new titles.

   ◦ Enlist school librarians, teacher leaders, literacy coaches, or other qualified school personnel to help you preview books.

   ◦ Establish your top three academic and social priorities for the school year and begin to find appropriate books to highlight these priorities.

2. Look for books that:

   • contain powerful language, vivid images, rhythm, a distinctive voice

   • include lines that stand alone and convey a message meaningful to educators

   • are short enough to read in one session

   • have beautiful illustrations that convey message, setting, character

   • are easily adapted for classroom use

   • feature a compelling story, well-developed characters, an interesting plot, and an evident yet subtle message

   • are the work of trusted authors (Kevin Henkes, Eve Bunting, Judith Viorst, William Steig, and Tomie dePaola are just a few.)

   • can be read and reread

   • reflect the diversity of teachers, parents, and students in the school as well as the challenges and issues faced by students (Aliki, Walter Dean Myers, Jerry and Brian Pinkney, Georgia Heard, Patricia Polacco, Allen Say, Arthur Dorris, and Ed Young are a few authors who do this well.)

   • inspire, motivate, and connect readers to one another and to the text (Jodi Hills, Bernard Waber, Langston Hughes, Mem Fox, Barbara Cooney, and Jean Little are some authors who fit the bill.)

   • connect to enduring themes, for example:

     ◦ *Collaboration and community*: *Stone Soup*, by Jon Muth; *The Quilt Maker*, by Jeff Brumbeau; *Hey World, Here I Am*, by Jean Little

     ◦ *Celebrations*: *I'm in Charge of Celebrations*, by Byrd Baylor; *Believe* and *I Am Amazed*, by Jodi Hills; *Hooray for Diffendoofer Day*, by Dr. Seuss, with some help from Jack Prelutsky and Lane Smith; *Julius, the Baby of the World*, by Kevin Henkes

     ◦ *Resolving conflicts peacefully*: *Recess Queen*, by Alexis O'Neill and Laura Huliska-Beith; *When Sophie Gets Angry—Really, Really Angry*, by Molly Bang

- *Gender issues: Horace and Delores*, by James Howe
- *Dealing with the pressures of standardized tests: Testing Ms. Malarkey*, by Judy Finchler
- *Change and transformation: Verdi* and *Stellaluna*, by Jannell Cannon
- *Honoring individual differences: It's Okay to Be Different*, by Todd Parr
- *Overcoming obstacles: Wallace's List*, by Barbara Bottner and Gerald Kruglik
  - ◆ carry universal messages (like the retold folktales that are familiar to most audiences)

3. Consider using the same book to begin and end the school year, thus allowing you to assess the year's growth by raising an issue in September to set goals and then revisiting them in June to assess progress and reflect on steps taken. (Some possible titles are *Ms. Rumphius*, by Barbara Cooney; *Courage*, by Bernard Waber; *The Brand New Kid*, by Katie Couric; *Wilma Unlimited*, by Kathleen Kroll; and *The Giving Tree*, by Shel Silverstein.)

4. Become familiar with how to write a powerful book-of-the-month cover letter:

- ◆ Address the letter to your specific audience. Using the personal, colleague-to-colleague *we*, tell why you selected this book and how the writer's story is connected to needs of the community.
- ◆ Celebrate the beauty and richness of the book's language by highlighting significant lines and phrases.
- ◆ Refer to other books with the same message, authors, or focus. Connect the book to an article, poem, current events, or an adult or professional book.
- ◆ Highlight the relevant message and make an inspiring call to action.
- ◆ Invite reader response: emails, letters, phone calls, conversations.
- ◆ Encourage readers to use this book and letter for their own purposes with their own community.

5. Become familiar with book-of-the-month protocols:

- ◆ Distribute the books in a consistent and predictable way so that they are eagerly anticipated and become part of the life of the community. They should arrive at the same time each month.
- ◆ Use them in connection with faculty conferences, principal meetings, retreats—any regular occasion in which the whole community gathers together.
- ◆ Display a copy of the book and the accompanying letter in a prominent place near your office. Include community members' comments as appropriate.

6. Read the book to your intended audience:

- Practice many times beforehand. Work on fluency, pronunciation, pauses, and eye contact.
- Think about how you will introduce the book and its author. Subtly refer to a community issue that prompted your choice, or tell how it is connected to your personal and professional story. The introduction should be brief, reveal a personal aspect of yourself in relation to the book, and make the listener eager to listen.
- Make sure everyone can hear you and see the pictures, especially if the group doesn't have a copy in front of them.
- Expand your reach by opening each parent meeting by reading the book of the month and encouraging parents to purchase the book to read at home with their children.

7. Plan for quality conversations:
   - Choose a setting in which audience members will be able to talk with one another immediately after the read aloud. Spaces with small tables are best; lecture halls are least desirable.
   - Allow enough time for the turn-and-talk conversations to be meaningful; participants should be able to both listen and speak.
   - Have some open-ended questions ready: *What personal meaning do you make from this book? How does this book connect to your present role? How might you share this book with teachers? students? parents? What language patterns linger in your mind?*
   - Walk around, eavesdropping on conversations. Expand the sense of shared meaning by inviting audience members to share their ideas and comments with the whole group.
   - In your closing remarks, quote especially relevant insights (thanking their originators by name) and transfer ownership to the members of the community.

8. Follow up:
   - Create a book-of-the-month bulletin board in a prominent place; include the book itself, your cover letter, and feedback from readers (teachers, students, and parents, as appropriate).
   - Chart the journey of the books of the month over time.
   - If you follow up in writing, invite a personal response. Don't require anyone to answer specific questions, respond to prompts, or fill in the blanks.
   - Continue to refer to the books when visiting classrooms and schools so they become part of the larger conversation.
   - Encourage members of the community to suggest titles of appropriate books. When someone's book is chosen, ask him to write the cover letter, read the book aloud, and collect and share responses.
   - Ask your local bookstore to display your books of the month and suggest it offer special discounts on them.

Avoiding Common Pitfalls

Choosing the right books—books that carry uplifting messages in line with your audience's needs—will engage the audience and demonstrate your passion. Choosing the wrong book—a book that is too long, too preachy, or poorly written—will derail the process. You need to choose books that reflect the needs of your community and match its readiness to connect to the message, characters, language, and meaning. If your audience is new to this experience or unfamiliar with the power of picture books, acknowledge their discomfort and explain why you have chosen to read this particular book aloud to them.

The power of the book of the month is the sheer joy of the reading experience, a reward in itself. Once the pleasure of connecting with others around a wonderful book is established and predictable, it will become an eagerly anticipated part of any community gathering. Be sure to ask audience members to extend and expand the experience by talking with the people seated near them about meanings and connections. Using the book as a skill-building tool or requiring fill-in-the-blank responses signals to the community that their time and choice of response are not respected or honored. Their pleasure will turn to dread.

Every book-of-the-month letter models the value you place on communicating effectively. A letter that has errors in spelling, punctuation, or grammar will undermine your effort to demonstrate the power of literacy. Always have someone with good writing skills proofread your letters.

Reread books that address sensitive and controversial issues several times before choosing them as books of the month. Remember that humor and a light touch go a long way in these situations. Always run books by a trusted colleague first. Mixing the security of familiar titles with the risk of new titles will keep the community engaged and excited about new discoveries.

After the book of the month is a well-established strategy, you will want to share the responsibility of choosing books and writing the letters with community members.

Evaluating Success

To verify that the book of the month has united the school community around literacy practices that promote and inspire continual school improvement, look for these kinds of evidence:

• Is the increased emphasis on read-alouds, independent reading, accountable conversations, and letter writing leading to more critical thinking and improved student achievement?

• Is there visible evidence of positive changes in student behavior? Are teachers changing to more student-centered and interactive practices? Is the community focusing on issues such as equity, gender, and community building?

• Are your values and beliefs evident in your selections? Are your daily actions predictable and aligned with your written and spoken messages?

- Are members of the community taking an active role as book advocates by visiting bookstores, reading book reviews, and subscribing to journals and magazines? Are they beginning to collect and display books in their classrooms or offices, talk about them during and after school, and share them with the community? Are classroom libraries growing? Is the principal's office a place to read and talk about books? Can principals demonstrate their increased knowledge of children's literature by recommending books for specific purposes to parents, students, and teachers? Are parents seeking guidance about books to purchase and sharing stories about the growing enthusiasm of their children as readers? Are the books being sold at book fairs and school bookstores of high quality? Has the community of readers expanded?

- Is the structure a vehicle for sharing books and continuing a dialogue within and across schools? Are principals and teachers beginning to create their own lists of books and share their cover letters with one another? Are books and letters exchanged so that everyone's libraries are enriched? Are books used to celebrate special occasions and benchmarks?

- Are the books being used to mobilize the community around problems and serious challenges? Do community members have the shared language and common purpose necessary to find collaborative solutions?

- Are book-of-the-month conversations inviting the unique response of all members of the community, especially those who have previously been silent?

- Are members of the community being affirmed and celebrated? Are teachers replicating this strategy with their students? Is the energy and focus in the school community moving from the top down and the bottom up? Is the flow constant?

- Has the enthusiasm for literacy extended to a wider audience such as school secretaries, lunchroom workers, and maintenance personnel? Is the community becoming convinced of your vision and values?

- Is the structure so embedded in the life of the community that others can replicate the practices? Will the practices continue when you are no longer part of the community?

Celebrate!

Dear Reader,

We were very fortunate to be guided at the beginning of our careers by principals who understood that we needed nurturing and affirmation. The feedback they provided was specific and timely—explicit recommendations for improvement that gave us energy to continue working and strengths to build on. We find it heartbreaking that talented people are leaving the education profession because they aren't receiving the personal acknowledgment they need. When we visit schools, one of the concerns teachers share with us is that that they feel little connection to their leaders, who seldom provide this kind of supportive feedback. Instead, teachers receive orders to carry out or are given a list of things they need to improve, usually without any appreciation for the things they are already doing well or any acknowledgment of their unique talents and strengths. Principals suffer the same lack of affirmation from *their* supervisors; most of the communication they receive is focused on meeting mandates and improving students' standardized test scores, with no recognition of their efforts or accomplishments.

The leaders we learned most from gave us written feedback that celebrated us both as people and as the educators we hoped to become. These personal communications motivated us to keep striving and kept us from becoming complacent. Their letters were benchmarks within the different phases of our lives and provided a balance between challenge and celebration. We still have many of these letters, vivid reminders of the mentors who took the time to notice our strengths, encourage our growth, and demonstrate the power of written compliments.

Timely feedback is a wonderful gift that everyone deserves, particularly feedback that affirms our character, beliefs, and professional expertise. Educators need individual recognition for their efforts, but they also need to feel part of a community. Being famous even for a little while raises the public worth of the individual, prompts conversation, and motivates improved performance. Compliments can be given orally and in writing, either privately or publicly, depending on the purpose and context. Although monetary rewards may also be involved, they are too often based on narrow criteria that do not reflect the collaborative values we want to instill. In some schools, the few teachers who become stars are afraid to take risks or share their good ideas for fear they'll lose their competitive edge. The other teachers see these few as the principal's pets and often resent them for the attention and praise they see as undeserved and unfair.

When leaders reward the taking of risks and sharing of ideas with compliments and celebrations, they model collaborative learning and bring out the best in every member of the staff. Principals who are celebrated by their superintendent will celebrate their teachers, who in turn will celebrate their students. A culture of celebration raises the energy of the community; what's more, community members can reread written compliments during difficult times when their energy and their spirits are low.

One story about the power of celebrations stands out for us in particular because it exemplifies the dramatic transformation possible when communities work together. In our new jobs as superintendent and deputy superintendent, we visited a large elementary school that was struggling. It had a large number of students, many of whom were English language learners; it had been included on the list of schools in the state needing improvement; and a strong union presence seemed to be encouraging complacency. The new principal was struggling to find her way around these problems. On our first visit, after she had somewhat apologetically shared the negatives she faced, we asked her to show us the classroom with the most promise. We happily discovered that the fourth-grade classroom she brought us to aligned with our goals. We celebrated the interactive learning environment with the students, complimented the teacher, and encouraged the principal to build on the strengths in this classroom by creating a corps of similarly minded teacher leaders who could study together, visit other schools, and begin to establish a collaborative school culture. We suggested that the principal write a letter thanking the teacher for her good work and talk with her about how she could share her expertise with the school community. The principal visibly relaxed: we had identified a strength she could build on and use as a model for other staff members. We told her honestly that the reorganization ahead would not be easy nor accomplished quickly but that we believed it could be achieved over time.

We also sent a thank-you letter to the staff highlighting the things that could be celebrated (see Figure 4.1). We deliberately used the *we* voice and tried to balance our honest feedback with encouragement and support.

Because of this letter, our school visits became less intimidating and more collaborative. We introduced the principal to a retired colleague who had run a school similar to hers and who was an expert in teaching English language learners. We also brought a literacy staff developer to the school to work with the teachers. Over the next three years the school changed its status; it was no longer a school in need of improvement.

Dear Colleagues,

Thank you for opening your classroom doors to us during our visit last week. As we walked through the building, we saw rich evidence of the pride you take in displaying student work and the steps you are taking to encourage the writing process. When we stopped by the parent room, parents shared their affection for the school and their appreciation for the work that all of you do each day. We were particularly impressed with the Spanish language lending library that is being set up in the parent room, which allows Spanish-speaking parents to demonstrate to their children their love of reading. We also noted the extensive after-school program to which many of you devote additional hours. We were heartened that several of you have joined the principal's breakfast study group and are reading Pauline Gibbons' *Learning to Learn in a Second Language* as a way to better help your students. We hope to join the group on an early-morning visit very soon.

Our focus this year is on interactive learning, and we were pleased to see such strong beginnings, especially in one fourth-grade classroom. We look forward to seeing many of you at our next professional development series, which will offer specific strategies for strengthening interactive learning, particularly in connection with English language learners. We also plan to support your professional development this year by encouraging intervisitations within your school and across the district. We know from experience how much can be learned from conversations with our peers.

We had several conversations with your principal about how we can support your effort to remove your school from the SINI list. We look forward to seeing more evidence of interactive learning, particularly student-generated writing, during our next visit. We know you will support one another in this area.

We wish you continued success in your very important work.

—Carmen and Laura

FIGURE 4.1 *Celebratory Letter*

Our stance was radically different from that of the previous supervisor, who had distributed lists of unsatisfactory ratings along with improvement checklists and threatened to place negative evaluations in teachers' files, while offering little specific support in turning the school around. His refusal to communicate directly with members of the staff and his punitive approach paralyzed people, sapped their energy, and made it impossible for them to think for themselves or take risks.

Celebrations of teachers and students are essential. They allow you to recognize progress, affirm your willingness to try new practices, build consistency, and unite the community around successes large and small. Celebrations also convey your expectation for constant improvement and invite everyone to join in that effort. They make successes public and allow the community to visit, compliment, reflect, and replicate practices that work. The energy created encourages the community to deepen its work, think positively, take more and more risks, and develop inquiring habits of mind.

Celebrations that involve everyone in the community level the playing field and encourage people to borrow ideas from one another and become invested in one another's successes. The letter in Figure 4.2 is one of the ways we invite our community to participate in celebrations.

—Carmen and Laura

Dear Colleagues,

Our book of the month, *I'm in Charge of Celebrations*, by Byrd Baylor, captures the joyful experience of celebration, an essential ingredient in building and sustaining energetic communities. In our determination to make sure students receive the best educational experience possible, our priority is to communicate clear expectations and reinforce best practices in teaching and learning. At the same time, we want to make sure we notice, affirm, and celebrate progress—the small steps along the way. Celebrations bring communities together around successes and reinforce positive and productive relationships. As Byrd Baylor writes:

Last year	I'm very choosy
I gave myself	Over what goes in that book.
One hundred and eight	It has to be something
Celebrations	I plan to remember
Besides the ones	The rest of my life
That they close schools for.	You can tell
I cannot get by	What's worth a celebration
With only a few.	Because your heart will POUND
I keep a notebook	And you'll feel like you're standing
And write down the date	On top of a mountain
And then I write about	And you'll catch your breath
The celebrations.	Like you were breathing a new kind of air.

I urge you to make celebrations a vital part of the life in your school community, creating opportunities to stop, reflect, and appreciate the gifts of each member of your team. Many schools use a hallway bulletin board to capture the best practices happening throughout the school. Inviting all members of the school community, including parents and students, to add their voice to this bulletin board makes real and visible the work that is happening in the school. This kind of community celebration reenergizes and reconnects community members to the positive forces within the school building. Writing celebrations and schoolwide events like reading pajama parties, student performances, award ceremonies, potluck dinners, and author visits are ways to share successes and generate excitement and energy.

Let's make a new year's resolution to keep a notebook and write down the celebrations that make our hearts POUND and let's agree to give ourselves 108 celebrations to remember the rest of our lives. Reading Baylor's book aloud to your staff will add more voices to the spirit of celebration, and sharing the book with students will make this truly a schoolwide effort.

Thank you for your willingness to be in charge of celebrations. I look forward to hearing about your special celebrations and sharing some of these celebrations with you in the coming year.

—Carmen

FIGURE 4.2

Why Do Celebrations Matter?

Celebrations are energizing and life affirming. Human beings are first and foremost social beings; they need to connect, be recognized, and feel affirmed in order to do their best work. Educators tend to live in a more isolated world than people in other professions. Classroom doors too often separate the adults from one another, and when adults do have the chance to meet, the time is often predetermined by others and comes with a structured agenda that seldom invites participation or a real sharing of personal qualities. The one place teachers can have spontaneous conversations is the teachers lunchroom, where the energy is too often negative, and complaining is the norm. Celebrations encourage teachers to widen their social network, interact with a variety of community members, dwell on what is working and why, and share and borrow ideas. Celebrations return the joy to the work we do.

Being a principal is the most difficult job in education. Principals must focus on instruction while being consumed by managerial tasks, often with too little support. Leaders who clearly demonstrate that people matter put the priority on the most important resource they have, the people in their community. Celebrations renew leaders' energy by forcing them to focus on successes, look for positive steps forward, and recognize achievements that go beyond numerical test scores.

Life in a school follows peaks and valleys and positioning celebrations throughout the year creates an even flow of positive energy and keeps morale and the inspiration for teaching and learning predictable and constant.

The long winter months can often cause people to feel weary. Planning a Valentine's celebration reminds everyone what matters most and restores the belief in the coming of spring. In New York City, Valentine's Day 2005 was We Celebrate Our School Day (see Figure 4.3).

Principals on the lookout for creative thinking, risk taking, and thoughtful and reflective practices are more likely to have a school with a positive buzz. These schools exude a palpable energy that can be felt the moment one enters the building. Teachers strive to do their best work, work with their colleagues well after 3 P.M., are excited about learning new practices, and invite others to join their community. Principals who spend time creating a culture of celebrations are more likely to retain staff—even in difficult schools with a history of rapid turnover.

Honoring milestones in the lives of the members of your community—major anniversaries of years of service, retirements, promotions—demonstrates your knowledge of them as people and the value you place on their personal contributions. Such public recognition affirms the life of each member, lays the groundwork for a smoother transition, and acknowledges the hard work of the community.

Celebrations encourage collaboration and best practice. When teachers work in a celebratory environment, they experience the joy of collaborating and are more willing to take on the role of teacher leader and future administrator. Teachers who are celebrated are more likely to share their practices with colleagues,

Dear Colleagues,

February 14, 2005, is We Celebrate Our School Day. While every school community can identify how best to do that, I want to suggest one activity that every school can undertake. Principals can dedicate a specific place in the school for everyone to post her or his own message of celebration. A bulletin board, a long sheet of paper on the main office door, a scroll in the front lobby—all are places suitable for personal expressions of appreciation like these:

- students lauding the teacher or guidance counselor who went above and beyond to help them

- parents acknowledging a person or activity in the school that helped them or their child

- staff members promoting one of their class activities or congratulating a principal or a colleague for her or his assistance or collaboration

- students thanking their parents for helping them to do better in school

- a principal talking about the dedication of the staff members

I look forward to hearing how each of you made your celebrations personal and appropriate for your community. Happy celebrating!

—Carmen

FIGURE 4.3 *We Celebrate Our School Day*

spend time recognizing the achievements of their students, and take risks to reflect and refine their teaching.

A school with a reputation for having a celebratory culture is more inviting to parents, teachers, and students alike. Visitors are eager to see for themselves what is happening, and principals and teachers are rewarded by positive feedback, career advancement, and the satisfaction of work well done.

Celebrations make your vision visible, spotlight steps along the way, and leave a lasting legacy of affirmation. We have always written letters to connect personally with school leaders, lift their spirits, and remind them that we understand their realities while keeping them focused on the work of teaching and learning. These letters communicate our unified voice and also help us maintain our visibility when we can't be physically present in every school. Carmen sent the letter in Figure 4.4 at a particularly low point during the year: Important tests during the spring term had just been administered and people were drained from working so hard. The letter gave them permission to celebrate themselves and invited them to respond when they were feeling refreshed and reenergized.

Getting Started: Step by Step

1. Invite new staff members to join you at a luncheon during the summer to share their personal histories, talk about why they became educators in general and why they joined your community in particular, and discuss their hopes and

Dear Colleagues,

I am a big believer in the importance of celebrations. Last week I celebrated my first anniversary as deputy chancellor. Perhaps the best moment came when someone said that I looked so much younger than I did when I took this job. This job is undoubtedly the most difficult and demanding of my career, but it is energizing at the same time. Hence my younger appearance!

Sometimes the first thing to go when you're short of energy is maintaining a dialogue with your staff. We all know how important that is, but as the inevitable spring demands of tests, reports, and plans for next year increase, conversations and celebrations are often the first things to suffer. Now is the time all of us, especially teachers, need to feel good about the work we are doing and recommit ourselves to the future. You can't take care of your staff if you are not taking care of yourself. I hope you will encourage your teachers to pamper themselves as well. Take a weekend off. Don't take any files home with you, don't return any calls or send any emails. Sleep, go to the gym, read a trashy-but-fun novel, cook some great meals, but mostly spend time with family and friends. Refuel. Celebrate your achievements. Then take that energy back to school on Monday morning. Send a thank-you note to your staff. Put out a platter of sweets in the break room. If you want your teachers back next year, make sure they know how much you appreciate what they do.

You might also send a letter to parents encouraging them to think of their children as whole persons, not only as students who bring home a report card. Every child deserves to be seen and appreciated by family and school as a sum of his or her strengths and challenges. It is important as leaders to reinforce all aspects of our mission—social, emotional, and academic. Highlighting this attitude for parents will assure them that you understand the value of celebrating each child.

As a principal I always gave a state-of-the-school address in May in which I highlighted our goals and celebrated our achievements. At the same time, I set objectives for the coming year and indicated how everyone was expected to participate in reaching these goals. I also commemorated milestones and the individuals who helped us reach them.

During March and April, I spent a lot of time thinking about the changes that I wanted to happen next year. I considered how I could begin the year differently, asked myself who in my building had untapped potential, thought about whether I was making full use of my staff's strengths.

By becoming more collaborative and celebratory and shifting instructional leadership to staff members who welcomed the challenge and could carry the day, I strengthened my community and gave myself time to get to the items on my to-do list that otherwise would have gone untended to.

Some people view being more collaborative as a drain on their time and energy. I have always found it to be just the opposite. I draw strength and inspiration from my colleagues. By inviting others to walk in my shoes even for a moment, I'm giving everyone a new take on this rewarding but difficult job of educating children. By celebrating events both large and small, we renew our community and ourselves.

When you're away on your no-worry weekend, send me a postcard. Just write, "Principal refueling here." I'll fill in the blanks!

Best Wishes,
Carmen

FIGURE 4.4 *An Invitation to Celebrate*

dreams for the school year. This meeting is very different from your first formal staff conference because it is smaller and more intimate and fosters the development of interpersonal relationships. The new staff members are able to connect with one another and form a network that will support them as new teachers; you are able to connect personally with the new staff members. It's a good idea to continue to meet with the new staff members periodically during the year.

2. Enhance the incentive to begin the new school year in a collaborative and exciting environment by distributing rugs, bulletin board paper, and other classroom supplies during an informal work day; you can also provide breakfast, lunch, and a motivating guest speaker. A day like this allows teachers to reconnect with colleagues and renews their energy and inspiration.

3. The first day of professional development sets the tone for the year. Providing turn-and-talk opportunities rather than lecturing in the school auditorium demonstrates the value you place on celebrating individual voices. Speaking with just one other person allows staff members to nurture relationships, clarify their thinking, reinforce new concepts, and perhaps practice leadership. Instead of sending your teachers to a seminar elsewhere, use the first day back to plan school-based events that unite the staff and promote collegial conversations. Honor staff members' accomplishments and personal milestones that have occurred during the summer: getting engaged, getting married, having a baby, going to summer school, writing a book. Beginning with the personal, both orally and in the conference notes (see the example in Figure 4.5), models the importance of celebrating and keeps everyone up-to-date.

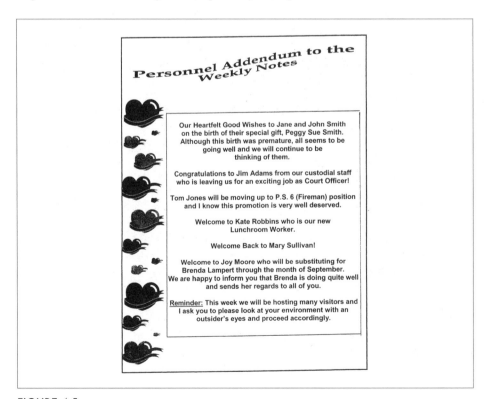

FIGURE 4.5

4. Form a committee to schedule celebrations throughout the year.

5. Send personal congratulatory messages every week via notes, bulletin board postings, and emails.

6. Publicly note the accomplishments of staff members in your weekly notes (see Figure 4.6). This encourages staff members to congratulate one another and keeps everyone informed of innovative and creative ideas. Things you might highlight include extraordinary accomplishments in working with struggling students, volunteering to serve on committees, coming in on snow days, participating in collaborative projects, and supervising extracurricular activities.

```
KUDOS

...To all of you for braving the elements and providing us with a full
   staff on "White Hurricane" Monday.
...Enjoyed reading and smelling the Bakery book.
   profits from sale went to Ronald McDonald House.
...Thank you to              ,              and              for
   providing visitors with a demonstration lesson on extremely short
   notice.
...Felicitations to          and class for an outstanding performance.
   Their "play about a book" was informative and educational.
... Our Chess Team won 2nd place in the New York State Chess Tournament
```

FIGURE 4.6

7. Circulate a birthday calendar each month. Celebrate each birthday with a card (actual or electronic), a lottery ticket, a single rose. Perhaps take everyone who has a birthday during a given month out to lunch, or order pizza or cake. One gift we found especially appreciated was covering the class while the teacher took a birthday coffee break (this had the added benefit of helping us get to know the students). When teachers' birthdays are honored and recognized, the practice becomes part of the school culture. Teachers whose principals celebrate their birthdays often celebrate their students' birthdays.

8. The day after parent-teacher conferences, when teachers are tired and stressed from the pressure of dealing with parents, celebrate with a staff breakfast. Hand out throat lozenges (to relieve throats sore from talking so much!), along with a letter thanking teachers for their time and efforts. Be especially supportive of teachers who had to deal with particularly difficult parents.

9. Create special stationery emblazoned with *Wow!* or *Bravo!* on which to compliment extraordinary efforts made by teachers, parents, or students or actions that touch the heart and mind. These notes need be only two or three sentences that capture the moment. (See Figure 4.7.)

FIGURE 4.7 *WOW Letter*

10. Create a "Random Acts of Kindness" bulletin board and invite the community to record anonymous actions undertaken to benefit others. This encourages positive behavior apart from school rules and regulations.

11. Create a citizen-of-the-week program. Have teachers nominate students who have provided a special service for the community and recognize them with a certificate.

12. Celebrate best practices with rave reviews. When teachers or administrators from other schools tour your classrooms, ask them to write down specific things they saw that they will replicate. Post a summary of these comments on a bulletin board or put a copy in everyone's mailbox. (See Figure 4.8.)

13. Once a year hold a thank-you assembly honoring the contributions of people who are often overlooked: the crossing guard, school volunteers, local politicians, bus drivers, local merchants, donors, and members of the district staff. Ask students to provide entertainment and write thank-you letters. You could also hand out certificates of appreciation (see Figure 4.9) or buttons that say, "I Make a Difference in the Life of a Child." A program listing the names of the

RAVE REVIEWS

DEAR STAFF:

IT WAS AN EXTRAORDINARY VISITORS DAY ON FRIDAY IN SO MANY DIFFERENT WAYS. HOWEVER I THINK MY PROUDEST MOMENT WAS WHEN SOMEONE ASKED, "WHAT DID YOU DO TO GET READY?" AND I SIMPLY REPLIED, "I TOLD THEM TO BE THEMSELVES." BEING YOURSELF MEANS ENCOURAGING CHILDREN TO BE INTERACTIVE AS WELL AS MAKING SURE THAT CHILDREN ARE HARD AT WORK IN THE LEARNING PROCESS.

- "CONFIRMING TO MYSELF THAT THE ATTITUDES AND DISCIPLINE OF STUDENTS IN UPPER MANHATTAN ARE NOT SIGNIFICANTLY DIFFERENT FROM STUDENTS IN BROOKLYN AND THE BRONX."
- "....GIVING AND SHARED THEIR EXPERTISE IN A WARM AND CARING WAY."
- "I WAS AMAZED TO SEE HOW WELL THE CHILDREN WORK TOGETHER ON AN INDEPENDENT BASIS."
- "HOW I WISH MY PRINCIPAL WOULD HAVE ATTENDED, TO SEE HOW TO RELATE AND SPEAK TO TEACHERS."
- "...RICH STUDENT CREATED ENVIRONMENT."
- "...THE INTEGRATION OF ALL SUBJECT AREAS. I WAS IMPRESSED WITH THE ENTHUSIASM OF THE TEACHERS IN RESPECT TO STAFF DEVELOPMENT."
- "ORGANIZATION AND COMMITMENT OF BOTH STAFF AND ADMINISTRATION HAS PROVEN AND SHOWED THE SUCCESS THROUGHOUT THE SCHOOL."
- "...VISITING ALL PARTS OF THE SCHOOL FROM TOP, (MUSIC AND ROOF-TOP) MUSIC AND ROOF TOP) TO THE LUNCH ROOM. ALL THE TEACHES WERE SO ENTHUSED ABOUT WHAT THEY WERE DOING."
- "...THE SCHOOL'S ATMOSPHERE. THE TEACHER'S COOPERATION."
- "...SEEING SO MANY IDEAS THAT CAN BE ATTEMPTED--MOST WERE NOT COSTLY."
- "....TEACHERS WERE VERY HELPFUL AND WILLING TO ASSIST ALL VISITING TEACHERS."
- "THIS SCHOOL HAS A WEALTH OF MATERIALS AND HARD WORKING STAFF."
- "....SEEING HOW THE DIFFERENT TEACHERS DEVELOPED THE SAME CONCEPT."
- "...TOURING THE 3RD GRADE CLASSROOMS. THE CHILDREN WORKED AS IF WE WERE ALWAYS THERE."
- "I THINK IT IS GREAT THAT THE PARENTS HAVE SUCH AN INTENSE KNOWLEDGE OF WHAT AND HOW THE SCHOOL IS RUN. THIS SHOWS HOW OPEN THE SCHOOL IS TO THE COMMUNITY."
- "...BEING TREATED AS A PROFESSIONAL."
- "THE WALL DISPLAYS INSIDE AND OUTSIDE THE CLASSROOMS AND IMPRESSIVELY MULTI-CULTURAL."
- "....PROLIFIC PRODUCTIVITY OF THE STUDENTS."
- "....ALL COULD EXPLAIN WHAT THEY WERE DOING."
- "THE OPEN AND WELCOME FEELING THAT WAS EVIDENT."
- "...THE SHARING."
- "THE BULLETIN BOARDS REALLY REFLECTED THE WORK THAT IS GOING ON IN CLASS."
- "...JUNIOR HIGH SCHOOL TEACHER AND I FOUND IDEAS THROUGHOUT THE BUILDING IN EVERY GRADE THAT CAN BE USED IN MY CLASSES."
- "....SEEING HOW TEACHERS CARRY OUT THE PROGRAM IN THEIR OWN UNIQUE STYLES."
- "....TEACHERS WERE RESPONSIVE AND IN TUNE TO THEIR CLASSES NEEDS."
- "THE OPENNESS OF THE WHOLE SCHOOL IS REFRESHING."
- "...A SCHOOL OF TEAM MEMBERS WHO ARE STRIVING FOR SUCCESS."
- "...SEEING STUDENTS INVOLVED AND NO DISCIPLINE PROBLEMS."
- "THE CLASSROOM WERE TRULY A JOY TO SEE. THE CHILDREN SEEM TO BE HAVING A WONDERFUL TIME LEARNING HERE."
- "...THE STIMULATING VISUAL AIDS IN THE CLASSROOM; THE TOTAL IMMERSION VISIBLE IN THE CLASSROOM."
- "...ABUNDANCE OF LITERARY MATERIAL, STUDENT INTERACTIVITY."
- "THE STAFF WAS MOST GRACIOUS IN ANSWERING ALL OUR QUESTIONS."
- "BEING ABLE TO GO FROM ONE ROOM TO ANOTHER AND NOT FEELING WE WERE DISTURBING THE CLASS/TEACHER. PARENT GUIDE WAS VERY INFORMATIVE AND GAVE A PARENT'S INSIGHT ABOUT THE SCHOOL, P/T INTERACTION AND EDUCATION."
- "THE WORK THAT THESE TEACHERS DO WITH THE CHILDREN IS PRETTY AMAZING. I LIKE THE FACT THAT THE TEACHERS DECIDE WHAT TO TEACH DURING DIFFERENT POINTS OF THE DAY AND THEY ARE NOT RESTRICTED TO TIME."
- "...THE CLIMATE AND ATMOSPHERE."

FIGURE 4.8

people you are thanking and the nature of their contributions is a nice touch. Invite the local media!

14. Hold curriculum celebrations of individual student projects, grade-level units of study, and whole-school learning. Include parents and other members of the community. Science fairs, art festivals, student musical and theatrical performances, and publishing parties are all occasions for bringing the community together to celebrate. Have students celebrate one another's work and share the joy of work well done. Inviting district leaders can help break down preconceived notions of what your students can achieve.

These comments by the teachers sum it all up!

•••"My volunteers are amazing! Great with kids - caring and patient, giving, kind women! They are a *huge help to me!*

•••"My volunteer has been with me for several years. She's terrific!"

•••"My volunteer is preparing a unit which she will begin in a couple of weeks. She's very special."

•••"My volunteer works with a shared reading group. She prepares materials, works with individual students on varied assignments and she even escorts the class on trips, although it's not her day to volunteer! What a help she is to me."

•••"This is my third year working with these volunteers and I would be lost without them! They bring so much to my classroom and my students enjoy having their help. They have become an integral part of my classroom!"

FIGURE 4.9

15. Celebrate your teachers' achievements. (Thanksgiving and Valentine's Day are perfect opportunities.) Keep a file of index cards, one for each member of the school community, and note excellent work and special contributions to be acknowledged when the occasion warrants. There are many picture books you can give as gifts to affirm your staff's contributions. *Guess How Much I Love You*, by Sam McBratney, accompanied Carmen's valentine to her teachers one year (see Figure 4.10). The staff valentine in Figure 4.11 invites staff members to join in!

16. Make sure holiday celebrations honor individual beliefs and recognize diversity.

17. Celebrate the end of a semester with a bring-a-dessert party or a potluck dinner in the school cafeteria. Include significant others; the people who matter so much in our private lives should get to know the people who matter so much in our professional lives. School communities that celebrate socially are cohesive and see their members through difficult times.

18. Say thank you in a very special way by hosting a party in your home.

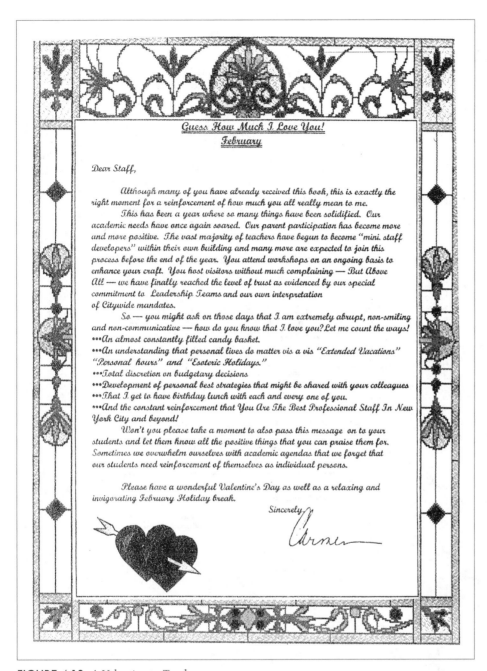

FIGURE 4.10 *A Valentine to Teachers*

19. On days when the weather or other circumstances make getting to school a challenge, have hot chocolate and cookies waiting.

20. Celebrate the day after standardized tests are administered. Play games or orchestrate some other kind of physical activity so students and teachers can release their tensions.

21. Display photographs of all your staff members (teachers, cafeteria workers, custodians, secretaries) on a bulletin board at the entrance of the school. Back each photo with special paper and include the staff member's job title and name

*"A Man is Rich in Proportion
to the Number of Things which he can
Afford to Let Alone,"
by Henry David Thoreau*

Dear Staff,

The above quote is so true at this time in our history. Although things are never left alone, I do feel that all of you are now busy doing different pieces of my job — from budgeting to staff development to building community. All of you have taken pieces of my job; thereby, making us truly more community driven and at the same time making my job a little easier. It is truly why I attempt to smile more often, not always successfully.

At this time, there is another piece of my job I feel is perfect for delegating. As Valentine's Day roles around I would like once again to send out special "love you notes" to the staff. Won't you help me by taking a name from the enclosed envelope and writing "••••A You are Special Because..............." note or card to a colleague. This will make our messages to each other doubly wonderful and obviously lessen my load by at least six hours. Should you wish not to do this, just pass it on. However, if you do, won't you please send it c/o me or Jan by February 8th.

Thank you for you everlasting cooperation and enthusiasm.
Carmen

Name of Person note is going to_____

Quote that you write about person_____

_____
You may remain anonymous, if you wish!

FIGURE 4.11 *A Staff Valentine*

underneath. You might also include their favorite book, favorite quotation, hobby, or other interesting fact. Parents, students, and visitors will be able to become personally acquainted with the names, faces, and special talents of each person. (It's helpful if all the photographs are the same size and attractively displayed, so that the aesthetic values are consistent.)

22. In the reception area (or the school library), keep a collection of photo albums that capture each year's history and accomplishments. Visitors to the school can see the school's journey toward excellence, and members of the school community can reflect on the past and chart the future. Ask the school librarian to assume the role of school archivist and enlist a team of students, teachers, and parents to take the photographs and write the captions.

23. Hold an alumni celebration to honor the school's history and keep in touch with alumni. Alumni are valuable sources of school history and are often eager to become mentors, career day and graduation speakers, and volunteers. They may also make financial contributions.

24. Have the teachers at each grade level host a series of breakfasts at which they talk about their curriculum and display student work. Particularly in large schools, with many teachers and staggered schedules, this is a way to encourage collaboration and make sure that faculty members feel part of a cohesive community.

25. Establish your office as a gathering place. Keep lots of professional books around, have a table with hot coffee and a big bowl of candy, and provide soft, comfortable chairs for private conversation.

26. Set up a system of buddy classes. Let teachers explore a particular curriculum area with a colleague at another grade level. For example, a fifth-grade teacher and a kindergarten teacher could focus on reading and writing, with the fifth graders becoming mentors to the kindergartners and the kindergartners being the audience for the fifth graders' writing. Over time this will lead to consistent schoolwide literacy practices.

27. Keep a shelf of books in your office that teachers can borrow to help their students celebrate changes in their life. For example, *Julius, the Baby of the World*, by Kevin Henkes, honors the sibling who has a difficult time coping with the birth of a new brother or sister. *Hooray for You! A Celebration of "You-ness,"* by Marianne Richmond; *The Quiltmaker's Gift*, by Jeff Brumbeau; and *Hey World, Here I Am*, by Jean Little, are other excellent books that celebrate uniqueness.

28. Appoint a student principal for the day. This helps students understand what you do all day and is a way for you to get to know students who need some extra attention and support. Have your teachers identify upper-grade students who are quiet in class and need an opportunity to shine in front of their peers. (In some schools, students write an essay about why they should be chosen and what they would do to improve the school during their daylong tenure.) Select a student (or a series of students) to spend a whole day with you. You can let this student decide whom you invite to lunch, make loudspeaker announcements, help resolve hallway altercations, deliver messages, and visit classrooms with you.

29. Celebrate outstanding academic performance, sportsmanship, civic-mindedness, attendance, and special gifts and talents at student honor assemblies. The criteria should be clearly articulated and publicly displayed so students know the exact path to follow to be honored.

30. Have fun and build school spirit with theme days. Themes that work well are Make Your Own Hat Day, T-Shirt Day (students decorate T-shirts to illustrate their personalities), and Stay in Bed and Read Day (students spend most of the day reading in a comfortable place). The theme can also be more serious. On Career Day, for example, parents and other members of the larger community talk about their jobs and answer student questions, bringing to life the connection between school and the real world of work. Scheduling theme days when many students are expected to be absent will increase attendance and add to the school spirit. (Encourage secondary students to create and plan their own theme days.)

31. Create a banner, quilt, or brochure advertising your school's accomplishments. Involve the whole school community: each class can make a different type of contribution, and the art department can provide professional finishing touches. A public display like this is a creative demonstration of school pride. (Figure 4.12 is a section of a school brochure.)

1994

P.S. 6 provides a nurturing environment for students, teachers, and parents that enables academic and social growth. This atmosphere ensures that each child reaches his or her full potential.

Writing/Research Skills
A strong emphasis is placed on oral and written fluency in language arts. Students from third grade and up are expected to complete an in-depth research project.

Science
The enriched science program provides a fully equipped laboratory for hands-on experimentation, an annual science fair, field study trips to the Poconos Environmental Education Center, professional science mentors, and a Career Day that highlights careers in mathematics and science.

Technology
A fully equipped computer laboratory offers computer instruction to all students. Individual classrooms have access to "mobile" computers which are shared.

Music
A comprehensive music program consists of regularly scheduled music classes as well as extracurricular programs that include junior and senior chorus, musical productions, and a dance ensemble.

Cultural Partnerships
New York City, with its many cultural institutions provides a wealth of learning opportunities for P.S. 6 students. Partnership programs with the Metropolitan Museum of Art, Metropolitan Opera Guild, Frick Museum, and the American Museum of Natural History help students integrate science, social studies and the arts.

Art
Art is an integrated component of the interdisciplinary instruction. It culminates in the traditional P.S. 6 outdoor Spring Art Show.

Reading and Writing
Emphasis on literature along with the writing process and Making Connections Program are factors that have made P.S. 6 the top school in reading in District 2.

Foreign Language
Spanish language instruction with an emphasis on Latin America and its cultures is provided to students in grades K through 5. Latin, which serves as a basis for learning other languages, is offered in grade 6.

Club Programs
Club programs offer students an opportunity to explore their own areas of interest. In-school clubs are electives which students in grades 3 through 6 may select. Clubs include cooking, law, sports, video, economics, art, oceanography, community service, and newspaper.

In addition, after-school programs are offered to students in grades K through 6. These programs include art, theater, jewelry, computer, chess, math, and science. Club programs in computer and Spanish are offered to parents.

OUR MANDATE......EDUCATIONAL EXCELLENCE!

Resources
A dedicated talented staff, a newly remodeled library with over 8,500 volumes, and a resource center for English as a Second Language are just some of the many resources available at P.S. 6. Others include an AV lending library, and the Peer Tutoring Program.

Staff Development
Ongoing staff development programs support a high level of innovation and improved techniques with emphasis on Communication Arts, Science and Mathematics. P.S. 6 serves as a model visitor site for administrators and teachers from the Tri-state area.

Physical Education
The Physical Education Program offers movement and physical education classes to the younger grades with an emphasis on skills. Classes for the upper grades focus on competitive sports. The program boasts an award winning track team and tennis pro instruction.

What "They Say"...

The NEW YORK TIMES – 8/24/94
"...P.S. 6 is a public school, a magnet school that draws from a wide and demographically diverse population, and none of its teachers get paid more than teachers at any other public school. Its success over the last century is clearly worth celebrating and worth studying."

"Every grade is being assigned a period in the school's history," explained Carmen Fariña, the principal. "Classes will interview old graduates and look up records. Our school newspaper will cover what we turn up about our past."

"Such stuff makes for tradition. It makes for pride. P.S. 6 has both. It also gives its pupils confidence."

The Intrepid New Yorker:
"The instructional program is rigorously academic, interdisciplinary, and centered around the study of literature. Science, math, social studies, writing activities, and projects emerge from the particular literature that children read. The arts are also an integral component of the children's projects: puppetry, mural, and original playwriting are a sampling."

The Spirit of '94.

FIGURE 4.12

32. Acknowledge contributions and accomplishments through affirmations, toasts, and shout-outs. Send a letter to the community highlighting plans and accomplishments (see the example in Figure 4.13). Try to get the letter published in the local newspaper.

Dear Parents and Community Members,

Celebrating our school successes is a vital part of our everyday lives. Over the last 5 years, we have strived to build a community of learners that can become an integral part of our society.

Our students, parents and staff have worked together to create and reach many successes. Recognizing these accomplishments is important in building the self-esteem of our students. We want to share with you some of our student accomplishments.

School Accomplishments:
- The implementation of small learning environments- three theme vertical academies with a uniform policy
- We received a Well Developed Score on their Quality Review
- On-going Professional Development for teachers to make teaching and learning more differentiated, student-centered and less teacher-directed.
- The development and implementation of six science labs supported by certified science teachers.
- After-school test prep classes for at-risk, enrichment in ELA, Math, Science, Social Studies, and extended day session
- Offering students Math A Regents Exam
- Saturday Preparatory Academy and SES Programs
- Hired F-Status Teachers for push-in and pull-out small group instruction
- 100 Book Challenge
- Hired Aussie Consultant, Princeton Review Consultants, Teaching Matters Consultant for the purpose of building school capacity
- The implementation of a 3 high tech computer labs supported by wireless laptops for mobile classroom use in all subject areas
- Elective courses offered to students- Choral Music, Journalism, Forensic Science, Law, and The Stock Market Game
- The implementation of a Clinical/Therapeutic Learning Environment-H.O.P.E. in collaboration with Columbia University Social Worker Internship Program
- Middle School Advisory Classes- targeting sixth grade students this year and to expand to the seventh grade next year
- New Teacher Retention Rate increasing every year

FIGURE 4.13

33. Present teacher-and-student talent nights and art exhibits. These events help everyone see the world from a different perspective.

34. Share inspirational or humorous poems, cartoons, and quotations, especially during challenging times. (*The New Yorker Bank Street College Book of New Yorker Cartoons* is an excellent source of cartoons with educational themes.)

35. Bring people together in an upscale setting for food, drink, and conversation—a tea (see Figure 4.14) or a dinner dance (see Figure 4.15), for example. (Local merchants may be willing to underwrite these celebrations.)

FIGURE 4.14

FIGURE 4.15

Avoiding Common Pitfalls

Choose which things to celebrate when. If you celebrate everything, nothing seems important. And don't postpone celebrations—making the effort to notice and affirm progress along the way will add energy and renew commitment to the work ahead. Last-minute celebrations often misuse the energy and resources of the community. Carefully planning a year's calendar of celebrations builds positive energy and forward momentum, uses time and resources wisely, and keeps everyone focused on the established priorities. Center your compliments on stated school priorities, and make sure everyone knows the criteria for being recognized.

You need to provide honest feedback. Compliments for the sake of compliments lower standards and encourage mediocre performance. Candor is an acquired but necessary skill that when used effectively makes your compliments mean something. Hand out compliments when they are well earned, not simply because they are expected.

Celebratory letters and notes are most powerful when they are timely. They should always be dated, signed by you personally, and delivered quickly enough to reinforce the complimented behavior. Leaders who devote a specific time each week to writing notes and letters show that they value writing and are committed to doing it well; their comments will also be prompt.

The community needs to be well aware of what you are celebrating, why you are celebrating it, and how you make decisions about whom or what to celebrate. Clear, public criteria serve as a road map that all members of the community can follow and will ensure that those you recognize are worthy of praise. You must also help members of the community feel comfortable suggesting how to make the celebrations more inclusive.

Make sure you honor equity and diversity. Everyone deserves to be respected and recognized. Traditional holidays may be directed only at a particular segment of the population. You need to address these challenges and generate inventive ways to include everyone.

Take the same tone with everybody—teachers will compare the notes you write them, we guarantee it! Naturally you will know, and like, some staff members better than others, but no one must be made to feel marginalized. Giving your personal friends undeserved praise or extra access will undermine the culture you are trying to create. (Withholding compliments is also a powerful tool, but it needs to be used judiciously and professionally.)

If you are new to the leadership role, give yourself a few months to observe the strengths and needs of the people you supervise before giving written feedback; first impressions can be deceiving. The complexity of human relationships and the depth of understanding they require are amazing. You also need to understand the traditions and history of the school and the role existing celebrations play. Don't eliminate a celebration the school has honored and valued for many years without finding out how various members of the community feel about it.

The work of improving schools is constant and never ending. Celebrations cannot be perceived as a mark of completion or a designation of perfection; instead, they are stepping-stones on the path, a source of energy. Compliments followed by next steps give everyone the opportunity to build on strengths and successes and avoid complacency.

Leaders who know each member of the community well recognize that celebrations belong to everyone and can be proposed by anyone, including parents and students. The true sign that a community has built a culture of celebrations is independence in and ownership of the process of celebrating all members of the team.

Evaluating Success

To determine whether the culture of celebrations has resulted in increased energy, improved student achievement, and the recruitment and retention of quality teachers, look for evidence like this:

- Is there more (and more meaningful) talk around the work of teaching and learning? Does this result in improved student performance? Does the talk focus on the work of moving students forward? Does this positive energy propel the community to initiate and own continual learning? Is the teachers' lunchroom a place where teachers talk about their work in positive ways, share materials with one another, and laugh together? Do teachers ask one another's opinion when they examine and analyze student work, match that work to standards, try new strategies, and plan for improved student performance?

- Is there evidence of more collaboration and less competition? Do teachers write curriculum units together and share resources and ideas? Do teachers work with one another after classes have ended for the day and come to school early to meet with colleagues? Are teachers eager to learn new strategies from one another? Do they visit one another's classrooms? Are teachers beginning to take on leadership roles?

- Is there evidence of successful teacher recruitment and retention? Do new teachers feel celebrated by the community? Do they feel supported and nurtured and want to stay? Is there a positive buzz?

- Are there more celebrations for students and parents? Are students recognized for their individual contributions in a variety of meaningful ways? Are they given the opportunity to celebrate themselves and one another? Is celebration a two-way street that everyone has an opportunity to drive on? Do parents take part in celebrations? Do celebrations have realistic goals and time frames? Do they result in increased commitment and effort? Does the community have its own internal system of evaluation that balances outside pressures?

- Is there evidence that the culture of celebrations will be sustained even when you are no longer part of the school community?

Supervise Creatively
and Evaluate Reflectively

Participatory Lessons, Teacher Portfolios, and Peer Coaching

Dear Reader,

In the late 1960s, when we first became teachers, principals were expected to be building managers—to make the school safe and orderly and keep everything running smoothly. The emphasis on conformity and following the rules applied to principals as well as teachers; often principals' evaluations rested on how well they were able to keep problems to a minimum and keep their constituents happy. The hierarchy of the principal as the all-powerful boss and the teachers as the acquiescing followers was very much the norm.

The relationship between principal and teacher often consisted solely of their professional interactions, which were limited to meetings called to review rules and regulations and react to pressing school issues, and monthly faculty conferences in which the principal often read verbatim from written notes. Teachers had little opportunity to have professional conversations or make suggestions about curriculum or teaching strategies. Principals controlled all the major decisions and, most important, the end-of-year evaluation, based solely on the observation of a single lesson. The only follow-up, if any, was a letter listing a few surface reminders—list the aim on the board, keep the blinds halfway up, keep the bulletin boards up-to-date. There was little or no ongoing support, little or no opportunity for the supervisor to get to know the teachers' strengths and needs.

Although the role of principal has changed dramatically and leaders are now expected to be instructional experts, this form of supervision and evaluation is still very common. As you read this chapter, supervisors all over America are walking into classrooms, checklist in hand, to observe a lesson. For many teachers, this onetime observation is a nerve-racking, high-risk experience that does little to improve their skills or generate reflective thinking. If the teacher is somewhat sophisticated, she has rehearsed the lesson with another colleague and prepared or even threatened the students to behave in the appropriate way. The lesson is often gimmicky or on a safe topic with a predictable outcome, the teacher's purpose to entertain rather than educate. For new teachers, this experience is often the most dreaded of the year, because so much depends on this one opportunity to prove their competence. Conversely, veteran teachers treat it as something to endure and expend as little effort as possible.

In many schools, there are few specific guidelines for this one-shot observation, and teachers are given little opportunity to reflect on their learning goals or evaluate their own progress. In addition, many administrators fail to provide timely feedback. As a result, teachers who have prepared for many hours for this experience derive little value from it. For their part, the leaders spend an inordinate amount of time conducting these observations, time that could be spent advancing their own learning or having meaningful conversations with teachers.

Our *aha* moment, when we realized formal observations yielded little practical information, occurred around the copy machine. We noticed a long line of teachers waiting to copy their lessons for the day, lessons they had formulated on the spur of the moment rather than as part of a cohesive unit of study. Then, stepping into classrooms, we noticed too much teacher-directed whole-class instruction. In many cases, the lessons were not differentiated or developmentally appropriate. It became clear that these teachers needed our help in planning lessons, focusing on small groups, and pacing their instruction to the diversity of their students.

We therefore began centering our evaluations of untenured faculty during participatory lessons in which we worked closely with them (and in doing so, we were able to develop a well-rounded professional relationship). This also allowed us to meet many of our own goals: ensuring schoolwide consistency, meeting the needs of the most struggling students, and integrating new initiatives with stated school goals. Our intimate engagement in the life of the classroom, our commitment to the success of every student, and our willingness to become colearners and risk takers spoke more loudly and clearly than any checklist or rating sheet ever could.

By the end of our second year at PS 6, we were hosting many visitors, and we wanted to be able to share our teachers' best practices in their own voices, in order to encourage other teachers to try these practices too and gain a deeper understanding of the craft of teaching. Therefore we set up our own version of teacher portfolios to take advantage of teacher expertise, enhance professional collaboration, and focus on student achievement (particularly that of students who had struggled). The portfolio topics were determined on the basis of our many conversations with the teachers, our visits to their classrooms, and their individual passions and interests. They ranged from straightforward issues like how to integrate social studies with literacy to issues that turned classrooms into research laboratories. One first-grade teacher wanted to eliminate Friday spelling tests but first needed to convince herself that alternative strategies could be successful. She tried a number of new ways to teach spelling patterns in her classroom, inviting her colleagues within and outside the school to observe.

Our third-grade teachers were the first to volunteer to participate in the portfolio program, because they were introducing an interdisciplinary approach to social studies called *Making Connections* and hosting most of the visitors. But we were surprised when a few senior teachers (previously resistant to participating in any professional development at all) wanted to turn their classrooms into portfolio laboratories as well. Our conversations with these veterans encouraged them to become more reflective thinkers and articulate their expertise in written and oral presentations. Eventually every staff member, including the principal and staff developer, created a portfolio. Developing these portfolios helped teachers understand the challenges of the writing process and model it for their students—capturing ideas in a draft, struggling to revise the draft, and celebrating the published product. Everyone related as writers and thinkers.

Peer coaching, like participatory lessons and portfolios, encourages collaborative rather than competitive strategies and promotes reflection, self-evaluation, and personalized and differentiated professional development. Peer coaching encourages teachers to invest in one another's success and creates a setting for positive interactions between teachers who might not naturally seek each other out. Teachers who have refined their practices in particular areas and developed successful new strategies are rewarded by being able to share their expertise with their colleagues, build a consistent culture of collaboration, and initiate new teachers into the school community.

Too often, schools are divided into two camps—the senior teachers versus the new teachers—who have little opportunity to share best practices or engage in deep conversations about teaching and learning. This separation can be felt in the faculty lunchroom and at school social events, as well as during department and grade-level meetings. Thoughtfully matching a senior teacher with a new teacher changes this social dynamic and leads to greater teacher learning, professional satisfaction, and increased student achievement.

Supervisors are also hungry for creative, differentiated reflection and evaluation. When we became superintendents, we were amazed at how few principals had experienced positive supervision or evaluation. Many told us horrific stories about abusive and unfair supervisors who tried to catch them by surprise, gave mixed messages about their expectations, and singled them out for punishment or praise based on unclear criteria. The most common complaints were the lack of thoughtful conversations about student achievement, the scarcity of differentiated support, and the unwillingness of superintendents to look at their own responsibilities for the failures of schools and districts.

Leaders, like teachers, need to have ongoing conversations with their supervisors that focus on essential questions, stretch their expertise, and trigger new learning. Superintendents who limit school visits to an examination of numerical data miss the exciting opportunity to expand their own learning, discover expertise in the ranks, reward best practices, and build a collaborative and trusting culture. Having thoughtful personal conversations about the learning in their schools' classrooms, developing portfolios based on their success and expertise, and coaching peers are all strategies that work as well with principals as they do with teachers.

For us, creative supervision and reflective evaluation require being committed to becoming learners ourselves, and much of the learning comes from talking, engaging in inquiry, and exchanging ideas with the people with whom we work. Creative supervisors understand that it is questions not answers, support not mandates, risk taking and innovation not complacency that create a culture of reflection and enduring energy. Leaders who establish a dialogue with their community develop a clear understanding of individual strengths that can support the professional growth of all members. Individual needs are the basis of differentiated professional development closely aligned to creative supervision. Targeted individuals or groups study one issue at a time and pilot new practices, and initiatives are modified and adapted based on what they discover. Equalitarian rather than hierarchal leadership ensures that all members are respected and valued and take responsibility for their own continued learning. Learning like this is professionally fulfilling. The joy of collaborative learning is passed on to the students, the direct and most important beneficiaries.

—Carmen and Laura

Participatory Lessons

A participatory lesson has three parts: plan, presentation, and evaluation. First the teacher, with the principal's guidance, plans the lesson, paying special attention to the active role the principal will play to support at-risk students. Then the teacher presents the whole-class lesson while the principal observes, after which the principal teaches a group of students using the plan the teacher has developed for the principal to follow. Finally, the principal evaluates how it went: the plan, the decisions made about at-risk students, and the lesson's appropriateness for the grade and subject area. This process ensures that schoolwide professional development uses a common vocabulary and consistent teaching strategies from grade to grade.

Why Use Participatory Lessons?

The participatory lesson is particularly helpful in working with new teachers to ensure that they are planning wisely and gathering rich evidence that their lessons are meeting student needs, are based on standards, and are congruent with school goals. Participatory lessons also let the community see you as a colleague and a teacher, someone who is eager to learn about student needs and classroom realities. They reinforce the perception of the classroom as the single most important place in the school.

Too often, leaders aren't able to participate in professional development along with their teachers. Going into the classroom like this, you become aware of the latest teaching methods and strategies and can better understand the challenges teachers may face. When you sit with students on the rug in a writing workshop or at a lab table in a science class, you are perceived differently; you receive a different kind of respect and are able to gather a different kind of information. Students connect with you personally and will be more likely to ask you for help.

You are also able to have more meaningful conversations with parents and teachers. Parents who have heard time and again about their child's needs from the classroom teacher will listen differently when you tell them about your personal experience with the child. Teachers appreciate having your hands-on support and knowing that you have seen what they see. You can present a fresh perspective.

You are able to notice patterns from class to class, particularly within a grade or subject area. This big picture helps you take next steps: plan effective professional development and identify issues to address in grade-level meetings and faculty conferences. Pondering questions and solving problems in the classroom make your job exciting and alive. Holding meaningful dialogues with your teachers about teaching and learning makes you a stronger leader and helps you hold on to the best teachers.

Getting Started: Step by Step

1. Send a letter to your junior staff members inviting them to a meeting introducing the participatory lesson concept (there's an example in Figure 5.1). It

---

To: Teachers with Less than Three Years' Experience
From: Carmen Fariña
Re: Participatory Lessons
Date: December 17, 1999

This year our participatory lessons, which are voluntary, will focus on either writing or reading and emphasize the following strategies:

1. planning
2. grouping
3. pacing
4. developmental appropriateness

I hope many of you will take advantage of this opportunity.

We will have a half-hour planning session at least two days before my visit. I'll let you know the date and time enough in advance for you to prepare, and I'll have someone cover your class. We'll discuss the focus of the lesson, how it fits into your yearlong literacy curriculum, its special features, and my role in it. Think about my role in advance, and be ready to give me a specific assignment related to your at-risk students (or any students you want me to work with). Your plan should include a preassessment and a postassessment of student needs and some details about how you will follow up after my visit. I will host an informational meeting on January 10 at 3:15 P.M. to answer any questions you may have.

Since planning is an essential part of good instruction, my evaluation will focus on your yearlong planning strategies. Also, please make sure the materials used in the lesson are appropriate to the subject and to your students' needs. I will be happy to help you procure the materials you need.

I know you are all working very hard, and I look forward to some wonderful learning experiences.

FIGURE 5.1

makes most sense to initiate this process in January; you'll have enough time between then and May to establish a trusting relationship and then plan, present, and evaluate the lessons before the end of the school year.

2. At the meeting, explain the purpose, plan of action, voluntary nature, and intended outcomes of this supervisory technique. Make sure there is enough time for conversation and questions. (Invite written follow-up questions.) Make sure teachers understand that both the content of and the strategies in participatory lessons should be based on already established school goals that the community is studying, practicing, and supporting.

3. After the informational meeting, allow at least two weeks for your staff members to talk about, think about, and plan their participation.

4. Schedule the lessons. Post the times you are available, and ask teachers to sign up for a time (first come, first served).

5. Arrange a half-hour meeting with each teacher two days before the participatory lesson. (Arrange for someone to cover the teacher's class.) This short turnaround time ensures that the lesson will be current and part of the larger plan for the unit. Discuss the intended lesson in relation to the school goals for the year; how the teacher plans to apply the priority strategies (planning, grouping, pacing, developmental appropriateness) during the lesson; and the specific students with whom the teacher wants you to work. Ask the teacher for a copy of the lesson plan, a list of materials to be used, and information about the students.

6. During the lesson, join the students as another participant, doing whatever is required of them. This demonstrates that you are there as a learner and an active listener.

7. After the whole-class portion of the lesson, join the small group of students assigned to you and follow the rest of the lesson plan the teacher gave you. Observe student behavior and reinforce some of the strategies used during the whole-class lesson.

8. Before you leave the classroom, thank the teacher and the students for their support.

9. Within a day or two, give the teacher your oral feedback.

10. Provide written feedback within the week. Refer to the lesson, the strategies covered, the insights you've gained, and your reactions to working with the small group. Suggest next steps. (Figure 5.2 is an example of such a letter.)

February 5, 2000

Dear _____,

Although you may not be aware of it, last year you set the standard for this year's participatory lesson. My visit to your classroom then showed me how much insight I could gain into student learning in a forty-five-minute visit. You opened my eyes to the role of nonfiction in our reluctant readers' lives. After your lesson, I was able to see things from the perspective of lovers of nonfiction and how powerful a tool nonfiction reading can be in motivating many of our struggling students.

This year you have moved from working with small groups to working with the class as a whole. This requires that you pay more attention to effective management strategies, especially transitions. During my visit, the transition from rug to tables and chairs was seamless; this is obviously something you have worked on. Congratulations! You have also become more confident using new strategies based on your work with the consultant from Teachers College. Language like "stretching out the talk," "jotting to the text," and "thought walks" is evidence of your new learning. Although this terminology was new to me (thank you for expanding my vocabulary!), the students obviously knew what you were asking them to do. Classroom management is really about having a bag of tricks that mix academics with behavior expectations, and your work with the consultant has helped you address both the classroom structure and the curriculum. (And I can now use the strategies and language you modeled for me when I visit other classrooms.)

In your introduction to the lesson, you consistently used a respectful tone that encouraged students to use this same tone with their peers. You also referred to students' previous work, which made it easier for them to transfer and apply new knowledge. Their success came from your careful planning, thoughtful grouping, and developmentally appropriate practices.

I followed all the directions you gave the students, jotting right along with them. Once I sat with my assigned group, I noticed a wide disparity between my group and the higher-performing students in other groups. The high-achieving students are adept at making inferences using personal experiences and evidence from the text. The members of my group had difficulty making the jump from the concrete, basic features of turtles to the inferred meaning of the text. I enjoyed working closely with Bob and plan to continue talking with him, since many other issues came up, especially his skipping his extended-day classes. Could you please check with his mother about his absences and urge her to make sure he attends? He was very adept at making meaning when I read aloud to him, so I know that with more support we can help him reach standards.

I suggest that the next time you introduce a short text you model how you use text-to-self connections to make inferences. Many of the students I spoke with could not relate any personal experiences to the text or move to inferential thinking. You might want to train some of your higher-performing students to model their own strategies for making connections and have them facilitate small-group conversations using picture books or the book of the month. One strategy you will want to continue modeling step-by-step is how to move from the concrete to the inferential.

Thank you for the wonderful lesson and for stimulating my thinking. I enjoyed working with you and learning so much about inferential thinking.

FIGURE 5.2

11. Affirm your support during the next few weeks by following up on the connections you made with the students and the teacher and celebrating the next steps.

12. In a notebook, list the students you have worked with and the specific support they need from the school's guidance counselor, reading specialist, physical education instructor, and so on. These notes will help you match students and teachers in future class assignments and inform the conversations you have with parents.

13. Keep notes on the lessons you participate in; focus on teacher expertise, noting strengths and areas needing professional development.

14. Share new strategies and vocabulary when you visit other classrooms, lead grade-level and faculty meetings, and speak with your staff in other formal and informal situations. Include them in written communications as well.

15. Make use of your more intimate knowledge of students when you greet them in the morning and run into them during the day. Ask teachers to let you know about each small success so you can celebrate it.

Avoiding Common Pitfalls

Starting with teachers who are eager to participate will give you the opportunity to demonstrate the positive, collegial nature of participatory lessons. Although they are primarily intended to be used with new teachers, other teachers may want to join in when they see the kind of support they will receive. Remember, the program should be invitational: teachers must have the right to say no thank you or to choose to get involved even when they are not part of the intended audience. It is a good idea to meet with representatives from the teachers union to explain the purpose and intended outcomes of this model and anticipate any obstacles before implementing.

An important value being modeled in participatory lessons is thoughtful planning. It is essential that you honor the appointments you make and make every effort not to reschedule. This demonstrates that what happens in the classroom is your highest priority. Each visit will require two hours of your time at a minimum, which includes a conversation before the lesson, the lesson itself, and a conversation after the lesson. Letters summarizing the experience also take time and are essential documentation. (If you are the principal of a large school, you may want to share this responsibility with the assistant principals.)

January is a good time to initiate participatory lessons. Earlier in the school year, the community is still getting to know the students, settling into the curriculum, and becoming comfortable with school practices. By January your staff will understand and trust your motivation. Also, teachers' energy is often low in January, and the lessons will build excitement and momentum.

Making the purpose, expectations, and intended outcomes of participatory lessons transparent allows the community to feel more comfortable about becoming involved. When the purpose and the focus of the participatory lesson match the priorities that have already been established, teachers will feel less overwhelmed and more supported.

Participatory lessons are intended to help your staff become better teachers; the lessons need to be part of a professional development environment in which they feel it is safe to take risks. Without this supportive atmosphere, the approach is a recipe for disaster. You should also make clear to parents the purpose of the participatory lessons, so they understand why you are spending time in their children's classrooms.

Evaluating Success

To determine whether your participatory lessons are having the desired effect, look for evidence like this:

- Does the community see you as a colearner? Are they more willing to follow your example in taking risks, trying new practices, reflecting on their craft, and having meaningful conversations with you and one another about strategies for continued student improvement?
- Do the patterns you discover during participatory visits lead to instructional and organizational changes that result in improved student achievement? Does identifying and supporting struggling students as part of your classroom visits encourage teachers to focus on these students as well as other students who would benefit from differentiated instruction?
- Are more teachers choosing to take part in participatory lessons, and do they see the value of this method in deepening their understanding of effective practices?
- Are you gaining a deeper knowledge of the struggling students? Are you better able to plan interventions and professional development support? Are the personal relationships among students, parents, and teachers leading to more meaningful dialogue and increased student support?
- Are you more confident about discussing teaching and learning strategies after experiencing them firsthand in the classroom? Are grade-level and faculty meetings becoming more practical and less theoretical as you are able to refer to things you have observed and the lessons you have learned in the classroom? Are your follow-up visits to classrooms more meaningful because of the context that has been established?
- Can you better affirm individual teacher strengths and better connect teachers with one another based on their expertise and needs? Has your supervision become less hierarchal and more personal? Do you see less jealousy, frustration, and burnout?
- Are teachers more competent in both short- and long-term planning? Are they able to identify and acquire appropriate resources?

Teacher Portfolios

Teacher portfolios encourage conversation about best practices. In this form of action research, teachers' classrooms become laboratories for reflecting on what they do and why they do it. With the support of the staff developer and the principal, they study a question related to their current teaching and become researchers using student work as evidence. They collect data, analyze it, formulate hypotheses, draw conclusions, and create an action plan to use in their classroom. Then they capture their teaching and learning strategies in writing so they can share these ideas with their colleagues. Portfolios are great vehicles for experienced teachers who are eager to share their skills with others.

Why Develop Portfolios?

Portfolios are valid, concrete, and educationally sound vehicles for creative supervision and can take the place of traditional observations. Through them, teachers' areas of expertise are pushed in new directions—they are prompted to think deeply about their own classroom practices and how they affect the shared goals of the community. Portfolios are an opportunity to refine practice and address each year's mandates (looking closely at student work, differentiating instruction, and focusing on cooperative learning, for example) in an integrated, practical way.

Portfolios invite every member of the school community to become a public expert—to share her expertise with her colleagues within the school and beyond. In creating a portfolio, teachers explain their best practices in their unique voices, tangibly fulfilling their shared responsibility for the school's success by functioning as de facto staff developers.

Portfolios foster collaboration rather than competition. They allow all teachers to lessen their professional isolation and implement new strategies at their own pace. Portfolios also turn teachers into writers; they become role models for students, parents, and visitors.

Portfolios are a way to appeal to teachers who are reluctant to participate in other forms of professional development. Because a portfolio is based on their strengths and passions as teachers and leads to the recognition of being published authors, many experienced teachers are more than willing to take advantage of this means of reflecting on their practices and reengaging as learners.

Finally, portfolios are excellent support material for grant applications, schoolwide assessments, and comprehensive planning.

Getting Started: Step by Step

1. Make everyone in the school community aware of the portfolio initiative: what is expected, what the payoff will be (in lieu of formal observation, extra money, more support, etc.), the criteria (expertise in a specific area, a special talent one wants to develop, a desire to take part in collegial self-improvement). Emphasize that the program is voluntary; it's important that teachers do not feel pressured or required to participate. You might distribute a letter like the one shown in Figure 5.3.

Dear Teachers,

As we look forward to our first meeting about portfolios, we thought outlining some possibilities would help clarify our expectations. Your portfolio might consist of

- a unit of study related to a theme or content area

- an investigation of possible answers to and reflections on a practical question about teaching practice:

    How can I incorporate essential questions in my social studies curriculum to insure transference of knowledge and deeper understanding of content?

    How can I use cooperative learning strategies in my math classroom to meet the diverse needs of my high achieving and struggling students and ensure problem solving and critical thinking skills grow stronger?

    How do I infuse writing in all content areas to help students deepen their thinking and improve their writing skills?

- strategies for connecting a personal interest with a curriculum area: a love of travel with a study of geography, a passion for art history with social studies

- an innovative teaching strategy or project that pushes student achievement to higher levels such as a new spelling program, an investigative approach to mathematical concept development, or a gender based reading structure.

    Every teacher has his or her own strengths, personality traits, and successful teaching techniques. Therefore, no two portfolios will ever be the same: each is a reflection of the teacher who created it. A portfolio is your opportunity to polish what you already do well, learn more about things that interest you, and share your ideas with others.

FIGURE 5.3

2. Engage in one-to-one conversations with a small group of teachers who you think are most willing and ready with exemplary work, assure them that they will have your support, and get their buy-in so that the plan can proceed. Identify at least five teachers who have the necessary expertise and are willing to begin the process.

3. Hold an informational meeting. Allow enough time for teachers to explore possibilities, ask questions, and voice concerns

4. Arrange to compensate teachers for the time they spend researching and writing the portfolio (or find ways to reward teachers by removing other responsibilities).

5. Create a system for helping teachers determine their portfolio topics, negotiating the writing process, and having ongoing conversations about their work.

6. Establish a system for publishing and distributing the portfolios.

7. Establish a time line for drafting, revising, and publishing the portfolios.

8. Talk privately with teachers who are reluctant to participate or seem overwhelmed by the process, and explore their issues and concerns.

9. Evaluate portfolios as part of the participating teachers' formal year-end assessments. This may be based on the Recommended Annual Supervisory Review Checklist, shown in Figure 5.4, or a similar tool already developed by your district or the state.

Recommended Annual Supervisory Review Checklist

1. The teacher has demonstrated an expertise in a curriculum area of her or his choosing. This area is developed in a detailed, in-depth portfolio that includes suggested lessons and a bibliography of research material that supports this educational philosophy.

2. The teacher has demonstrated a willingness to share this professional portfolio with others and welcome visitors into the classroom to observe teaching demonstrations.

3. The teacher understands that what happens in the classroom must reflect and support curriculum goals. The material in the portfolio fulfills professional curriculum responsibilities in regard to the area of expertise.

4. The teacher demonstrates the ability to assimilate new classroom practices and is on the alert for strategies that result in improved student achievement. The teacher requests and accepts supervisors' assistance in improving classroom instruction.

5. The teacher knows the ability levels of the students and is fully aware of how to motivate and support students to achieve their potential. The teacher respects each student's individual learning style and is able to accommodate individual needs.

May be copied for professional use. © 2008 by Carmen Fariña and Laura Kotch from *A School Leader's Guide to Excellence* (Heinemann: Portsmouth, NH).

FIGURE 5.4

10. Have the staff developer help individual teachers focus and narrow their topics and begin drafting their material, provide feedback on the ongoing writing, support those who struggle with putting thoughts on paper, and monitor scheduled completion dates. Teachers may find the tips in Figure 5.5 helpful.

11. Be sure teachers have the materials they need to conduct their research. Put a list of proposed topics in every teacher's mailbox to encourage collaboration and the sharing of information and materials.

12. When the portfolios are well along and have been revised on the basis of conversations with the staff developer, send a letter to the writers inviting them to share their drafts and their learning with you. The letter in Figure 5.6 illustrates a colearning stance and an invitational tone that work well.

13. Arrange for school personnel to help teachers design a cover for the portfolio, choose internal organizational features, and make copies for colleagues and visitors.

Talk and Listen

Share your work with a colleague; ongoing feedback and support are essential. You might even create a joint portfolio. Begin by discussing all the possibilities:

- What do I do very well?

- What do I love to do either as a teacher or as a learner?

- What issues do I worry about as I travel to school in the morning?

- What would I like to learn to do better? How can this learning enhance my school community?

- What new ideas am I eager to try?

As you share the answers to these questions, possible directions will begin to take shape. Don't feel you have to make a choice in a hurry. Give it a lot of thought. Often the best portfolios begin with a nagging question that won't leave you alone. Choose the issue that interests you most, which will also probably teach you the most.

Collect, Collect, Collect

Once you've decided on a topic, start your research. Keep a working folder of articles, ideas, resources, experts, conferences to attend, and so on. Begin making *jottings*—informal notes on questions, theories, experiences, experimental lessons, and observations. Your colleagues will contribute information if you let them know your area of focus. Sharing like this creates a community of teachers learning together.

Outline the Contents of Your Portfolio

- *A letter to the reader*: An introduction like this helps you identify your specific audience and explain who you are, what you believe about teaching and learning, what experiences you've had that have brought you to this point, and how you've learned what you know. Many teachers find it helpful to write this letter first, although it may be also be the most challenging part of the portfolio.

- *A description of your classroom*: Include a map of your classroom or list the key areas in the room. How does the focus of your investigation influence your decisions about the environment? How are your library and meeting area arranged and why? How are the children's desks arranged? Where are the materials kept to promote independence and responsibility? What study centers have you set up? A close look at the environment helps you see your classroom in new ways. It encourages you to rethink key decisions.

- *Replication tips*: Help readers understand the issues in your classroom so they can replicate or adapt your practice with their own students. Provide details about grouping, structure, scheduling, and planning. So often we rely on instinct without thinking deeply about what we do and why. Going step-by-step like this allows you to slow down and reflect.

- *Resources*: These include materials you use in the classroom, like novels, picture books, read-alouds, math manipulatives, and handouts, as well as any teacher references and guidebooks. Tell readers how they can gather similar resources.

- *Research*: Provide the reader with the current research that supports and documents the practices you are promoting. Also include the counterarguments to help prepare for questions and concerns of the audience. List the professional references and

FIGURE 5.5 *Tips for Creating a Portfolio Successfully (continues)*

resources you've consulted in order to know what to do. These may include books, magazine articles, journals, websites, and so forth.

- *Artifacts*: These are things that document your classroom practice or are produced as a result of it: student projects, student writing, audiotapes, videotapes, letters from parents, newspaper articles, and photographs. As your portfolio grows, case studies from a diverse group of students will be added to illustrate the evidence of the work you are doing. You'll want to add evaluations and reflections from students and teachers in the form of letters, surveys, and anecdotal jottings.

Draft the Portfolio

Begin with whatever section seems easiest. The hardest thing is forcing yourself to sit down and write. Sharing your thoughts with a supportive colleague will help you get started. Scheduling a sizeable chunk of time just for drafting works better than trying to fit it in around your other activities. The most important thing is to begin and give yourself permission to write a *rough draft*; you can revise it later. Focus on what you can do, and silence the doubts and negative feelings (*I can't do this*).

Revise Your Work

Your partner can help you recognize where revisions are necessary. These questions may help:

- Is my topic too broad or too narrow?

- Are my thoughts clear to the reader?

- Did I say what I intended?

- Do my thoughts follow a logical sequence?

- Is there a better way to organize the parts?

- Is my language clear?

Publish Your Portfolio

After you have completed your revisions and another writer has reviewed your final version, you are ready to publish—to share your portfolio with an audience. Make sure the writing is legible and easy to read. If you can, celebrate your work publicly and bask in the recognition of your community.

Grow Your Portfolio

The best portfolios grow over time and change as you add artifacts, revise your thinking, and refine your work.

FIGURE 5.5 *Tips for Creating a Portfolio Successfully (continued)*

Dear Colleague,

I would like to begin our conversations about your portfolio, since you are now almost ready to publish it and there is so much learning for us to share. In our time together, I hope we can discuss these questions:

• What are you finding in the course of your research or investigation?

• How are you sharing this information?

• How is this new way of working affecting your students (average, above average, and those with difficulties)?

• What adjustments have you had to make to accommodate different learning styles?

• Where do you hope to go from here? How can I help you do that?

Please select the time you would like to meet with me (see below); whatever time you choose will be uninterrupted.

       __ preparation period

       __ after school

       __ lunchtime

Thank you for your cooperation and professionalism. I look forward to our meeting.

FIGURE 5.6 *Sharing the Portfolio Learning*

14. Celebrate the completion of the portfolios and display them in a public place.

15. Send a "Dear Author" letter to all teachers who have completed a portfolio (see Figure 5.7).

16. Arrange audiences for the published portfolios by scheduling visits, workshops, and opportunities for teachers to teach one another what they have learned through this process.

17. Encourage teachers to become mentors for each other. Match those who have published portfolios with those who have not yet become involved. Continue to encourage all members of the staff to participate in this process by noticing and affirming expertise.

18. Think about how you can expand the portfolio program to meet new school needs.

Dear Author,

Congratulations on your published portfolio! It has been a delight to see the ongoing effort you have made to complete your study. Your dedication, enthusiasm, and professionalism shine through. Learning is an ongoing process, and I hope that next year you will expand the portfolio as you continue to deepen your knowledge and focus on our schoolwide goals.

At our celebration next week, all the members of our community will receive a copy of your portfolio. Please also have your portfolio available for each visitor who comes to your classroom and spends time with you. You might also present your portfolio at parent workshops, teacher workshops within our district, and professional conferences (applications are available on the respective organizations' websites).

The time you have spent researching your topic, the student work you have provided, your focus on meeting the needs of struggling students, the clarity of your writing, and the passion of your beliefs all make your portfolio very powerful. I know that this work was sometimes a challenge, requiring many revisions as you narrowed your topic and focused the work. Your determination and relentless pursuit of excellence will be a powerful model for your students; I hope you have shared your struggles as well as your successes with them.

I know we can count on you to share your expertise with our new teachers as they begin their careers here with us next year. Would you consider inviting a colleague who has not yet participated in the portfolio program to be your coauthor of a portfolio next year?

Once again, I want you to know that you have my sincere admiration. Congratulations!

FIGURE 5.7 *Dear Author Congratulatory Letter*

Avoiding Common Pitfalls

Knowing your staff well is the most important prerequisite. Establish a firm, trusting relationship with your staff before embarking on this initiative to ensure that you will have volunteers for this initiative.

Clearly define the criteria for who should and should not participate. Teachers whose classroom skills are inadequate, who are poor communicators, or who are not knowledgeable about curriculum content will undermine the program if they are allowed to participate. Support teachers who want to participate but are unable to name their area of expertise.

This process is very time-consuming. Principals, staff developers, and whoever else is supporting professional development will support the work best by spending time in the classrooms talking with teachers and observing evidence of expertise firsthand. Have continuing conversations with the staff developer, and align the portfolios with the professional development on which the school is focusing.

Portfolios need to be an entity on their own, not added to other initiatives. You will need to support a portfolio program over a period of many years to ensure real benefit and deepen the work over time. Teachers who create portfolios need to be paid for this extra effort or compensated in other ways. The staff developer will need to plan his time in advance to ensure teachers get the support they need.

Be flexible about teachers' participation. Keep in mind that there will be a natural tension during the first year of the program, when some teachers are celebrated and others are not.

Remember that portfolios need audiences. You must be willing to create them in whatever ways you need to.

Evaluating Success

To determine whether the creation and dissemination of professional portfolios has deepened conversations, promoted reflection, encouraged teacher leadership, promoted writing as a vehicle for critical thinking, increased collaboration, and positively affected student performance, look for evidence like this:

• Is this close look at teaching practices and student learning leading to improved student achievement? Are the diverse needs of students addressed in ways that allow them to achieve rigorous standards more quickly?

• Has teachers' ability to write and publish portfolios successfully led to the introduction of student portfolios as an evaluation for learning? Do the opportunity and ability to reflect and self-assess also extend to students?

• Are teachers becoming writing models for their students? Are they better able to relate to struggling writers? Are they better able to help students improve their writing?

• Has creating professional portfolios provided an opportunity for teachers to become active learners and teacher researchers? In a profession where time to reflect is often difficult to come by, has writing portfolios helped teachers clarify their beliefs about teaching and learning? In this time of inquiry-based assessment, have portfolios encouraged teachers to articulate their practices and connect them with evidence of student achievement? Are teachers experimenting with new ideas, investigating lingering questions, and rethinking existing practices?

• Are teachers who are recognized and celebrated by their colleagues and others demonstrating renewed energy, increased self-confidence, and improved competence?

• Are teachers applying for more grants, writing professional articles, and forming enrichment classes and clubs?

• Are teacher portfolios encouraging collaboration? Are they a rich resource for community learning? Are other schools taking advantage of this expertise and visiting classrooms to borrow ideas? Are parents viewing the teachers as intellectual thinkers?

• Are more teachers becoming teacher leaders in various roles? Are more teachers taking advantage of this evaluation tool to reflect on and analyze their practices and become independent decision makers and self-evaluators?

• Is the community eager to engage in inquiry-based professional development, with its commitment to meaningful conversation, reflective thinking, and extensive writing and revising? Are more teachers creating portfolios each year and encouraging colleagues to participate as well? Is this practice becoming part of the school culture?

The following comments from teachers speak to the power of professional portfolios:

> The process of writing a portfolio was a somewhat spiritual experience in terms of my teaching. I was able to clarify in my own mind what I had accomplished, how I did it, and whether it was successful. Essentially my teaching philosophy as well as my teaching methods were put into print. When I completed my portfolio and read it, I felt proud of my accomplishments and excited about the thought of what I can accomplish next year.

> Having someone to clarify my ideas and guide my thoughts to fruition was so satisfying.

> The most valuable thing I learned from my portfolio is the reflection. Not until I sat down to type it did I really reread and make connections and see the actual growth in my class. It helped boost my self-confidence when I wasn't sure if what I was doing was correct.

One Teacher's Portfolio—Assessing Reading and Writing Using Response Letters

A fifth-grade teacher who was experimenting with ways to teach reading wanted to use his own thinking about reading as a model to deepen the understanding of his students. He did not want to rely solely on formal reading evaluations and was committed to getting to know his students based on their thinking about the books they read.

The professional development sessions he'd attended often confused him and led him to question both his own and his colleagues' practices. He wanted to puzzle out his thinking and prove to the administration and his colleagues that exchanging weekly letters with students did enhance their reading ability and that becoming more aware of each student's current reading and writing abilities helped him create individual teaching plans as well as lessons geared to the whole class.

His portfolio discusses why the strategy of response letters was generated, gives specific directions so that other teachers can replicate the practice, shares his frustrations and challenges, and gives examples of letters written both to and from his students. It also includes a summary of what he learned from his investigation and recommendations for follow-up work.

The portfolio, which was developed more than fifteen years ago, is just as timely now, because it demonstrates the power of teachers as researcher and tells the honest story of one teacher's journey to connect with the students in his class as reader to reader, which was his passion. The teacher's introductory letter, shown in Figure 5.8, outlines what he wanted to study and why and generates interest in and support for his topic. Figure 5.9 outlines his response letter strategy.

Steve wrote a letter to his fifth graders explaining the purpose of the response letters and the connection he had forged with them through the letters (see Figure 5.10). The letter validated Steve's own thinking and encouraged his students to dig deeply into the text they were reading and respond with their own thinking. Steve used his own search for meaning to show his students the strategies of lifelong readers and writers.

Steve's reasons for recommending this approach to his colleagues, which are listed in Figure 5.11, offer crucial support for his belief that evaluating students involves a personal connection and is so much more than their test scores.

This portfolio was the basis of many impassioned conversations Steve had with his colleagues and with us about the need for multitiered assessments that capture the complexity of student learning and build on individual talents and strengths. The learning documented in this portfolio demonstrated the depth of Steve's commitment to knowing his students well. The personal connections he made with his students and the things he learned about them from their weekly letters made his report card comments and parent-teacher conferences extremely powerful and satisfying. We used his expertise in workshops for new teachers on how to write meaningful report card comments and to help them plan insightful parent-teacher conferences.

Dear Colleague Readers,

I'm attracted to ideas. I like discovering them from other people, and I love coming up with my own.

Ideas mean different things to different people; I tend to think of them as thoughts that are new for whoever has them. Certainly there are a wide range of ideas, influenced by the age of the thinker, his prior knowledge and experiences, his facility with language, and many other factors. There is also a very great range in the quality of ideas. I want to distinguish ideas from facts and information, though I realize a well-known fact for one person may be a great discovery for someone else.

The role of teacher is wrapped up with the concept of ideas. We struggle to come up with our own ideas for addressing the staggering number of problems that need solving; we need to introduce the ideas behind our curriculum; and we would love to find a way to enable our students to leave our care with a sharper ability to come up with their own ideas and be more able to spot the great concepts of others.

Unfortunately, much of our time is spent showing our students how to meet basic grade-level requirements and assessing whether they are doing so. How, you might ask, can I cover my curriculum and assessment needs and at the same time satisfy my wish to give my students a stronger relationship to ideas, particularly their own?

I don't have the definitive answer, but I am confident I have made a start. Reading response letters, which are the subject of this portfolio, are not my idea (I'm not sure who started them or when), but I've used them regularly over the years and to an even greater extent this year. I feel it satisfies a number of issues for the teacher concerned with teaching higher-level thinking, introducing students to quality literature, and assessing their reading. The following pages describe some of the procedures for getting started. I consider this a work in progress; there is room for much refinement and new ideas.

FIGURE 5.8 *Portfolio Introductory Letter*

- A reading response letter is one or two pages long and is addressed to the teacher, the author, or a character in the story. In the letter, students are expected to share ideas, concerns, questions, and observations from and about the book.

- The letter is an open-ended assignment allowing the student to branch off in a variety of directions but always highlighting personal connections.

- The letters are never expected to be summaries or retellings but rather to stress a personal connection to the text. There is no right or wrong way to do the letters as long as they have a personal voice.

- Implicit in this strategy is the idea that writing response letters is how adults respond to rich ideas in a community of literate readers.

- Steps in creating response letters:

    - Read the text and think about the personal meaning you take from it.

    - Take notes about your ideas, the questions raised in the text, and the theme the author is conveying.

    - Discuss your ideas with a partner to clarify your thinking.

    - Begin your first draft with the reader in mind (the teacher, the character, the author); speak personally to the reader.

    - Reread your draft for meaning and clarity; make sure there is evidence from the text for every idea.

    - Revise, proofread, and give to the teacher every Friday.

- The teacher reads each letter and responds personally to each student.

- The teacher selects model letters that illustrate best practices for others to follow and shares them with the class.

- The teacher provides strategies for improving response letters, such as writing more clearly, staying on point, using evidence from the text, asking the important questions, and avoiding generalizations.

- The teachers presents minilessons matched to the needs of the students.

- The teacher writes a letter to the whole class modeling effective strategies that address student needs discovered during the weekly letters. For example, if students seem to be struggling to organize their thinking into big ideas, the teacher's letter would model how this is done so that they might do the same.

FIGURE 5.9 *How to Use Response Letters*

Dear Student Readers,

I've been finding myself, more than ever before in my teaching career, enjoying the writing of my students. I think this is because as fifth graders you are able to write substantial letters, full of ideas, opinions, and observations, instead of repeating what I already know. Children in the younger grades often have trouble making even the simplest points. (Since it wasn't too long ago, some of you remember that feeling well.) Today all of you are busy putting down ideas of your own, helping me in two ways: one, I get to know you better, and two, I learn more about the material we are reading.

How do I learn more about our novels through your writing? One way, of course, is when someone notices something I paid little attention to. Tom, in his letter, observed that characters in Katherine Paterson's contemporary novels often call their parents by their first names, something he found to be quite strange. I appreciate his point because I'm reminded how different our culture can be from the culture of a character we are reading about and how such customs come and go. (When I was a senior in high school everyone I knew all at once began referring to their parents by their first name, as if we were all one big group of chums.) I end up seeing the novel a bit more deeply through such insights. I become more aware of what details an alert fifth grader can notice.

The second way I gain deeper understanding is through questioning and wondering. Last Friday, Lucy said that she is enjoying *Bridge to Terabithia* and doesn't know why, since the beginning seems to lack action. I hope she can find the answer to this question and, since it is one she's asked before, perhaps reframe it. That's what thinking is about. But at the same time it's an intriguing question, one I puzzle over myself: why *do* kids like this book so much? Without action, what is the appeal? On Friday, I put Lucy's question into my mental trunk of cluttered wonderings to let it simmer for a while. I had some theories to consider but I wanted to give it some time.

Lucy of course must answer this question for herself; no one can do it for her. As I try to answer the question for myself, I can't be certain what moves kids most about *Bridge to Terabithia*, but I do have a theory. And the theory sprang from your letters. All of you touched on the power of imagination. Sally wrote, "Leslie's and Jesse's imaginary kingdom makes you want to forget everything around you." Jon said, "Terabithia is a private place."

I suspect kids appreciate the creativity of Leslie and Jesse in inventing a world of their own to play in, and they recognize that same creativity in themselves. Ms. Paterson supplies just enough details to make this world come alive in the reader's mind, from the ritual of arriving in Terabithia to the speeches of the natives. I think these examples touch us because we love the mystery and the power of the imagination, especially our own.

I have enjoyed reading this book with you and reflecting on the power of our questions to trigger an inquiry while also looking for sources to support our theories.

Sincerely,

FIGURE 5.10 *Teacher's Letter to Students*

- Quiet students who may never be comfortable expressing their thinking in a conversation are able to communicate their thought process and their personal circumstances in writing.

- They reveal students in a way that can be very different from the way they appear in the classroom.

- They contain clues to the students' reading habits and preferences. The teacher can then stock the classroom library accordingly and give the students more ownership over what they read.

- They make the reading-writing connection concrete and help students transfer strengths from one area to another. They provide an authentic reason and concrete audience for writing.

- They are a window into the students' comprehension strategies and can elevate the level of student conversation.

- Reading and analyzing the letters lets the teacher get to know the students well and group them more effectively.

- They move students toward independence. The more capable students can become peer tutors while the teacher supports the students who struggle most.

- They connect students with one another and help strengthen their sense of community. They also connect the teacher with each student as a coreader and a model.

- They document student progress and help students assess themselves and reflect on their goals.

- They are a source of specific and personal feedback during parent conferences and meetings.

FIGURE 5.11 *Why Reading Response Letters Are a Powerful Assessment Tool*

Peer Coaching

In peer coaching, two carefully matched teachers are given many opportunities to meet and plan together for their mutual benefit. They visit each other's classrooms, identify practical next steps, and provide specific feedback. Discussing teaching decisions and curriculum implementation with a compatible colleague makes the process of planning more meaningful, promotes reflective thinking, and builds consistent schoolwide practice. Matching curriculum expertise is essential, particularly in secondary education, where content area knowledge is as valuable as strategies for managing discipline, classroom routines, and organization.

Peer coaching is a particularly valuable way to help teachers who haven't had the experience of teaching as students or interns, and the more experienced teachers who coach them benefit by acquiring skills that help them move up the career ladder: they learn leadership strategies and how to become supportive colleagues. They also have the satisfaction of being recognized as master teachers.

Through peer coaching, teachers become committed to the success of their peers and the larger community. It is also a great way to introduce people to the pleasures and challenges of leadership. Principals who implement peer coaching demonstrate their trust and confidence in their teaching staff and empower them to help others and take their own learning seriously. Peer coaching, supported by study groups, retreats, and conferences, strengthens the social network, builds a collaborative culture, and leads to greater teacher satisfaction.

Why Use Peer Coaching?

Peer coaching is a venue for collaborating and sharing expertise; it fosters unity of purpose. It ensures that knowledge, history, and culture are passed from one generation to another. It is a way to recognize experienced staff members and solicit their help in becoming familiar with curriculum areas outside the leader's expertise while other pressing issues are addressed.

Through peer coaching, teachers build trusting relationships that allow them to ask questions and air concerns that might not be appropriate in other contexts. Peer coaching demonstrates the value you place on your teachers' expertise and the confidence you have in their ability to lead.

Finally, parents are often apprehensive when they feel that an inexperienced teacher is working with their children; knowing that an experienced teacher is supporting the neophyte is reassuring.

Avoiding Common Pitfalls

Peer coaching is a more equalitarian than mentoring. Teachers are not placed in hierarchal roles; rather, both teachers benefit equally. Therefore, teachers may be matched in ways other than years of experience or academic credentials. If you establish transparent criteria—expertise in a particular content area, a reputation as a successful classroom teacher, willingness to participate, strong interpersonal skills—everyone will understand that the partnership is one of equals. Unsatisfactory teachers need another kind of supervision.

You and the partner teachers need to determine confidentiality and privacy parameters at the start, so that everyone's rights are respected and no one becomes the subject of school gossip. Training led by an expert may be necessary to help peer coaches understand that their roles are supportive, not supervisory. Ultimately, you are responsible for decisions about ratings and staff retention.

Peer coaches need time, training, and monetary compensation or other rewards. As with any relationship, peer coaches will experience ups and downs; they need the constant support of a supervisor who can troubleshoot problems, give advice and affirmation, and realign partnerships when necessary.

Evaluating Success

To determine whether the support provided by peer coaches is leading to improved teaching practices, more teacher satisfaction, and greater student achievement, look for evidence like this:

• Are curriculum expertise, department and grade expectations, and pedagogical practices more consistent?

• Are teachers who participate in peer coaching more invested in school initiatives and energized to commit to school renewal and reform?

- Are new teachers more easily acculturated into the school community? Are more teachers staying at the school longer?
- Is there more sharing and inquiry-based dialogue?
- Are you demonstrating your commitment to distributive leadership and your confidence in your staff's expertise?
- Are your teachers becoming more interested in their own learning and taking advantage of teacher leadership opportunities?

Develop a Culture for Sustainable Professional Learning

Dear Reader,

When we became part of the community of District 2 under the leadership of Tony Alvarado and Elaine Fink, we saw firsthand their powerful commitment to professional development and the impact this sense of urgency had on the entire district. Tony's belief and support for adult learning and his bottom-line expectation that principals and teachers would participate in professional development side by side were revolutionary and helped make District 2 a model learning community.

The principals' conferences there were dramatically different from most meetings we had attended in the past. We looked forward to hearing Tony speak at the beginning of each session; he shared his passion for improving instruction, his latest professional reading, and his conviction that together we could change teaching and learning for all students. He challenged us to address issues of inequity and low expectations; later, in small groups, we planned how we would follow through in our own communities.

Our priority at these meetings was to increase our understanding of teaching and learning through collaborative inquiry. Administrative issues were relegated to a half hour, usually just before lunch. In afternoon study groups, principals and staff developers had inquiry-based discussions on topics chosen by the participants and led by facilitators. During these sessions we often visited schools, discussed professional reading, and examined student work.

As a result of this serious study, the more than thirty schools in the district, serving students in kindergarten through grade 12, were able to build consistent practices. These conversations and support materials allowed us to extend our thinking and share our learning with others. The meetings, often hosted by arts organizations or businesses, were held in welcoming, comfortable places that made us feel honored and respected. Informal networking during tasty breakfasts and lunches helped us form bonds with our colleagues and lessened the sense of competition. Professional development, with its premise that learning never ends, helped us focus on instruction and push ourselves to do more and do it better.

We took all the good ideas about professional development we learned in District 2 and adapted many of them to meet the unique needs of District 15. We carefully planned a year's calendar of monthly principal meetings based on what our principals (during one-to-one conversations, in surveys, and on feedback forms) said were their most pressing issues. Principals contributed their expertise in leading these conversations and opened their schools to visits. Small study groups formed around diverse needs and interests. Each session included time to practice strategies with colleagues while working closely with staff developers.

We looked forward to these monthly meetings because they were our opportunity to make our support for learning public, encourage networking and collaboration, celebrate success, and pose new challenges. We spent the month between the meetings planning, gathering materials, and anticipating surprises, then opened each session by talking about our mission for the schools, highlighting the day's learning, and doing our best to inspire leaders to confront their particular challenges and obstacles with courage and confidence. We connected with each principal personally, observed their interactions, apologized for any missteps we made, and followed up with phone calls.

Many of the structures and rituals that were effective with principals—study groups, curriculum development meetings, special-interest and advocacy groups, lab sites, classroom visits, school walk-throughs, and professional development courses and institutes—were also effective with teachers, administrators, staff developers, and parents. The result was a common language, consistent practices, and an increased capacity to learn. These structures and rituals were the glue that held all members of the community together, inspiring and energizing them to continue their collaborative learning. They made the learning personal and compelling and helped the community feel supported and comfortable.

Excellence in teaching and learning requires that professional development become a way of life. Our definition of professional development is very different from the passive, one-shot, product-based, vendor-driven programs too often encountered in schools. For us, professional development is an interactive, process-based context for new learning that is practical (for both students and adults) and transferable to the real world. Professional development works best when it is based on high expectations for students and adults alike, invites critical thinking, encourages decision making, and moves everyone toward independence. It is not skill drills, formula-driven memorization, or instruction in how to prepare for standardized tests.

Professional development can be measured by the quality of the peer-to-peer conversations, the questions participants ask, and the new practices and strategic thinking it generates. It is most meaningful when it is rooted in classroom practice and the examination of student work. The most important investment leaders can make to introduce and sustain school reform is effective and consistent professional development in which all members of the community are invited to see themselves and one another as curious and proactive learners. Leaders who are willing to model their own learning invite others to join them, thereby establishing leaders for tomorrow. Professional development linked to well-established structures and predictable and exciting rituals bonds people together. The transfer of learning then becomes the responsibility of the community.

A principal's job can be lonely and isolating, but undertaking meaningful learning with like-minded colleagues transforms the experience. The trust established promotes honest conversations, risk taking, and collaborative decision making throughout the school community. Principals who are fully engaged in their own learning study their school's effectiveness, research best practices, visit successful schools, and replicate and adapt effective strategies. Collaborative learning stimulates deep thinking about teaching and learning and ensures that our students are prepared to be active participants in a global world.

—Carmen and Laura

Why Institute Professional Development?

Professional development is an opportunity to incubate new ideas, inquire into big questions (how best to implement new strategies and integrate them into existing programs, for example), and come to a consensus about how best to proceed. Introducing controversial initiatives successfully depends on ongoing conversations and abundant support. All members of the community, including parents, need to know that thoughtful research and learning are part of every decision and action. Professional development reminds the community of the leader's focus and invites ownership and responsibility.

It is also a concrete link to classrooms. It focuses on student work and on assessments of both teacher and student performance, ensuring that both eager and reluctant learners meet rigorous standards.

Professional development encourages and enables new members of the community to become leaders and ensures a smooth transition when these new leaders take the helm. It is a context for linking new initiatives with existing ones and ensuring that teachers incorporate new methodologies and practices. When continually assessed by the community and evolved from community members' recommendations and expertise, professional development prompts the energy and enthusiasm needed to sustain learning over time.

Getting Started: Step by Step

1. Begin by assessing a wide range of student achievement data, previous professional development efforts and results, and classroom practices.

2. Conduct a survey (see the example in Figure 6.1) to determine professional development priorities and the readiness and willingness of the community to embark on them.

3. Examine when professional learning has taken place in the past. How important is professional development to the community during school hours?

Principals' Professional Development Survey

Directions: *As we begin to rethink professional development for principals for next year, we would like to tailor our offerings to better meet your needs. In that vein, we are asking that you take a few minutes to complete this survey about your own professional development this year. Feel free to attach additional sheets as necessary.*

1. In which professional development activities, workshops, study groups or seminars did you participate during the 2003-2004 school year? [*Circle all that apply*]

   Principals Conferences   Summer PD
   Study Groups   April Institutes
   Saturday Seminars   Middle School Symposium
   Network/cluster meetings   Teachers College Principal Conference Days
   Intervisitations   Reading professional books
   Walkthroughs

2. In what ways was the professional development helpful to you in your work with faculty and staff?

3. a) What would make professional development offerings richer?

   b) Do you have ideas for topics you would like to see addressed next year?

4. Which formats do you find most productive/useful/helpful?

5. a) As you reflect on the year, what did you find most challenging, and in what ways can we support you next year?

   b) What can you contribute to the professional learning community?

Name: [Optional]_____   *Years as principal:* [Circle]   1-3   3-5   5+

Level: [Circle]   Elementary   Middle   Secondary   High

FIGURE 6.1

after hours? Be aware of possible contractual issues and work closely with union representatives.

4. Meet with small groups to discuss the learning priorities and possible structures and plan next steps.

5. Align professional development efforts with the stated goals for the year and gather necessary resources.

6. Plan a series of conferences for members of your community and decide which predictable and continuing rituals will anchor the learning. Choose the books of the month to distribute at each meeting. Prepare a system for organizing the distribution of materials at each conference for efficacy, predictability, and uniformity. (We always used the same color folder with a quote on the cover that matched the conference theme, with professional development materials on one side, and the administrative materials on the other.)

- During the summer, distribute a schedule of meetings for the year (see the example in Figure 6.2). You will want to choose a predictable time (the first Wednesday of each month) to ensure that calendars will be marked accordingly. Meetings should never be canceled except in dire emergencies. Keeping to the schedule demonstrates the importance of this time in

---

<u>Principals' Conferences</u>

September 25 – Best Practices in Literacy

October 23 – Best Practices in Intervention/Enrichment
Meeting the Needs of Diverse Learners – Looking at Student Work

November 20 – Best Practices in Mathematics –
Meeting the Needs of Diverse Students - Looking at Student Work

December 18 – Best Practices in Technology –
Meeting the Needs of Diverse Learners – Looking at Student Work

January 22 – Best Practices in Literacy for English Language Learners–
Meeting the Needs of Diverse Learners – Looking at Student Work

February 26 – Best Practices in Student Support Services/Guidance Strategies –
To Prevent Academic Failure – Highlight: Student Leadership

March 19 – Best Practices in Inquiry/Research for Science/Social Studies
Meeting the Needs of Diverse Learners – Looking at Student Work

April 30 – Best Practices in the Arts
Meeting the Needs of Diverse Learners – Looking at Student Work

May 21 – Sharing Best Practices for Leadership
Looking at Student Work

FIGURE 6.2

the life of the community and your commitment to ongoing communication in sustaining both social and academic goals.

◆ Choose a setting that is conducive to conversation and allows people to interact with a minimum of distractions.

◆ Establish norms of behavior: respecting confidentiality and different opinions, taking notes, turning off cell phones and other wireless devices.

◆ Be respectful of participants' time. Announce meeting start and end times in advance, and hold to them.

◆ Limit the number of participants to foster intimate conversation, and give every participant an opportunity to talk. Break a large group into several smaller groups if necessary.

◆ Differentiate support according to unique needs and interests. Participants with more experience or expertise can support those who have less.

◆ Circulate an agenda in advance of each meeting, highlighted by an appropriate quote that sets the tone and inspires participation. Pose clearly defined topics as questions participants can think about ahead of time. Allot an amount of time for each topic, and honor it. See that the topic is resolved; don't carry agenda items over from meeting to meeting. Figure 6.3 is an example of an agenda that holds all members accountable for contributing their ideas and achieving stated goals.

It is one thing to write like a poet, and another thing to write like a historian. The poet can tell or sing of things not as they were but as they ought to have been, whereas the historian must describe them, not as they ought to have been, but as they were, without exaggerating or hiding the truth in any way.

-Miguel de Cervantes

Monthly Instructional Conference
Wednesday, January 16

8:30 – 9:00	Breakfast (Networking)
9:00 – 10:45	Implementing Social Studies Curriculum
	Consistent, Rigorous, Thought-provoking
	Reading – Writing Core
	Why?
	How?
	What?
	When?
11:00 – 12:00	Tour of African Exhibit
12:00 – 1:00	A Proactive Approach – Planning for Next Year

- Student & Teacher Recruitment
- Use of Time – Scheduling – Rigor
- Budget

Extended Conversation – Everyone Welcome

Tuesday, January 22, 2002
12:00 – 2:00
District Office

FIGURE 6.3

◆ Begin each meeting by sharing a *short* inspirational text—a poem, a page from a picture book, an article, an essay, a short story, a cartoon, a vignette. Criteria include beautiful language, a compelling message, and content appropriate to the specific audience. We keep a file of texts that we use again and again. Two of our favorites are "To Be of Use," by Marge Piercy, and *Courage* by Bernard Waber. *Teaching with Fire: Poetry That Sustains the Courage to Teach*, edited by Sam M. Intrator and Megan Scribner, contains lots of other wonderful possibilities. The simplest way to share these short texts is to give each member of the community a copy and read the piece aloud while everyone follows along. Or you could ask the audience to read the text silently first, marking their favorite lines; then begin reading the text aloud and have members of the audience join in on their favorite sections. So many voices, with different cadences and timbres, reading as one turn the piece into an anthem representative of the diversity and unity of the community. Participants can then turn and talk about the text, sharing their personal reflections. Hearing these different perspectives makes members of the community more open to one another's ideas, better listeners, and more accepting of one another's personalities and motivations and sets the tone of interactive learning for the rest of the meeting. Using the same text for different audiences is perfectly OK: it allows people to talk about the piece from a wider range of perspectives and prompts deeper and more lasting energy and inspiration. Giving each member of the audience their own copy of the short text allows them to begin their own collection to share with their community and expands literacy to a wider audience.

◆ Collect administrative issues—compliance data and other requests for information, updated rules and regulations—under a single, brief "keeping current" agenda item. Prepare a supplemental color-coded handout (see the example in Figure 6.4) that is both an easy reference and a legal document conveying the responsibility of being aware of and complying with the items noted.

◆ Distribute carefully chosen professional articles related to the meeting topic to affirm current practices and stretch participants to think more deeply. Provide time during the meeting for participants to talk about these articles.

◆ Share best practices via voices from the field. In this part of the meeting, members of the community lead discussions about their curricular areas of expertise; courageous decisions they've made (integrating special education students into the classroom, for example); strategies for working with English language learners and their parents; strategies for forming study groups; strategies for mentoring new teachers; collaborations with colleagues to support new initiatives; and so on. Rotating this opportunity so everyone gets a chance to be an expert creates a spirit of collaboration, not competition. Highlighting people for their strengths creates a collegial environment; over time, these people are eager to share instructional information in person, on web pages, and in chat rooms.

Keeping Current - August

Confidential Student Information

It is essential that records be disposed of in a way that protects the confidentiality of information both to protect individual privacy and to comply with the law. Student records, for example, must be treated as confidential under federal state law. It is obvious that such documents must not simply be left for regular trash pick-up in open containers outside of a school building.

You must retain student records and other information in accordance with the Board's record retention policy. Documents may be requested for investigative, audit or monitoring purposes, long after children or employees have left your school. In that regard, in February the Office of Legal Services, issued a specific instruction that any documents relating to health related services, such as speech therapy, occupational therapy, physical therapy, counseling, special transportation, and nursing, provided to children in special education be retained.

September 11

I know that you will be planning appropriate activities in consultation with school leadership teams. Do not allow reporters, cameras, etc. to interview, photograph any students, classrooms on September 11. As a district, we will observe a moment of silence at 9:00 a.m.

Special Education Supervisors

In order to support their curricular leadership, this year all special education supervisors will have their own curriculum development added to their monthly meetings. I especially recommend they attend selected professional development during selected Fridays. I expect special education supervisors to be visiting classrooms and promoting appropriate classroom practices and environments.

Suspensions

If we are truly to serve our students, we must make a greater effort to put preventive procedures in place to lessen our suspension rate. This year, we will be focusing on this issue and look forward to sharing successful strategies.

FIGURE 6.4

◆ Serve food. It needn't be elaborate, but eating together encourages social interaction.

◆ Acknowledge successes (large and small) at the end of every meeting. These shout-outs are best when they are very specific, not just a generic "Good job!" Examples include academic achievements, personal benchmarks, challenges overcome, service to others. You should model this ritual initially, being sure to acknowledge every participant at some point. Later you can encourage community members to "shout out" compliments to one another.

◆ End each meeting by asking for written feedback on whether the meeting was effective and how it might have been improved; be sure to follow up on these recommendations.

7. In addition, set up consistent and predictable small-group structures that help make professional development the focus of life in your community. Examples include the following:

◆ *Professional development team meetings*: The professional development team—made up of school-based staff developers, outside consultants, teacher leaders, the principal, and the assistant principal—assesses the learning taking place in a school through conversations, surveys, walk-throughs, and examinations of student work. The team supports the principal in laying out the year's plan, including the professional development focus, the structures that will best support this focus, how best to differentiate support, and how to assess and celebrate progress toward established benchmarks. Teachers may be offered a variety of options: participating in lab sites and demonstration lessons, taking courses and attending institutes, working in study groups, and participating in walk-throughs and intervisitations. The team also establishes procedures for monitoring progress, evaluating what is working and what adjustments need to be made, and troubleshooting problems. Leaders often write a letter to the community at the beginning of the new school year to communicate the goals and expectations of the year's professional development initiative, the roles and responsibilities of the staff developer and the participating teachers, and the urgency of working to improve teaching and learning for all students. (A sample letter from a superintendent to principals is shown in Figure 6.5; principals can write a similar letter to their teachers.)

Dear Colleagues,

We begin a new school year dedicated to working together to strengthen our professional learning community, building on each member's unique strengths and uniting around a shared vision. We count on you, as the model learner, to make sure professional development is the center of life at your school. Your direct involvement in planning, scheduling and implementing professional development will model its importance, move initiatives forward, farther and faster, and build school-wide momentum.

The district **literacy and math staff developers** (along with Teachers' College, CCNY and AUSSIE consultants) will be essential supporters in establishing clear expectations and strengthening best practices for teaching and learning in your school. They will:

- Serve as leaders of your math and literacy team.
- Provide demonstration lesions for groups of teachers.
- Build the capacity of teacher leaders through coaching, study groups and intervisitations.
- Facilitate grade meetings to analyze student work and plan effective instruction.
- Walk the building with you and assess strengths, needs and next steps.
- Meet weekly with you to provide specific feedback to help you notice and affirm teacher growth and alert you to areas of concern so that you can follow up.
- Connect you to learning opportunities within our district and beyond.

The district staff developers have demonstrated their ability through a rigorous selection process and will strengthen their content knowledge, peer coaching skills and accountability through bi-monthly professional development. Directors of professional development will be working closely with you and your staff developers to address issues and concerns and ensure success. They will be contacting you to arrange visits of new staff developers to your school, and to support you in planning short and long term initiatives, scheduling time and helping to forge a strong beginning. The urgency of using time well requires careful thought. Staff developers' schedules should be posted on a professional development bulletin board, along with topics of weekly demonstration lessons, articles and study group meetings. Please keep the following ideas in mind as you create schedules:

Teachers' College leadership participants, ALPS interns, social studies liaisons, classroom cluster teachers, mentors, paraprofessionals and parents can all be powerful resources. Each school will establish their professional development team and meet regularly to keep the focus on established goals.

Teacher leaders are also essential members of this team. They will have an expanded role this year and will be asked to plan with you as to how their per session allocation will be utilized (see attached form). We will continue our effort to recruit teacher leaders, especially for special education (posting enclosed).

Thank you, in advance, for your time and energy in getting the most from the professional development structures we have put into place for your school. We appreciate your contribution to our learning community.

Sincerely,

Carmen Fariña
Carmen Fariña
Community Superintendent

FIGURE 6.5

◆ *Cabinet meetings*: A cabinet is a small group of people with whom you share your instructional priorities and who help you lead the school. Cabinet members should be committed to the school's mission, have leadership potential, be divergent thinkers, be willing to take on extra responsibilities, and be able to make wise, thoughtful, confident decisions. Members might include the assistant principal, a guidance counselor, an in-house coach or outside staff development consultant, a teacher leader, a parent leader, or any other person who can assist in conveying and implementing the school's mission and the professional development plan by which this mission is accomplished. Predictable, consistent, interactive weekly cabinet meetings with focused agendas and timely follow-up ensure that you are not leading alone. Listening to cabinet members' opinions keeps you from becoming complacent and encourages you to reassess professional development action plans and school goals. Being a cabinet member is excellent training for new leaders and provides practical experience in communicating and implementing policy. Sharing your leadership responsibilities and decision making with a well-informed cabinet gives you more time to visit classrooms and focus on educational priorities. A well-functioning cabinet is empowered to disagree when necessary, is able to reach consensus, and leaves each meeting speaking with one voice and promoting the school agenda.

◆ *Grade or department meetings*: In these weekly meetings, teachers work on common issues and concerns, focus on school performance data, develop curriculum units of study, examine student work using a variety of assessment tools, generate strategies for differentiating instruction, discuss obstacles and pose possible solutions, and share best practices. You should attend at least one of these meetings every month, supporting teachers and assessing their progress. Grade and department meeting agendas work best when they are consistent for the whole-school community (see the example in Figure 6.6). For example, during October, all agendas might focus on the rigorous pacing of instruction. Ideally, you will attend the first meeting of the month to review the items on the agenda, provide background information and rationale, and outline the intended outcomes for each grade or department. In the following weeks, teachers have in-depth conversations about the agenda items (such as how to pace learning so that homework extends the understanding reached in class), examine student work, develop an action plan, and determine strategies for moving all students forward. Keeping the same schoolwide agenda for the whole month fosters in-depth learning and provokes across-grade conversations, which could never take place if every grade were doing something different. Teachers are responsible for contributing to each meeting, reading any related material provided, and practicing the recommended strategies in their classrooms.

◆ *Grade or department leader meetings*: Grade and department leaders need to be respected by their peers, be well organized, be effective communicators, and demonstrate an understanding of the school's mission. These

GRADE AGENDA *(all grades)*

- Standards/Assessment/Best Work Criteria (rubrics)

- Parent Meetings (dates, agenda, workshop)

- Testing (preparation materials)

- Report Cards (placement issues)

- NYSTL ordering

- Restructuring

- Closets - inventories

- Respect for others (<u>all</u> students, <u>all</u> adults)

    --tone in classrooms
    --grouping
    --discipline
    --enrichment vs gifted

Meetings will be held in grade leader's rooms and we will need the *full* hour, so be on time with lunch - 11:15 - 12:15   12:15 - 1:15

Classes will be held longer in recess if necessary.

FIGURE 6.6

leaders represent you to the community and represent the community to you. Some of the issues that may be discussed at monthly grade or department leader meetings include strategies for integrating new staff members, strategies for communicating with parents, conversations about curriculum and ways to assess implementation through the examination of student work, and strategies to achieve consistent practices across grades (homework and field trip policies, for example).

◆ *Articulation team meetings*: Teachers need to understand what the grades before and after theirs are doing to support their efforts. Articulation teams for each content area—composed of one teacher from every grade—build schoolwide consistency and reduce gaps and redundancies in a specific curriculum area. Choose teachers for these teams who demonstrate expert curriculum knowledge and exemplary classroom practices. Articulation teams foster a sense of community among teachers and help put an end to the blame game that too often gets in the way of meaningful collaboration. The articulation team creates a schoolwide mission statement, prepares a comprehensive educational plan, researches best practices and visits other schools to see these practices in action, and develops a yearlong curriculum calendar and a common vocabulary. It might also hire consultants, develop after-school programs and/or lunchtime clubs, look at student work using teacher-created rubrics, and raise questions and concerns for the principal and the school community. Your ultimate goal is to have every teacher serve on an articulation team over a period of time. Since you need to oversee each articulation team personally, and these meetings eat up a lot of the team members' time, it's best to start small. Begin with a single curriculum area such as reading or writing or mathematics and add a new subject area each year. Articulation teams begin meeting in April; one of their important functions is to prepare the school for June planning (see Chapter 8). Figure 6.7 is an articulation team agenda, which was used for all grades; Figure 6.8 shows the minutes from a writing articulation team meeting.

◆ *School leadership team meetings*: Participants in school leadership teams usually include parents, teachers, and members of the community at large. If there are anticipated problems, talk with each individual before the meeting to understand their point of view and elicit their support and to ensure that the team members are working in the best interests of all students, not promoting their own special interests. Bring supporting materials (statistics, research, and evidence of successful practices) to the meeting that demonstrate the efficacy of your vision and to help members

---

ARTICULATION MEETINGS

▸ Discuss Readings to be distributed by April 10 (see Chairperson)

▸ Consultants to be invited (as per your request)

▸ Mission Statements for CEP, include Standards work, Accountable Talk, Common Vocabulary, Strategies

▸ Test Considerations for ind. Curriculum

▸ After-School Workshops to Enhance Instruction

▸ Lunchtime Clubs to Enhance Instruction

▸ Year-Long Curriculum, Plan By Grade

    ▸ Example (Social Studies)

    ▸

	September	October/November	Etc.
GRADE 1	Community Building (Specifics)	Unit Study Outcomes	
GRADE 2			

FIGURE 6.7

Notes from Writing Articulation Meeting 5/20

Questions/Concerns to address on 6/2:

1. How do we make sure we are implementing the standards in writing workshop?

2. How can we prepare children to write to an assigned topic? (ie. PAM test) We discussed the plan of the 5th grade to pick 4 topics across the year. How should the lower grades be preparing students?

3. What are the writing issues that writing workshop doesn't address?

4. What are we doing across grades about spelling?

5. What genres are studied across grades? - We discussed the possibility of "assigning" specific genres to specific grades to minimize repetition of genres.

6. What new genres can we consider doing?

7. What is the profile of a child who needs extended day writing? What would promote writing best in the building in an extended day program?

8. What writing process strategies should all teachers teach regardless of whether or not they are doing writing workshop?

9. Penmanship - possibility of an after school program for primary students to focus on "writing readiness" activities.
            - discussion of lack of use of cursive writing after 3rd grade.

FIGURE 6.8

reach consensus. End contentious meetings by inviting everyone to continue the dialogue; this signals that you respect their opinion and are willing to accommodate and compromise. Follow-up questions might include *What would make you feel better about this decision? Is there any other evidence I can supply for you? Would you like to read or study more about this topic or visit a classroom?* People appreciate the opportunity to be heard and respected.

◆ *Advocacy group meetings*: Advocacy groups have a special interest and agenda and usually want to confront an existing practice or perceived problem, like the math wars or textbooks versus inquiry learning. These meetings can be volatile, and you may want to invite a seasoned colleague who has gone through a similar experience to provide moral support.

Having teachers who support your point of view present demonstrates a united community firmly committed to the mission. Question-and-answer sessions need to be carefully monitored, preferably by someone other than you. Keep a record of promises made and immediately follow up on them. Convening a small group to continue the dialogue is a good way to show that you are committed to resolving issues. (Never have a controversial meeting like this on a Friday; it spoils the weekend, and unresolved issues have two days in which to fester.)

◆ *Meetings of specific constituencies within or across schools* (speech teachers, guidance counselors, physical education teachers, or art teachers, for example): Too often these educators are isolated from one another. They need the opportunity to socialize, share best practices, and form collaborative relationships with others with the same job description. At the district level, team members might include assistant principals, teaching coaches, supervisors of curriculum areas, teacher leaders, or new teachers. Holding these meetings regularly lets district leaders discover the strengths and needs of their community, support curriculum mandates, and establish collaborative community norms. Figure 6.9 is an invitation to assistant principals and special education supervisors to participate in a

Dear Assistant Principals and Special Education Supervisors,

Welcome back to a new school year. I hope the summer provided opportunities for you to rest, read, reflect and enjoy your time with family and friends. Providing differentiated, meaningful and quality professional development using each leader's expertise and uniting the community around a shared vision is our top priority. We used the feedback you provided to us last year outlining your specific needs to develop a multi-tiered approach focused on strengthening leadership skills, deepening understanding of literacy and mathematics instruction and building community through shared learning.

The structures we have designed for you parallel the principals' activities and include:

New Leaders Support Network
- Monthly after school meetings with expert senior assistant principals and special education supervisors to problem-solve, share effective practices and discuss issues and concerns (see attached schedule of dates).

State of the District Meetings
- Half-day meetings at the district office focused on hearing the superintendent's priorities and sharing information from principals' conferences. 8:30 a.m. – 11 a.m.
  o November 25, January 27, March 24

Focused School Visits
- Led by exemplary assistant principals in their own school, visits will include walk-throughs of teacher leader classrooms to observe best practices, discussion of leadership implications and study groups focused on literacy issues. Partnerships will be formed within each group to follow-up on curriculum conversations, visit each other between sessions and become critical friends. Teams of leaders from visiting schools will be linked with teams of leaders from host schools to study organizational structures and communication systems (see attached outline of leaders and participants; specific dates to follow). 9 a.m. – 12 N.
  o October 2002, December 2002, February 2003, April 2003

One-to-One Conversations
- Beginning in October, leaders will meet to discuss plans for the year. Leaders will participate in frequent walk-throughs with the deputy superintendent to assess progress and plan next steps. Mid-year visits will focus on demonstrating leadership, particularly in planning and leading grade level meetings.

Shadowing District Office Staff
- Additional support in budget, guidance issues, meeting the needs of diverse learners, etc. with district office leaders

We look forward to learning with you this year. We welcome your comments about this plan.

Sincerely,

Carmen Fariña
Community Superintendent

FIGURE 6.9

variety of professional development offerings to ensure that they are fully informed about instructional priorities and can support their schools.

◆ *Town hall meetings*: Use these open-forum meetings to inform the community about instructional matters and elicit its support. Opportunities for dialogue are essential. When a new curriculum initiative is being considered, a town hall meeting at which a panel of experts answers questions honestly and recommends adjustments when warranted is a proactive way to explain the plan of action and lessen the negative feedback and rumors that can often undermine such an effort. Town hall meetings alleviate concerns, reassure the community that teachers and principals are united in their vision, de-escalate public outcry, and often lead to a smooth transition from crisis to resolution.

◆ *Faculty conferences*: It's best to focus each meeting on an instructional issue with which teachers and students are currently grappling. Your vision needs to be apparent, and activities include sharing best practices, looking at student work, and determining how best to move students forward. Teachers need to know their voices are being heard and that their time is valued and grouping them according to their interests and needs will foster rich conversations around essential questions. The notes from these conversations can then be disseminated to the entire community to extend the learning and prepare for next steps.

◆ *Off-site retreats*: Gathering staff members for longer chunks of time in a relaxed and pleasant atmosphere with few distractions is very beneficial. Plan the time carefully to balance social and academic activities. When retreats require extended time away from families, inviting spouses and significant others, as well as the executive board of the PTA, to the culminating celebration is a wonderful way to provide an audience for the work achieved and inform the community about next steps.

◆ *Courses, workshops, institutes, curriculum-writing sessions, and certification programs*: These professional development offerings are all excellent ways to build teacher knowledge and increase teacher effectiveness but only if the participating teachers are willing and ready to learn and eager to apply the new thinking in their classrooms. All teachers don't need to study the same things in the same way. Staff developers can help you match appropriate offerings to individual teachers so that they extend and deepen their learning over time. Inviting teachers to learn with their colleagues works best when the material is relevant to the needs of their students and can be applied the next day. If you group teachers by grade level and/or years of experience and help them adapt new ideas to their already existing practices, they will be more likely to embrace change. Professional development should always be linked to existing instructional initiatives so that teachers remain focused and don't become overwhelmed. There should be a clear expectation that teachers who attend these offerings will implement the practices in their classrooms and share them with their colleagues.

- *Study groups*: Study groups stimulate adult learning and collaboration, engage learners in authentic inquiry about issues of immediate concern, and broaden social connections. The best study groups use inquiry to challenge preconceived notions, acquire new knowledge, and come up with innovative ways to improve student achievement.

  - Issues studied work best when they are related to the specific needs of the community, and aligned to the current professional development focus. Members read professional articles and texts, conduct research, engage in conversations, visit classrooms, and attempt new strategies. A whole school or district might study one issue, with small groups focusing on different aspects. For example, when investigating differentiated instruction, one group might study accelerated learning, another could look at grouping options, and still another might study student work to identify learning styles. They might all read the same professional text but through slightly different lenses.

  - Before you set up study groups you need to be knowledgeable about the basic tenets of the subject being studied and be able to articulate the big ideas, the philosophy of the underlying research, the rationale for studying this particular area at this time, and the anticipated outcomes. Model your own learning by investigating a key resource, discussing your reading and your questions, and sharing your resulting action plan. Asking teachers to choose issues of interest from a predetermined larger menu lets you balance personalities, interests, strengths, and desired outcomes when forming groups.

  - Time frames need to be established before members commit and should be long enough to produce concrete results but short enough to sustain interest.

  - Members are responsible for actively participating and completing assignments. Roles include facilitating, taking notes, reminding members of meeting times and responsibilities, planning culminating activities, and being responsible for the logistics of each meeting.

  - Provide necessary resources and experts, sufficient time, and a setting conducive to achieving the goals.

  - Each study group might begin by determining the big questions it wants to investigate, the end result to be achieved, the action plan to follow, and the way the learning will be disseminated within the study group and in the larger community. Groups must establish clear and explicit accountability measures so that members and leaders can evaluate the learning. (Figure 6.10 offers some guiding questions to consider.)

- *School walk-throughs*: A focused, in-depth tour of a school can reveal what matters most in the school community and what next steps are needed to ensure schoolwide consistency. Walk-throughs are an opportunity for the whole community to focus on the issues most important to teacher learning and student rigor. (They are not flybys, emphasizing checklists, man-

Study Group
Guiding Questions

- How have you communicated your school's literacy vision?
  o School Handbook
  o Weekly Letters
  o Beginning faculty conference and notes
  o Grade meetings
  o 1 – 1 Conversations and
  o Observations
  o Parent Workshops
  o PTA Meetings
  o Other

- How have you aligned your professional development to your stated vision?
  o Early Morning *Extra Time*
  o Plans for Mondays
  o Election Day
  o Study Groups
  o T.C. Calendar Days
  o Other

- How are you creating literacy leadership in your building?
  o Cabinet Meetings
  o Teacher Leaders
  o Staff Developers
  o Intervention Team
  o Inter/Intra visitation
  o Other

- How are you developing both intervention and enrichment strategies in your building for all students?
  o Use of Time
  o Use of Support Staff
  o Lunchtime and After School Clubs
  o Saturday Courses
  o Paraprofessionals
  o Use of Technology
  o CBO and Parents
  o Other

- What do you want to learn and how will you make your learning public?
  o Participation in T.C. Study Groups and administrator's Wednesdays
  o Professional Reading
  o Letters to Staff
  o Study Groups
  o Other

- What support do you need from District, from each other?

FIGURE 6.10

dates, or surface details.) Focusing on a specific grade or subject area allows time to look at student work, teacher expertise, and consistency and will yield important information about what is already going well and what reforms are beginning to take hold and need support. Walk-throughs are particularly powerful when focused on the following:

- *Use of time*: How are teachers planning instruction so that students can practice and apply their learning to authentic and meaningful tasks? How much time do students spend listening to the teacher and how much time do they spend on interactive learning? How much time are students able to spend reading, writing, thinking, and problem solving? Is pacing differentiated to support individual students? How much time is devoted to whole-class teaching versus small-group instruction?

- *The work students produce*: What kinds of texts are students reading and how are their increased stamina and volume monitored and supported? What kinds of texts are students writing? How is their writing improving over time? What kinds of work do students produce and why? Are expectations consistent within each grade? Are there increasingly higher expectations as students move from grade to grade? Is there evidence of rigor and challenging work? Can students articulate their purpose and process for learning?

- *Teacher learning*: Is the focus of teacher learning clear? Is it linked to professional development initiatives? Is there evidence that teachers borrow ideas from one another? Are teachers planning and assessing their work together?

- *Resources*: Are there abundant materials for student learning? Are these materials used appropriately to promote student independence? Are teachers sharing these resources?

- *Practices and curriculum*: Are teachers within each grade and throughout the school using the same language, methodologies, expectations, and strategies? Are teachers learning from one another and building student learning? Are there consistent ways to evaluate student work? Are there high expectations for all students?

After each walk-through, share what patterns you discovered, what excellent practices you observed, and the next steps for professional development. Figure 6.11 outlines the steps of an effective walk-through by district supervisors.

- *Intervisitations*: Visits to other classrooms and schools make theory visible and let learners borrow practical and replicable ideas from one another. Often the best work happens when company is coming. Leaders have a wonderful opportunity to highlight their vision and articulate the learning journey of their community. The entire community is energized, affirmed, and motivated to continue learning at a higher level. Successful intervisitations may trigger mentoring or coaching relationships and ongoing collaboration within and across schools. Here are some things to keep in mind:

  - Visitors need a clear focus, an explicit purpose. They should develop essential questions before the visit and protocols for their behavior both during and after the visit. They need to be respectful, ensure confidentiality, provide appropriate feedback, and express appreciation for the hard work and efforts of the community. There should not be a rush to judgment.

  - There must be clear, public criteria for who participates in the visit and who hosts the visit. Everyone needs to understand respective responsibilities. Choose participants who are open to innovation,

```
Questions to Ponder During Walk-Through

Conversations with School Leader(s)
        (before walk-through)
    •   What are you most proud of?
    •   What has been the focus of professional development?  What are the
        structures that afford time to learn?  (grade meetings, study groups,
        courses, lab sites)  Who are the change agents?
    •   What are the bottom-line non-negotiables?  How are they communicated?
        What evidence will we see?
    •   What are your concerns?  How can the District support you?

Focused Walk-Through
(Look for....these together as co-learners)
    •   Where are the strengths?  How can consistency be developed?
    •   What kind of print is displayed?  Whose words?  Process?  Content?
    •   How is time used?  Flow of day?
    •   What is the quality and quantity of student writing/reading?
    •   Classroom library?  Nonfiction materials?  Variety?  Organization?
    •   Student Talk - Partnerships?  Small Group?  Whole class?
        -Can students articulate what they are learning?  How and why they are
        learning it?
    •   Can teachers articulate what they are teaching and why?

Conversation with School Leader(s)
(After walk-through)
    •   Articulate the strengths – list beginning steps in very specific language
    •   List the "threads " – outside eyes notice repeating patterns that insiders
        may overlook
    •   Discuss next steps – (short term) Define plan for building on strengths
        Begin to think ahead –what can District do to support school in next
        months?
```

FIGURE 6.11

willing to share their learning, and eager to adapt and implement practices they have observed. Visitors will want to bring notebooks and pens to record their learning during the visit and take pictures to share with colleagues on a bulletin board summarizing the visit.

• Plan the visit carefully; find the right match. The model school should not be so far ahead as to be intimidating or too different from what is already in place, particularly in terms of student population and teacher readiness for change. A coach, an assistant principal, or the principal can accompany teachers on the visit and support them as they implement the new practices they've observed.

• A shared breakfast on the day of the visit sets a personal tone and allows you to preview what teachers will see and talk about how these results were achieved. Teacher leaders might take the role of leading the conversation and practice sharing the story of the school's journey using the *we* voice. This opportunity provides additional investment in the progress made and offers visitors insight about the change process. After the visit, discuss any issues, concerns, or questions in order to clarify misconceptions and plan next steps.

• The visiting principal will want to send a prompt rave-review letter. The host principal will want to thank the teachers for opening their classrooms to visitors and share the feedback with them (see Chapter 4).

- Next steps to extend the learning include reflecting on the visit, affirming what is already in place, noting needed changes, providing additional professional development, and perhaps sending another group of teachers to visit the school.

Avoiding Common Pitfalls

Learners must be matched with the most appropriate type of professional development, targeted and differentiated to honor the knowledge, learning style, and prior experience of each member of the community. If you only rely on sign-up sheets to enlist participation, most of the community will probably choose comfortable formats rather than take risks. When you know your community and have developed trusting relationships during one-to-one conversations, you can encourage participants to challenge themselves to explore areas that will deepen their work.

Community members will take their own learning seriously when they recognize you as the head learner. Learning alongside teachers and supporting staff development efforts demonstrate that professional development is your top priority. Your active participation is essential.

Your administrative team also needs to model collaborative learning. Too often, community members feel that assistant principals and other administrators don't require professional development, that their time is better spent keeping things running smoothly. However, their active involvement as colearners with the principal and the teachers raises their visibility as curriculum leaders, gives them a common vocabulary, and enables them to support teaching and learning in the classroom.

Bringing in a trendy guest speaker once a month may be inspirational in the short term but does not build insider's expertise. Preview what guest speakers plan to say, and give them background information about the audience and the current area of study so that they can focus on the specific needs of the community. Presenting a guest speaker who delivers an impersonal message and doesn't engage the audience will undermine your teachers' faith in you.

Professional development that lacks coherence and is imposed without regard for the community's needs is an isolated, one-shot event that wastes time and never becomes part of the fabric of school life. Professional development should be coherent and reflect established priorities over time. Knee-jerk reactions to political pressures should be avoided at all costs. The community can easily become overwhelmed when too many professional development initiatives are undertaken simultaneously. Prioritize, align, and find common threads that will allow the community to study one compelling issue deeply. Review past agendas and explore how to revisit topics in new ways that deepen learning. If you are a new principal, you may want to evaluate your predecessor's successes and blend them into new initiatives.

Without resources and support, professional development often fails. Providing books, videotapes, and consultants to support the community as it inquires together through established and predictable structures immerses the community in exciting new ideas and removes barriers to learning. Empowering committees and study groups to order appropriate materials for their own learning demonstrates your commitment to honoring teacher input and ensures that materials will be well used. (Thoughtful use of technology can greatly enhance learning, but make sure there is the right balance between presentation and active participation.)

Every community has negative members, and you need to know who they are and how best to handle them. Separating naysayers from the group or balancing them with more positive voices is a sign of a good leader. Honesty and a good sense of humor can effectively deflect negative energy. Favoritism is perceived when community members are not clear about the criteria for participation in a meeting or study group and the same small group is always involved.

The best insurance for successful meetings is thorough planning: keeping to stated beginning and ending times, asking for suggestions, making your intentions explicit, and being willing to hear feedback, even when it is negative. Meetings without agendas, action plans, or minutes appear purposeless, and the time is often wasted. Without a written record, the conversations that take place are subject to different interpretations and spur rumors, misunderstandings, and mixed messages. Written evaluations help you revise and improve professional development. Failing to take feedback seriously demonstrates that you do not value the voice of your community.

Evaluating Success

To assess whether professional development is fully embedded into the life of the school and results in greater teacher expertise and ownership and improved student achievement, look for evidence like this:

• Are professional development structures and rituals aligned with school and teacher needs? Is there sufficient time for in-depth learning? Are members of the community clearly aware of anticipated outcomes and empowered to participate fully?

• Are teachers sharing their practices and building schoolwide consistency, thus ensuring that time is well used and gaps and redundancies are eliminated? Do teachers trust one another to set high expectations for all students?

• Are the community's new members easily acculturated and supported with predictable and consistent professional development opportunities that allow them to focus on teaching and learning? Does professional development increase new teachers' success and prompt them to continue teaching? Are senior staff members challenged and stimulated to continue their learning and share their expertise? Are more reflective teachers recruited and retained?

• Does the predictability and continuity of professional development give teachers ownership of and responsibility for their own learning? Is future learning determined by past successes and new challenges? Do teachers replicate professional development rituals in their own classrooms and invent new ones to increase their own learning?

- Do all members take turns leading meetings and carrying out the purpose and intended outcomes of professional development? Has the ownership for learning moved from the administrators to the teachers?

- Do teachers value professional development as a means to move into leadership positions?

- Are leaders becoming more confident of teacher expertise and focusing their time on new initiatives and supporting those who need more help?

- Are professional development conversations, networks, study groups, and school visits creating a more collaborative culture? Is time before, during, and after school devoted to professional development? Are teacher unions supportive of the professional development initiatives?

- Are parents supporting professional development based on their confidence in the progress of teacher learning and increased student performance? Do parents support new initiatives and promote budget expenditures for these professional development initiatives?

- Is there greater participation in professional development and more enthusiasm and energy for new learning?

- Do predictable rituals and structures sustain professional development during leadership changes? Are changes instituted by new leaders occurring within a well-established framework and therefore more likely to succeed?

- Is professional development viewed as a valued vehicle for dealing with challenging issues and taking risks? Are members of the community researching complex issues so that all students can be successful?

- Do school leaders see professional development as valuable and productive for themselves? Are they willing to fight for more time to engage in in-depth learning?

Nurture Teacher Leaders

Dear Reader,

Our own experience as teacher leaders began when we were invited by our principals to participate in our district's writing initiative in collaboration with the Teachers College Reading and Writing Project, led by Lucy Calkins. The first time we saw Lucy give a demonstration lesson was a revelation: She was doing things we'd never seen before. She crouched down and looked into a student's eyes, listening intently while the student shyly explained that she would never eat pistachio ice cream again because her parents told her they were getting a divorce the last time she had it. Lucy put her arm around the girl, asked if that statement would be the lead in her piece of writing, and then encouraged her to write it down before she forgot it. All the books and articles we had read could never teach the way being in the presence of an expert and passionate teacher could. Lucy made ideas visible and concrete and compelled us to action. We rushed back to our classrooms to try these techniques with our own students.

It was risky and lonely work; we needed the support of colleagues to take this leap of faith, to believe we could teach like Lucy and produce the same results. The network we formed within our schools started with just a few interested teachers sharing our small successes, comparing our many challenges, and urging one another on. The biggest risk we took was opening our classrooms to one another and turning them into lab sites. The conversations we had after each demonstration lesson included practical feedback about what was going well and suggestions for next steps. As a group, we talked late into the evenings about the professional books we were reading, attended every writing conference we could, and continually revised our practices as our understanding grew. We talked honestly with one another, admitting our failures and our worries and gaining strength from those learning alongside us.

Observing this new way of engaging students, our principals became enthusiastic colearners committed to change. They made time for us to visit one another's classrooms and talk about what we saw and encouraged other teachers to join our study. Experiencing the power of teacher-to-teacher learning and the importance of collaboration affirmed our belief in transforming schools from the bottom up with top-down support.

When we became a principal–staff developer team, we knew the catalyst for change was to nurture teacher leaders. Identifying a small group of the best and brightest teachers was the first step in modeling our commitment to teacher collaboration and excellence. These core teacher leaders were eager for targeted professional development, excited about developing curriculum, and ready to turn their classrooms into lab sites. We recognized their courage in taking on this new role, in standing out from the crowd.

We encouraged these teachers to learn from one another and from outside experts. We then talked with them about what they'd learned so we could learn more ourselves, modeling our belief that learning is social, ongoing, and intended for all members of the community. Working closely with these teacher leaders, we demonstrated our support for the whole community and our commitment to learning as an avenue for all teachers' development. Affirming the leadership talents of our teachers, we took advantage of their strengths, their social and emotional intelligence, and their organizational and administrative skills. As we grew more comfortable delegating responsibility, we had time to move on to new initiatives and pressing problems. Our teacher leaders became the advocates for the community's buy-in and commitment to our mission for change.

As district leaders, we encouraged principals to identify teacher leaders who could help lessen teachers' sense of isolation, create a sense of urgency and excitement about trying new strategies, and build a collaborative culture. We worked closely with principals to help them see the power of mobilizing a small group of talented and dedicated professionals to help them communicate their vision, establish consistent practices, and improve instruction for all students. We provided professional development to help teacher leaders grow into their new role. This network of teacher leaders met monthly to highlight strengths and encourage growth.

Support like this provides a career path leading to future staff developers, assistant principals, and district leaders. Conversation with teacher leaders in other schools expands knowledge, develops collegial support and friendly competition, and builds networks of expertise and interest. Teacher leaders raise their expectations for themselves and their students and see their own work from a broader, more multifaceted perspective. Nurturing cadres of teacher leaders extends the learning of the whole community through the creation of customized units of study and professional portfolios.

As we visited schools and noticed the talents and strengths of principals who were eager to share their expertise both large and small with others, we put them in touch with one another. Just as networks of teacher leaders support the intellectual growth of each member, networks of principals leaders do the same. The more educators can articulate their thinking and share their ideas, the more likely they are to keep growing, refine and reflect on their thinking, and become risk takers.

Teachers contribute to the life of the school in many ways. Nurturing teacher leaders allows us to recruit and retain the best and brightest teachers and keep the most experienced professionals engaged and challenged. Teacher leaders help us promote intellectual curiosity, collaborative conversations, and empowered decision making. School leaders who publicly demonstrate their commitment to cultivating leadership in others ensure that their work will become embedded in the culture, sustained over time, and part of an enduring legacy.

—Carmen and Laura

Why Nurture Teacher Leaders?

Recognizing the importance of teacher leaders and creating structures to support them help attract and retain more thoughtful and reflective professionals. Teacher leaders are vital to distributive leadership and to the stability of school life. Including teacher leaders in a variety of decision-making committees (cabinet, professional development team, and school leadership teams, for example) helps provide continuity in a school's instructional practices, lets school leaders know what's going on in classrooms, and ensures a plan of succession. In addition, serving as teacher leaders helps educators articulate their thinking, advocate their vision, and use their passion for teaching to bring about change. Teacher leaders can help create and implement each year's comprehensive school plan, promote ownership and responsibility, and publicize shared expectations.

Teacher leaders help the principal and district leaders disseminate the latest pedagogical information. When new initiatives are implemented, teacher leaders conduct action research, trying the new practices in their classrooms first and recommending necessary changes. This ensures that any problems are recognized and quickly resolved before a program is implemented schoolwide. Teacher leaders can also alert principals to problems that may be brewing in the school community before they become major issues.

By modeling interactive and ongoing collaborative learning, teacher leaders promote a consistent approach to problem solving and shared learning. They make new ideas and strategies visible in their classrooms so that colleagues who have not read the research or attended a workshop can still replicate these practices.

Teacher leaders make the whole community smarter and illustrate the expectation that teaching is an intellectual pursuit. They are constantly challenged to adjust their expertise, reflect on their practice, and develop their skills in order to support their colleagues' learning, push their thinking to new levels.

Publicly recognizing teachers' expertise by expanding their responsibilities helps school leaders retain staff members and gives staff members a way to advance their careers. Once the community realizes that successful teachers are given the opportunity to become coaches, district staff developers, curriculum writers, and assistant principals, word spreads quickly. Schools that offer opportunities for leadership are high-energy learning communities that support students and teachers more effectively.

Effective teacher leaders can often take the place of outside consultants, giving school funding more flexibility, and take on administrative responsibilities, which lets school leaders spend more time in classrooms and become more visible members of the learning community. In addition, a collaborative culture eliminates the need for an outside agency to resolve conflicts.

A cohesive learning network of teacher leaders within and across schools promotes a positive spirit of competition and challenges the community to exceed expectations. It stimulates personal learning and offers a structure for assuming new positions over time. Schools that may not have been viewed as places of excellence in the past receive renewed respect.

Getting Started: Step by Step

1. Articulate your goals for nurturing teacher leaders by analyzing the strengths and needs of your community. Academic needs should receive priority, especially new initiatives in a particular curriculum area. You may also want to address the school climate, the social and emotional needs of teachers and students, and administrative needs such as scheduling. In large schools, you may share this responsibility with an assistant, but it must be seen as one of your personal priorities. Figure 7.1 is an example of a letter to school principals defining

---

Dear Colleague:

We share the belief that professional development is our most important initiative. We know that building teachers' knowledge and expertise and creating structures to share best practices is crucial in strengthening our community of learners. We are pleased that teacher leaders have been recognized in so many schools and hope that our goal to establish two teacher leaders in each school will be achieved by the end of this school year. If your school doesn't already have two teacher leaders and you feel you have teachers who are ready to become teacher leaders, you may post the enclosed vacancy notice for your staff. We will then schedule interviews for candidates who apply.

As you know, teacher leaders must demonstrate success as practitioners in particular grades and subject areas. Their classrooms should serve as models for teachers on your staff to visit and observe best practices. Teacher Leaders will:

- Model exemplary whole class, small group and individual student lessons within the workshop structure;
- Meet regularly with the staff developer to plan and assess units of study;
- Meet regularly with participating teachers to share their planning process and support team building;
- Meet regularly with literacy/math team to assess progress and plan next steps;
- Develop a professional portfolio;
- Keep a reflective notebook of ongoing work with staff developers; and
- Attend professional development calendar days whenever possible.

In order for teacher leaders and participating teachers to take full advantage of the model classrooms they need your support in scheduling time for ongoing visitations, demonstration lessons, and study groups. Teacher Leaders will meet monthly to strengthen their knowledge and develop professional portfolios. We've budgeted for each Teacher Leader 50 per session hours for this purpose as well as five sub days for visiting other teacher leaders.

Thank you for your continued support in providing opportunities for teacher learning and sharing of expertise. We appreciate all that you do to nurture teacher knowledge and talent, and provide quality learning opportunities for your community. Finally, we'd like to share two pertinent articles on this topic for your professional reading.

FIGURE 7.1 *Defining the Role of Teacher Leaders*

the expectations for teacher leaders, the kind of support they will receive, and the selection process.

2. Get to know each member of the school community through one-to-one conversations, classroom visits, and teacher surveys. Identifying teachers' strengths and affirming them by suggesting teachers share their expertise at faculty conferences and grade-level meetings will create a buzz and make the community excited about distributive leadership.

3. Build a foundation for developing teacher leaders by actively listening and following up on what you hear so everyone in the community feels valued and supported. This takes time and cannot be rushed or delegated.

4. Have private conversations with the union leader, teacher mentors, and other senior members of the school community to alleviate any concern they may feel and gauge their readiness to embrace this initiative.

5. Decide how many teacher leaders you hope to support each year (we recommend a minimum of two so that they can work as partners and model collaborative conversations), what role they will play, and how they will be compensated (additional salary, compensatory time, professional development opportunities, college credits, or reduced teaching responsibilities). Be flexible. Begin with the areas of greatest need and expand the number of teacher leaders and the roles they play in future years.

6. Announce the initiative publicly. Invite the community to a meeting at which you define the initiative and answer questions and concerns.

7. After the meeting, formulate and post publicly a list of teacher leader criteria based on input from those who attended. Criteria might include
- strong knowledge of curriculum as demonstrated during at least three years of classroom practice
- willingness to
  - collaborate with others within and outside the school community
  - attend additional professional development and participate in action research
  - open one's classroom to visitors within the school community and beyond
  - share one's learning at grade-level and faculty meetings
  - contribute to newsletters to share expertise (see the example in Figure 7.2)
  - assess one's own progress as a teacher leader and the professional growth of the teachers one mentors
- ability to conduct workshops for teachers and parents in one's area of expertise

Leadership Network Newsletter

Issue #1, January

News

I'm in the group whose focus is craft. We began by planning our writing curriculum for the year, balancing both genre studies and focus units, while forecasting probable publishing dates through June.

We also have been looking closely at teaching craft. We have focused our work on showing students how to notice text so that ultimately they can independently look at any text for craft intentions.

In addition, our group discussed how to choose appropriate texts so that they can be used across units of study.

Inspired by Katie Woods' interest in Cynthia Rylant, each member of our group picked an author to study with his or her class. I have picked Jane Yolen and our class study of her work has been wonderful.

I would love to share with anyone interested, strategies for yearly planning, as well as discussing both the craft and structure studies I have completed.

****

PLEASE NOTE:

Future Newsletters will keep you up-to-date on the work of our groups.

In addition, we will be setting up a file box in Room 125, where you can find print-outs of some of the inquiry work of the groups.

Please feel free to contact any of these teachers to find out more about a specific reading or writing issue.

****

FIGURE 7.2

◆ strong interpersonal skills in communicating and collaborating with other adults

8. Clearly state that the opportunity is voluntary. Teachers should never fear punitive steps if they choose not to participate. Being a teacher leader may be a step up the career ladder, but choosing *not* to be one should not prompt a negative evaluation.

9. Meet with well-qualified but reluctant teachers to determine what incentives might make them change their minds.

10. Form a small committee to select or help select teacher leaders. Interview candidates and visit their classrooms to ensure transparency and fairness. If someone lacks one or more criteria or needs additional support (in the ability to write, for example), tell him where he needs to improve and encourage him to reapply when he has made the appropriate changes. Alternatively, he may still fulfill a teacher leader role with your or another mentor's support. Or two teachers may share one teacher leader position.

11. Take an informal poll to be sure the community will react positively to the chosen candidates.

12. Determine teacher leaders' specific roles and responsibilities: whom they will collaborate with and how, how they will be compensated, how they will participate in meetings and professional development, how they will share what they learn (projects, final products like portfolios, presentations, demonstrations), how they will communicate findings and concerns, how confidentiality issues will be handled, and how their expanded leadership role will affect the students in their classroom. (A list of possible responsibilities created for one school community is shown in Figure 7.3 on page 128. Teacher leaders were asked to choose those responsibilities that fit their expertise.)

13. Announce the names of the teacher leaders and the roles they are to play.

14. Send a congratulatory letter to the teachers selected, defining the roles they are to play and the training they will receive and inviting them to a kickoff celebration. (See the example in Figure 7.4 on page 129.)

15. Hold the first meeting. Distribute the schedule of future meetings and classroom visits. Hand out copies of a log or form for the teacher leaders to complete each month (see the example in Figure 7.5 on page 130). In addition, you may ask them to complete a simple survey like the one in Figure 7.6 on page 131 to help them remain focused and help you keep track of their work.

16. Create a yearlong calendar of professional development that focuses on deepening pedagogical and curricular learning as well as the skills of active listening and effective collaboration.

17. Support the initiative by listening to teacher leaders, changing their schedule when necessary, supervising them, and setting clear leadership parameters. Quickly resolve any professional jealousies or conflicts that arise.

18. Support your teacher leaders' decisions both publicly and privately. The rest of the community needs to know they are speaking with your authorization.

19. Assign teacher leaders to the school cabinet, school leadership team, and similar leadership groups as appropriate.

Teacher Leaders: Promoting Excellence

1. Early Bird Group for New Teachers (hold classes until 9:00 AM)
   - Classroom management
   - Creating the classroom environment
   - Scheduling
   - Handling "new teacher" anxiety
   - Inviting question/answer session
   - Planning for report cards
   - Planning for parent-teacher conference
   - Planning/curriculum (short and long term)
2. Group Course/Study Group (AM/PM)
   - Literacy
   - Leveling libraries
   - Books on the grade
   - Writing process
   - Professional Books
      - *On Solid Ground*
      - *The Art of Teaching Reading*
   - Developing a genre study
   - Interdisciplinary Social Studies
   - Developing accountable talk
   - Portfolios children
3. Demo Lessons
   - Math (followed by question/answer session)
   - Literacy—minilessons/share/independent
   - Conferencing with students
   - Accountable talk
4. Invite Teachers in Your Room
   - Flow of the Day (how you manage a day)
   - How to display work in your room
   - Run grade meetings
5. Parent Workshop
   - Running parent workshops to explain/demonstrate various school initiatives
6. Curriculum Guide
   - Units of study for a project
7. Organizing Schoolwide Events to Build Community
   - Celebrations
   - Fundraising drives for books
   - Promoting success
   - Writing schoolwide newsletter
8. Creating a schoolwide needs survey to include everyone in the decision-making process of what a teacher leader might be able to offer.

FIGURE 7.3 *Suggested Teacher Leader Responsibilities*

[Teacher Name]
Address

Dear :

Thank you for applying for the position of teacher leader in your school. We appreciate the time you took to discuss your educational philosophy and share your many accomplishments.

Congratulations! You have met the selection criteria for teacher leader in the current school year. Your expertise in creating a model classroom and sharing it with your colleagues will be invaluable to the professional growth in our Region. Teacher leaders will study together and receive ongoing support in adult learning forming a strong learning network. They will work with the coaches in their building to plan and facilitate professional development for teachers. In addition to building instructional and leadership capacity in individual schools, teacher leaders will also help build capacity region-wide by sharing best practices at conferences, contributing to a quarterly newsletter or creating a video library of model lessons.

We are excited to launch the teacher leader program with a gathering at
       on   , from   . Elementary literacy teacher leaders will actually begin their learning with a meeting with   Deputy Director of Reading for Teachers College Reading and Writing Project on   **, from**
       at   .   will provide insight as well as information on the rules and responsibilities of being a teacher leader. At our kickoff event on   , we will provide a calendar of monthly meetings for all teacher leaders as well as any full-day conferences.

Please RSVP to the kickoff event to indicate that you are accepting the position of teacher leader. We are looking forward to further discussion about your leadership role in this important area.

Sincerely,

FIGURE 7.4 *Congratulatory Letter*

20. Have each teacher leader mentor at least one colleague, so that person can become a teacher leader next year. This sets up the expectation that all teachers will one day grow into the role of teacher leader.

21. Assess teacher leaders' fulfillment of their role by observing them in the classroom and evaluating their portfolios, professional articles, photo-essays, and any other data that demonstrates increased student performance.

22. Meet with each teacher leader individually to evaluate the year's learning and determine next year's participation, which might be a new focus or a deepening of the current research. Use the log of the year's activities, any projects the leader created, action research conducted, learning analysis, learning shared with colleagues, and student progress to assess effectiveness. Determine whether the person is qualified to continue in the program.

23. Celebrate your teacher leaders at the end of the year. You might list their names and qualifications in a brochure. Have each teacher leader give a short presentation on her unique learning experience and how she has influenced the learning of others. Examples of possible teacher leader achievements include establishing a math resource center along with workshops in how to use it; discovering the importance of intervention and helping teachers identify and support at-risk students; identifying, leveling, labeling, and distributing new books;

TEACHER LEADER MONTHLY
PROFESSIONAL DEVELOPMENT PLAN

Activity: _____   **Dates:** _____

Participants: _____   **Hours:** _____

Focus & Rationale:

_____

_____

_____

_____

_____

Total hours requested: _____   **Principal's approval:** _____

Date Submitted: _____

FIGURE 7.5 *Teacher Leader Monthly Log*

helping teachers use assessment tools and adapt teaching strategies accordingly; conducting action research on the effectiveness of heterogeneous grouping; and integrating technology into units of study.

24. Encourage teacher leaders to share their learning with parents, other schools, and national conferences and to write articles for professional journals. Acquiring National Board Certification can be a natural next step.

TEACHER/LEADER

1. I am interested in developing a portfolio in the area of

    _____

    _____

2. I have developed a portfolio in the area of

    _____

    _____

    and would like to add

    _____

    _____

3. I would be interested in sharing my expertise with colleagues in:

    ☐   After School Workshop (Mondays)
    ☐   In classroom assistance
    ☐   Other schools (mentored, etc)
    ☐   Morning Coffee Talk

4. I would like my expertise described as follows:

    _____

    _____

    _____

    _____

5. I would like to be compensated by:

    ☐   Per session
    ☐   Prep period
    ☐   Comp time

    Name _____

FIGURE 7.6 *Teacher Leader Survey*

Avoiding Common Pitfalls

The choice of which professionals are selected to become teacher leaders is very important, especially when the positions are linked to additional compensation or used to recruit teachers in math and science or in high-poverty urban schools. If the number of positions is limited and a trusting culture has not yet been established, jealousies and resentments may derail the process. Public criteria, a transparent selection process, and a forthright statement of why individual teacher leaders were selected and the specific role they will play are essential, especially if you are implementing this program without district support. Don't select teacher leaders because they are your favorites, because they are the most senior staff members, or because they are the most vocal and powerful. If you choose candidates who lack the necessary credentials, have poor interpersonal skills, or fail to convince the community of their ability to support their colleagues' work, the initiative will surely be unsuccessful. Likewise, making the position mandatory or treating those who reject the opportunity in punitive ways will undermine the trust that is necessary for success.

To ensure the community respects your teacher leaders, don't let them make policy decisions on their own, evaluate their peers, reveal confidential information, select curriculum without inviting opinions and suggestions, or speak for you unless you know what they are going to say and give them the authority to do so. Overburdening teacher leaders with too many responsibilities, changing their responsibilities without their knowledge and consent, or failing to recognize and affirm their contributions is a recipe for burnout. Trusting teacher leaders to learn even when they make mistakes is an important part of leadership training.

Help teacher leaders develop communication skills such as speaking with poise and authority, writing effectively in a variety of forms, listening to and understanding differing points of view, respecting diverse opinions, working with difficult personalities, reaching consensus, and encouraging people's strengths instead of telling them what to do.

Choose only the number of teacher leaders you are able to support with professional development and coaching. Take the necessary time to learn from them and publicly acknowledge their role in making you smarter. Talk with them about problems and progress, but don't micromanage them when they are working with their colleagues; doing so will limit their effectiveness, and stunt their growth as leaders.

Be sure to reward teachers for taking on the position of teacher leader. Monetary rewards are certainly much appreciated, but there are other forms of compensation as well: offering them professional development opportunities, celebrating their achievements, and providing compensatory time. Recognizing and rewarding teachers' talents steers them toward excellence. And even when teacher leaders leave for positions in other schools, smart leaders let them go with willingness and grace, happy that their protégés will still be bettering the field of education and confident that they can recruit competent replacements.

Sending the message that teacher leadership is an end in itself negates the real purpose of this role, which is to model that everyone in the school community is a proactive learner, a researcher who is constantly refining and deepening his craft. You need to provide an audience with whom teacher leaders can share their expertise so that learning within and beyond the school community increases and teacher leaders receive feedback about their work.

The community should understand that all teachers will be invited to become teacher leaders when they are ready. Although academic leadership should be given priority, there are a variety of other roles teachers can play that use their unique talents and benefit the school. Senior teachers, in particular, need to be given the opportunity to be recognized and contribute. Remember, too, that leaders who assign too many of their responsibilities to teacher leaders or don't consult often enough with those who have accepted the responsibilities may give the impression that they are not doing their job and find their leadership undermined or challenged.

Finally, parents need to understand the role teacher leaders will play and the impact this will have on their children's academic life, especially when the new responsibilities involve time away from the classroom. Also, be certain parents know that you are not using this initiative to evaluate your teachers' performance or rank them competitively.

Evaluating Success

To determine whether teacher leaders are stimulating the professional environment, improving teacher and student performance, and helping you develop a cohesive and productive instructional plan, look for evidence like this:

- Are academic benchmarks continually being raised through teacher leader conversations, demonstration lessons, and research projects? Is student performance increasingly rigorous?
- Are teacher leaders stimulating and sharing reflective practices and deeper insights into student behavior and performance? Is the collaboration that teacher leaders model resulting in positive competition and increased morale? Do teacher leaders want to continue in their role, and do more teachers volunteer to become teacher leaders each year?
- Is your interaction with teacher leaders increasing their knowledge and understanding of the school's climate and its instructional and organizational goals? Are teacher leaders learning through inquiry? Are you acting on this information to improve school performance?
- Is your collaboration with teacher leaders leading the whole community to embrace a shared vision in which the idea of *we* is emphasized and honored? Do you feel confident teacher leaders have developed a partnership with their colleagues and that the community is supporting their initiatives and decisions?
- Can you focus more deeply on important issues because of the support and expertise of the teacher leaders? Is time for instruction better used?
- Do teachers seek one another's support as resident experts in formal and informal ways, thereby stretching limited resources? Do teacher leaders feel more comfortable giving advice about policy decisions? Are they moving from

self-interest to an interest in what is best for the entire community? Are potential nay-sayers encouraged to use their knowledge and expertise productively?

- Are you supporting and nurturing your teacher leaders' careers? Do you have a plan of succession?
- Are the products that teacher leaders create used by the teachers in your school and other schools to increase learning, replicate best practices, and take new risks? Do members of other communities seek your teacher leaders out for classroom visits, workshops, and model lessons?
- Will the teacher leader initiative endure if you are no longer at the school?

Teacher Leader Case Studies

There is no one correct pathway teacher leaders must follow; the decisions made regarding this position must be closely aligned with your goals and the community's strengths and needs. The following profiles illustrate how one school community defined the role of three teacher leaders. Various talents and expertise were aligned with school goals and the principal's vision for improving the culture and academic standing of the school.

Mathematics Teacher Leader

BACKGROUND AND RATIONALE FOR THIS LEADERSHIP ROLE

New mathematics mandates were being imposed, and resistance was anticipated from teachers as well as parents. Since the principal was not yet proficient in this new approach, a highly respected mathematics teacher needed to convince colleagues to take this new path and help the principal become aware of the specific challenges. This teacher leader could also analyze how best to proceed, including which grades would most likely be able to implement the changes successfully and how to supplement mathematical content areas not covered in the new curriculum.

HOW THE ROLE PLAYED OUT

The teacher leader's input and expertise were essential in helping the district committee examine possible programs and share its findings with the principal. After the district chose a program, the teacher leader was able to lessen teacher and parent anxiety. Although the teacher leader was an expert in mathematics, she needed the principal's coaching in communicating effectively with her peers as well as dealing confidently with people in power who did not agree with her.

While other schools in the district faced major parent opposition to the new program, this school did not join the chorus of dissent. Because the parents in the community already knew the teacher leader in the role of successful teacher, they trusted her to lead them in workshops introducing the new curriculum. Her relationship with parents convinced them that this program was worth implementing, that it would be phased in slowly, and that their concerns would be taken into account.

The teacher leader's willingness to conduct ongoing parent workshops, offer professional development for teachers, and develop and coach a team of mathematics teacher leaders ensured growing schoolwide proficiency in the new approach. (The teacher leader also trained a team of student mathematics leaders.) During the first year, while teaching her own class, she visited other classrooms in the school and conducted demonstration lessons. During the next several years, she obtained her supervisory license and became a full-time mathematics staff developer and is now a school principal.

JOB DESCRIPTION (OVER A THREE-YEAR PERIOD)

- Attend all district professional development meetings dealing with mathematics instruction and relay this information to the principal and staff.
- Inform principal of problems teachers are experiencing and propose possible solutions.
- Order materials, set up schedules, and conduct ongoing professional development.
- Create a model mathematics lab where teachers can observe exemplary practices.
- Visit colleagues' classrooms to model, coach, and observe.
- Create a course of study in mathematics for teachers.
- Develop a FAQ sheet for teachers to distribute to parents.
- Conduct parent workshops to explain the new standards and the resulting changes in curriculum.
- Lead teachers in looking at student work and developing rubrics, linked to standards, for evaluating student work and implementing changes in practice.
- Accompany teachers on visits to exemplary classrooms in other schools, discuss what has been observed, and plan next steps.

PROJECTS UNDERTAKEN

- Led the school mathematics team in developing the comprehensive school plan.
- Created a monthly newsletter that highlighted new learning and shared the community's expertise.
- Created a photo-essay summarizing the best practices being used in the school and in other schools.
- Selected professional articles about current research for the staff to read.
- Created a mathematics club for students.

Administrative/Organizational Teacher Leader

BACKGROUND AND RATIONALE FOR THE LEADERSHIP ROLE

When the principal of the school assumed her position, she inherited a haphazard teaching schedule, set up to fulfill stipulations in teachers' contracts rather than take advantage of their expertise or maximize student learning. During a one-to-one conversation, one senior teacher talked about her prior business experience and about setting up schedules when she taught in another school. She had a passion for solving organizational challenges, wanted to help the new principal create a departmentalized program in which teachers' schedules were determined more fairly and efficiently, and had earned the respect of her colleagues as a leader. The principal wanted to take advantage of this teacher's talents. However, since the scheduling position required additional and more varied experience, two other teachers were also assigned to the role: it became a team effort.

HOW THE ROLE PLAYED OUT

In the following weeks, the team created a draft schedule based on instructional priorities and consistency and teacher input, defusing the contentious nature of previous schedules, which had been presented as faits accomplis. The senior teacher who headed the team then became an advocate for further innovations, convincing other senior teachers to join her in accepting them.

JOB DESCRIPTION

- On the basis of detailed conversations with the principal, meetings with groups of teachers, and research about best practices, create a departmentalized school schedule that maximizes student learning, incorporates flexible block programming, and includes electives and clubs.
- Troubleshoot all scheduling issues that arise during the school year, listening to individual concerns and modifying the schedule when necessary. Keep the principal informed of issues and concerns.
- Train the administrative team and grade-level leaders in best practices related to scheduling.
- Meet with parent leaders about scheduling issues and adjust the schedule accordingly.
- Meet with leaders from other schools to discuss scheduling strategies; help them modify and adapt their schedules if appropriate.
- Keep current on professional reading related to using time well and share this information with the community. Attend conferences to increase scheduling expertise.

PROJECTS UNDERTAKEN

- Created a flexible and transparent yearlong schedule, available on the first day of school, demonstrating to all staff members that their time was valued and predictable structures were established.
- Developed procedures for dealing with scheduling changes more effectively and efficiently (hiring substitutes when teachers were absent, for example).
- Created a workshop for teachers in which effective strategies for using time well were demonstrated.
- Created a yearly staff survey to assess schedule effectiveness and identify any necessary changes.
- Created a newsletter for sharing best practices in scheduling.

New-Teacher Mentor

BACKGROUND AND RATIONALE FOR THE LEADERSHIP ROLE
In this school in the past, experienced teachers had been hired whenever possible. The new principal wanted to balance this existing expertise with the fresh ideas of teachers just starting out. She needed someone to mentor these new staff members and reassure current staff members and parents that educational goals were still being met. One very experienced teacher loved working with student teachers and was happy to extend this passion to working with new teachers. Her credentials were impeccable: she lived in the community, had taught several generations of the families who lived there, could recommend local cultural and social resources, and could alert new teachers to potential pitfalls. In addition, her taking on the role of mentor signaled her willingness to support the recruiting of beginning teachers.

HOW THE ROLE PLAYED OUT
Every year more new teachers were brought onto the staff in an almost seamless transition. This teacher leader became their surrogate mother and instructional supporter. The relationships she fostered benefited her as well: she learned to embrace new ideas and take risks and became knowledgeable in curriculum areas that were new and somewhat uncomfortable for her. This model of shared learning helped create more collaborative relationships throughout the community and supported schoolwide cultural changes.

JOB DESCRIPTION
- Help new teachers adjust by having one-to-one meetings with them, observing their classrooms, and providing historical background about the school and the community.
- Help new teachers forge positive relationships with parents by role-playing challenging situations and preparing them for parent-teacher conferences.
- Offer new teachers workshops in writing positive report card comments.
- Help new teachers with classroom management and discipline.
- Be the go-to person for all issues related to new teachers. Troubleshoot as necessary.

PROJECTS UNDERTAKEN
- Developed a handbook for new teachers listing dos and don'ts and community resources.
- Planned and facilitated monthly new-teacher meetings to address concerns and provide ongoing support.
- Set up a regular monthly meeting with the principal to discuss new-teacher issues and concerns.
- Created a newsletter for new teachers celebrating successes and highlighting learning.

Plan for September in June

Dear Reader,

One of the things we've always loved about being teachers is the chance to forge new beginnings and reinvent our lives as each new school year begins. The colors of the turning leaves trigger our renewed hope, energy, and expectation. We look forward to replicating the successes of the previous year and adapting and modifying things that didn't work so well. In schools across America, teachers return to their classrooms bursting with new ideas to try out but are often distracted by additional mandates, uncertainty about what students have learned in previous years, and lack of support from their grade-level colleagues.

Unfortunately, most school communities still skimp on thoughtful, comprehensive schoolwide planning. Teachers are often frustrated by not having the books and resources they need, being expected to adhere to misaligned schedules, and having no time to plan curriculum with their grade-level colleagues. Too often they sit at home alone on Sunday nights, the weekly lesson plan (a burdensome requirement) in front of them, trying to create lessons that will be approved by the principal and meet the needs of their students. This kind of planning focuses on isolated skills or daily lessons and requires little reflection or collaboration among teachers. Each teacher does her own thing, and curriculum, pedagogy, and pacing vary from class to class. Consistency is impossible. Each new school year begins with reviewing content and reteaching routines, skills, and habits of mind rather than with presenting exciting new challenges that build on the previous year's learning.

In our present environment, in which mandate after mandate drives instructional decisions and accountability pressures continue to mount, teachers are forced into uniformity. They have no opportunity for thoughtful conversations about their students' needs and have no motivation to practice their craft with energy and enthusiasm. In classroom after classroom, teachers conduct the same scripted lessons, putting their creativity on hold. Enlarging standards and rubrics and posting them on classroom and hallway walls without thoughtful conversations about what they mean for *this* community defeats their purpose. Concern about imposed standards has turned into a heated debate about autonomy versus consistency. We believe that when standards are linked to meaningful teacher conversations, not only do autonomy and creativity not have to be sacrificed to consistency, but they can actually be enhanced: collaboration results in both improved teaching practices and increased student achievement.

Principals are challenged to find a balance between the teachers who embrace lockstep conformity and the lone rangers whose only concern is protecting their autonomy. Building consistency within each grade and from grade to grade requires leaders who are willing to provide the time and resources for teachers to be able to talk with one another about content and practices while constantly assessing the needs of individual students, the progress of an entire grade of students, and continuity from grade to grade.

Group planning sessions in June enable teachers to reflect on the past year's performance and develop their own curriculum units and rubrics by grade or subject area while still adhering to state and national standards and scope-and-sequence outlines. This ensures that appropriate foundations are established. These schoolwide conversations make each year's expectations public: transitions are smooth, pacing is appropriate, and there are few gaps and redundancies.

During these June planning conversations, teachers can respectfully disagree and then work toward a consensus about units of study to be taught. They no longer have to plan alone but can share ideas about field trips, homework policies, and parental involvement. Together, all the teachers at a grade level or in a subject area can prepare and sign a letter to parents about next fall's curriculum, necessary supplies, books to be read, and homework expectations to lessen summer-vacation anxiety for parents, teachers, and students. Parents are assured that a smooth transition will take place and that their children will receive an equitable education with a consistent focus.

June planning also pushes teachers to look at the big picture, ask essential questions, and determine overarching goals (*What do I want to accomplish this year? What do I want my students to be able to do by next year? What do I need to learn to support them in accomplishing these goals?*). This outcome-based planning allows teachers to follow a step-by-step path of scheduling, pacing, teaching strategies, assessments, and resources. The conversations foster meaningful teacher interaction, thus forming a collaborative team that embraces and personalizes the standards to ensure student success. Problems of isolation, fragmentation, and distrust are gradually resolved. Teachers are able to use the summer to incubate ideas, take trips, read books, and conduct online searches centered on the established framework.

Summer becomes a time to think more deeply and productively about the coming year.

In a school where June planning is an established procedure, new teachers are welcomed into a collegial environment that will guide and support their adoption of a clear, detailed pedagogical framework. New teachers experience a smoother transition into the school community both personally and professionally; they can even reach out to other teachers during the summer should they have any questions or concerns.

In this time of federal and state oversight and the application of negative labels that are often based on the single criterion of standardized test scores, schools need to develop internal mechanisms to evaluate their own progress and motivate continual improvement. The June planning frameworks from each grade and subject area, which include teacher- and student-created rubrics, make up the school's comprehensive educational plan. This becomes a written, public document—a road map, a contract between the parents, the students, and the school. It is a living professional development guide, constantly revisited and revised and linked to school needs and student performance by the teachers who authored it. Teachers use this plan to anchor their teaching, assess student learning, and make necessary modifications. Parents no longer feel driven to request specific teachers. Teachers' concerns about losing their autonomy are reduced: they have had an important voice in developing instructional consistency, and they have experienced the support that comes with collaborating with their peers. Students benefit from the common language that has been developed and the clear expectations that have been established for each grade.

Leaders who sit at the table as active participants during June planning days demonstrate firsthand their commitment to conversations and comprehensive planning as the major tools for school improvement. Leaders who excuse teachers from their classrooms for an entire day or more or compensate them for the extra time in other ways demonstrate how much they value teachers' expert opinions.

June planning is an essential tool in building community. All teachers have the opportunity to engage in the most meaningful form of professional development—conversations with their peers. They own the decisions that are made and the curricula that are developed. The school becomes an intellectually vibrant professional community that respects teachers as decision makers and principals as facilitators.

—Carmen and Laura

Why Institute June Planning?

Expressing the school's mission by means of a visible, public framework means smoother and easier transitions for students and their families. Schools can evaluate their progress against this framework, make continual and timely changes, and articulate student progress in terms of concrete evidence. The result is an intellectually curious community that improves student achievement.

June planning encourages professional dialogue that leads teachers and parents to support and promote school goals. As teachers become more comfortable joining their colleagues in reflective thinking and intellectual discourse, they in turn model this behavior for their students, who then follow this kind of critical thinking as a way of life.

June planning results in a more collaborative team. Specialists (math, science, art, physical education, ESL) have an opportunity to support instruction, align their curriculum with that of the basic classroom, share their expertise and knowledge about student learning, and recommend appropriate materials. New teachers receive a positive introduction to the school community and begin their career on an inspirational note. A smooth transition in connection with any last-minute hires is assured.

Leaders glean important preliminary information about where their teachers stand on controversial or challenging issues like heterogeneous versus homogeneous grouping, the structure and purpose of report cards, the use of technology, and homework requirements. They can take the steps necessary to attain school-wide consensus before sharing school polices with the wider community.

June planning builds schoolwide consistency, results in fewer curricular gaps and redundancies, and establishes shared habits of mind. Teacher collaboration leads to more productive classroom instruction and improved student learning and achievement. There is less teacher isolation and negative competition; there is more positive sharing, respect, and support. Teachers are able to influence their professional development and help decide what and who will best support the work they are doing. Teacher leadership grows.

June planning gives the school's principal and leadership team an opportunity to introduce new initiatives in the meaningful and practical context of interactive conversations. They can order the right materials and be confident that they will arrive on time. They can schedule classes to students' best benefit.

Observing the way teachers perceive and relate to one another during these planning sessions helps leaders identify relationships that need to be smoothed and staff members with untapped talents and skills, so they can better assign teachers to classrooms and committees. The active involvement of leaders in June planning demonstrates, practically and concretely, their belief in distributive leadership and commitment to teacher ownership of the curriculum.

June planning transforms the end of the school year, often a time of low energy, to a time of new beginnings and renewed energy. Summer becomes a time to prepare for the new school year, an incubation period in which to attend professional development seminars and workshops, plan units of study, and shop for appropriate materials.

Getting Started: Step by Step

1. In April, write a letter introducing the concept, purpose, and intended outcome of the June planning sessions. Then convene a whole-school faculty conference, explain the process, and invite comments and suggestions. This incubation period is essential: planning like this requires thorough preparation and active participation. You might give your staff members copies of a professional book that discusses thoughtful planning (*Backward Design*, by Grant Wiggins; *Mapping the Curriculum*, by Heidi Hayes Jacob; and *Strategies That Work*, by Stephanie Harvey, are three good ones) so that they come to the June meetings with a common vocabulary and enough background information to engage in insightful conversations.

2. By the second week of May, determine which teachers will teach which grade or subject area next year and distribute a new organization chart. If possible, hire new teachers early enough so that they can also participate in the planning meetings.

3. With your cabinet, review the current year's comprehensive school plan, examine segmented student achievement data, and determine priorities for each curriculum area. Address any other schoolwide concerns.

4. Review parent concerns such as too much homework, too few physical activities, insufficient communication about remediation, too little parental participation in class activities, and promotion requirements. Compile and distribute these concerns to grade-level or subject area leaders so they can be discussed at preplanning meetings.

5. Review the subject area articulation teams' notes. (Articulation teams are discussed in Chapter 6.) Incorporate these suggestions and concerns into the June planning meeting agenda.

6. Convene grade-level or subject area meetings focused on making the best use of the June planning sessions and formulating teachers' ideas in persuasive and convincing ways.

7. Meet with grade-level or subject area leaders, listen to their concerns, and include them on the agenda. Examples might include having students read different titles each year, dealing with a wide range of student ability, assessing student learning, forming partnerships with other teachers and classrooms, taking appropriate field trips, and lunchtime issues.

8. Create a universal June planning agenda (the same for each grade level or subject area; an example is shown in Figure 8.1 on page 144). Include any new schoolwide initiatives as well as recommended teaching strategies.

9. Publicize the dates and times of the June planning meetings. Clear your calendar so that you can participate in all meetings.

10. Arrange to cover teachers' classes for the day their meeting will be held (unless the meeting is taking place over a series of evenings or on a weekend).

Planning Day

1. Welcome letter to parents
   - Goals, materials, trips, money*
2. Specialists/lunch/planning time
3. Standards (rubrics for teachers, research project, heterogeneous)
   - "All Children Can Learn"*
4. Teacher portfolio/Student portfolio
   - Past/present/future
   - Updates
   - Assessment (self, parents)
5. Club/mentor programs/products
   - (3/4)
   - (5/6)
6. Articulation
   - Visiting other grades/schools
   - Technology initiative

*Lunch to be provided (menu to be sent)

Only teachers scheduled on Organization Sheet for specific grades should be part of the planning session.

FIGURE 8.1 *June Planning Agenda*

11. Identify convenient spaces in which to hold the grade-level or subject-area meetings that are conducive to conversation and free from distractions and interruptions. If the meeting is being held at a site other than the school, make sure each grade has a private space. See that these spaces are supplied with charts and markers for taking notes; standards and scope-and-sequence outlines for each content area and grade; textbooks and other curricular materials; educational catalogs; a computer with an Internet connection; a list of websites helpful in extending curriculum knowledge and supporting the diverse needs of students; and appropriate professional books and journals.

12. Send a letter to parents explaining the June planning meetings. Include the dates of the meetings and the names of the substitute teachers who will be covering their children's classrooms. Figure 8.2 illustrates the tone and content of this letter.

13. Make arrangements to provide breakfast and lunch on the scheduled date and place these orders well in advance. (While the teachers are eating, encourage them to share their summer plans and the successes they experienced during the year; socializing is also important.)

Dear Parents,

As you may know, our school is committed to comprehensive planning that results in consistent language, content, and teaching strategies within each grade and across all grades. We publish this comprehensive plan each year in order to communicate to you our instructional purpose and our expectations for your children and to give you the opportunity to support these efforts at home.

In order to plan in a thoughtful and reflective way, each teacher will meet for a full day in June with grade-level or subject area colleagues as well as specialists. We have carefully considered how best to cover your child's class on that day so that instruction will continue. The attached sheet lists the date of each grade's planning day and the teacher covering each class.

On the last day of school you will receive a letter prepared during these planning meetings, signed by the teachers of your child's grade level next year, telling you the materials he or she will need, the instruction that will be presented, and ways you can support your child at home.

We are excited about this opportunity for our community to join together to think deeply about how our school and curriculum might be strengthened to serve our students better and address the concerns you and other parents and caregivers have voiced throughout this year. Your support in this endeavor is greatly appreciated by all the professionals in our community.

FIGURE 8.2 *Letter to Parents Explaining June Planning*

14. In advance, give teachers an agenda listing the expectations for the day and specifying materials they should bring from their own classrooms: samples of student work, resources they have found useful, paper and pens for taking notes. Also ask teachers what specialists (a data analyst, a literacy expert, an outside curriculum consultant) they would like you to invite to help them with their work. For each grade-level or subject area meeting, appoint a chairperson (often the grade-level or subject area leader) to take the minutes and highlight areas of disagreement that require your follow-up.

15. During each planning day, visit the grade-level or subject area meeting at least three times to assess the emotional climate of the community and provide assistance in any way necessary. This is the time to introduce and explain the rationale of a new school initiative, explain its ramifications for each grade level or subject area, and invite the teachers to air their concerns and make suggestions and recommendations. If the meeting is hitting roadblocks that cannot be overcome by the chairperson, step in and actively guide the group toward consensus.

16. At the end of the day, collect the materials the group has produced:
- chairperson's minutes (see Figure 8.3 for an example)
- curriculum calendars (If your school is just beginning June planning, it might make sense for each grade-level group to focus on one—mathematics, reading, or writing, for example—so that teachers are not overwhelmed; more experienced grade-level groups can work on more than one.)
- requests for professional development

Notes From Second Grade All Day Planning Meeting

Reports From Articulation Teams

INTERDISCIPLINARY
Focus on millenium- how different cultures/areas of the world will celebrate
- 2nd grade focus on neighborhoods of N.Y.C.
*Chinatown
*Harlem/Spanish Harlem
*Little Italy
*Lower East Side/Eastern European

Each class will study a neighborhood:
-take a trip to neighborhood
-investigate the history of neighborhood/culture
-research landmarks in neighborhood
-investigate any sights to see or events in neighborhood

Culminating Activities
-each class will have a cultural festival with food from their neighborhood
-we will prepare a second grade newsletter - each class will contribute info on their
neighborhood: recipe, calendar of events, pictures/photos, listing of restaurants, listing of books
from culture, poems

SCIENCE

- we will work with   from Central Park
- we need to ask around 5 parents from each class who will commit to 2-3 days of workshops
and trips
- we can study birds, history of park (then and now)
- Fall - Winter - Spring
- each of us will work with a Central Park Mentor

WRITING
Discussion of second grade genres:
Memoir, 1 other narrative genre, 1 informational genre

- Spelling - to be decided
We will hold kids accountable for 1st grade word list right away
- New second grade word list is being developed
- 4 times a year write to assigned topic

READING (Meeting 6/14)

What we need:
- explore more reading strategies to teach kids
- how does guided reading change with kids who are fluent readers
- management:
        - partnerships - how they change over the course of the year
        - keeping different aspects of reading going on at the same time (partnerships, guided,
        strategy lessons)
        - leveled library
        - what are the units of study we want to do

an assessment for kids who are already at level 6 ECLAS
what should writing response to reading look like

MATH

- we intend to do things out of district order
- we need to clarify what we need to do   Order and district

Team teaching for math
- we'd go to the district to learn book, etc.
- we'd look at book together, plan homework extensions
- we'd pick 1-2 days a week to plan math at the same period, so we can pull out kids who are
accelerated. (Group work)

Math Staff Developer - lab sites
                    - lunch time conversations

Possible order for TERC
1. Mathematical Thinking - number stuff only
2. Coins and Coupons
3. Shapes, Halves and Symmetry
4. Putting Together Taking Apart
5. Does It Walk Swim or Crawl

FIGURE 8.3 *Chairperson's Minutes*

- lists of children's books and other resources
- a calendar of field trips matched to study units
- themes for gradewide events
- strategies for working with both high-functioning and struggling students
- homework policies
- student assessments and a schedule for administering them
- a welcome-back-to-school letter for parents
- plans for parent outreach
- expectations for student performance linked to the school comprehensive plan

Teachers may also submit requests for schedule changes necessary to implement their goals. Teachers' suggestions relative to school scheduling, needed materials, professional development, lunchtime clubs, and after-school programs can be submitted on a form like the one in Figure 8.4.

Class Placements

•Let me know if you wish to have extra (per session time) to review class placements (2:30 p.m. to 4:30 p.m.)

MINUTES

1. Scheduling concerns to further instruction (cycles — to be held on Thursdays, intervention, arts,math, grouping, etc.)

_____

_____

_____

_____

_____

2. Materials

A. Rugs, faceless paper, color? chart tablets

_____

_____

_____

B. Books

_____

_____

_____

3. Curriculum Decisions

Time-Line for Writing/Reading/Math

(Attach to Minutes)   Please be specific.

_____

_____

_____

4. Staff Development - Special Assistance/Support - Video - Taping

_____

_____

5. Lunchtime Clubs

_____

_____

6. After-School Suggestions

_____

_____

May be copied for professional use. © 2008 by Carmen Fariña and Laura Kotch from *A School Leader's Guide to Excellence* (Heinemann: Portsmouth, NH).

FIGURE 8.4

16. Be flexible about the time the day will end, and make provisions in advance should the teachers be willing to stay late or continue the meeting on another day. Compensate them for the additional time, either monetarily or in some other way.

17. Take comfort in the knowledge that these planning meetings will become more effective and productive as teachers grow more comfortable collaborating with one another. Figure 8.5 is the agenda for one school's June planning meeting held eight years after the policy was initiated; notice the growth in teacher responsibility and expertise.

<u>June Planning Days</u>

Please be sure to take notes on all relevant discussions and give to me ASAP.

<u>8:40 a.m. Breakfast in Room ~~125~~ 329</u>
Order breakfast day before

<u>Articulation Team Reports</u>
Develop a year long calendar of units for each subject area.

Discuss testing implications for each grade.

<u>Science</u> — Collaboration Sites

After-School Programs

<u>Math</u> — Homework Units, **gaps**, (facts)

Role of Math Staff Developer

<u>Reading</u> — Author Studies

Library (use of..........)

Genres

<u>Writing</u> — TC Calendar Days

Discussion of **Spelling** (grade list)

Penmanship (place in the curriculum)

<u>Social Studies</u>

Themes/Time Frame/Research Projects

<u>Intervention</u>

There will be changes in intervention personnel. Please make <u>every</u>
effort to have assigned personnel attend at least a half hour of your day.

<u>Challenge Programs</u>

•After-School suggestions

•Lunchtime programs for Acceleration

←————————————————→

•Homework (time/value/appropriate work)

•Specialists (Annenberg initiative)

•Author Studies/25 book list (Review/Delete/add)

•Progress Reports (Do we need to redo?)

•Buddy Classes (Purpose/change of Grades — k/3, 1/4, 2/5)

•Trips (Value/permission, etc.) All Day / End of Year

•Use of Teaching Assistants/Student Teachers (one hour lunch)

•Closets (new procedures, clean-up, keys)

•Testing (Implications of ECLAS, E-PAL, ELA)

on instruction, evaluation, personnel

FIGURE 8.5

Common Pitfalls

June planning is an opportunity for teachers to hear about your vision for the school and discuss their suggestions and concerns with their colleagues in a very personal way. If you don't participate, you will undermine both the purpose and the outcomes of these discussions. (Many leaders train a second in command who is able to fill in should an emergency arise.) Remember, too, that if you invite teachers to become decision makers in formulating the school comprehensive plan and then don't allow them to implement that plan, they will be reluctant to participate in your other initiatives.

Naysayers can undermine the best good intentions. Know who they are and do everything you can to encourage their willingness to cooperate and collaborate. When all else fails, separate them from one another to contain their negative influence. When the naysayers outnumber the positive voices in your community, it may be best to pilot test June planning with one or two grade levels or subject areas so the initiative gets off to a positive and constructive start.

Senior teachers or others who feel their opinions are more important than others can sometimes dominate the conversation. Choose expert facilitators and see that they receive training in understanding and orchestrating effective group dynamics.

Schedule sessions when most teachers can attend, and hold them in places that are conducive to conversations and have few distractions. The goal of June planning is consistency, not rigidity. Foster creativity and engagement by asking teachers to reflect on pedagogical standards as opportunities for thinking deeply and asking open-ended questions, not simply as dicta to be posted on the wall. Demonstrate your respect and trust for teachers—never hold them to an absolute and rigid timetable, in either their curriculum or their day-to-day teaching.

June planning requires that details, both big and small, be thoroughly planned. Lack of foresight in providing food, hiring substitutes, reserving a location, providing appropriate materials, or assigning facilitators can lead to failure.

Evaluating Success

To evaluate whether June planning conversations lead to thoughtful reflections about teaching practices, the creation of an intellectually curious school community, and improved student achievement, look for evidence like this:

• Is the school comprehensive plan developed and implemented collaboratively using appropriate data? Can all members of the community articulate the purpose, the practices, and the anticipated outcomes? Are all members of the community sharing the responsibility for student achievement?

• Is the quality of the written, public document produced during June planning improving each year? Do teachers understand the need to revise and deepen their practices?

• Are the expectations for student learning increasingly rigorous? Are necessary adjustments made to meet each student's needs? Are teacher-created rubrics used to evaluate student learning, ensure equity, and make expectations transparent to students and parents? Are student-created rubrics produced and valued? Do teachers spend time at each meeting examining and evaluating student work based on these rubrics?

- Do teachers value the opportunity to use one another as planning resources? Can they use the time effectively to deepen the planning of all curriculum areas and take on difficult challenges like meeting the needs of every individual student?

- Do these planning conversations continue beyond the designated time? (At one school, teachers requested that June planning become a three-day retreat!)

- As parents begin to see the impact of the written curriculum framework, do their conversations move from individual concerns or requests to discussions about schoolwide improvement?

- Do the best and brightest new teachers seek to work in schools where June planning is the norm? Do the best and brightest teachers remain at these schools?

- Does June planning jump-start the new year? Is there a smooth transition from the previous year? Are teachers spending less time reviewing? Are there fewer curricular redundancies? Is a common language used within and across departments and grades?

- Does the document created through June planning highlight opportunities to apply for grants?

- Does June planning provide a context for replication? Does it lead to school- and districtwide consistency, improved morale, and improved student achievement?

Encourage Parent and Community Engagement

Dear Reader,

A guiding principle in our parents' lives was their respect for schools and the value they placed on education as the pathway to success. They cared deeply about our education and made sure we did our best work. They celebrated when we came home with good report cards and papers on which our teachers had jotted compliments. For them, school was a place of power and authority that neither needed nor sought their participation. Visiting the school was intimidating—they always felt they were being judged and found wanting. They therefore relied on the school to function without their physical presence.

They supported the school in their own way—baking cookies, sewing costumes, making sure we attended each day. They used their acquaintanceship with other parents to stay informed but seldom attended parent-teacher association (PTA) meetings and never served on a committee. They did attend parent-teacher conferences, but these meetings were often hurried and impersonal.

Our parents' experiences have convinced us that participation comes in many forms and that schools need to respect all parents and meet the needs of the various socioeconomic statuses and diverse cultures that make up our school communities.

When our own children were born, selecting the right school was one of the most important decisions we made. In our dual roles as mothers and teachers, we found we now understood and were more empathetic with parents when they forgot to pack their children's lunches, did not sign the appropriate papers on time, brought their children to school late on rainy days, failed to keep appointments because of family illness, or let their children leave the house with pants that hung around their hips. We were experiencing similar issues and were well aware that raising children was not as easy as it once seemed. Our connection with the parents of our students was personal and deep and enriched our classroom experiences. Because the normal venues for parent involvement—chaperoning class trips, becoming class parents, volunteering for school committees, joining the school leadership team—were impossible for us, it was important to find other ways to impact the life of our children's schools. The challenge was complicated even more because we both taught in the schools our children attended.

Wanting to make good use of our positions as insiders, we (with the help of our colleagues) initiated practices that would involve parents in the life of the school more fully: curriculum nights, expanded parent-teacher conferences, parent workshops and study groups, school tours, parent newsletters, parent-teacher committees, meet-the-author events, artist residencies, parent libraries, classroom demonstrations. Parents began to participate in areas that had previously been the sole dominion of teachers. Our schools became known for their parent-friendly atmosphere, which attracted both parents and teachers and demonstrated the power of parent involvement in raising student achievement and forging a positive school climate.

When Carmen became the principal of PS 6, the dynamics of parental involvement there were very different from those we had been used to. A small number of parent leaders, who were also very successful fund-raisers, made many important decisions, including hiring and firing staff. Their power over how the money they raised was spent affected curriculum decisions, administrative policy, and school goals. Too often, these decisions and policies benefited a select few.

The language used to describe the students held largely to ethnic lines; it was common to hear terms like "the janitors' class" applied to children whose parents were doormen, housekeepers, or held other service jobs. A small but prominent group of parents was speaking for all parents, when most of the other parents never attended meetings or joined committees. Clearly, we needed to communicate our policy of an expanded role for *all* parents in a fair and transparent way.

In this environment, teachers were often pitted against teachers, and they were eager for a leader who would set clear parameters for making parent involvement a positive part of school life without distracting them from their teaching. Over a period of ten years, we instituted many of the practices described in this chapter, giving parents a more equitable voice, inviting the full participation of a diverse group of parents, improving student achievement, and forming productive partnerships between parents and teachers.

Later, when we took on leadership roles in the larger New York City school system, we knew that one of the most important issues leaders face is redefining what parents need from the school and seeing to it that the school serves those needs. At our first parent advisory council meeting, a parent advocate voiced the concern that as more and more immigrants enrolled their children in city schools, the language barrier and the school communities' lack of specific knowledge about these diverse cultures prevented these children and their parents from being fully integrated into the life of the schools. In response, the department of education arranged for translators in eight languages, hired bilingual parent coordinators, and created school lunch menus that met the dietary needs of specific cultures.

At one of our first town hall meetings, we realized that the majority of the caregivers in the audience were grandparents concerned about the narrow definition of parent: even those with legal custody of their grandchildren were often prevented from participating in school life. They suggested we invite them to work with students on oral histories, create grandparent days, and add books to class libraries that would expand the definition of parent.

Several single parents with nine-to-five jobs were frustrated because school meetings were often held during school hours and those that did take place in the evening did not provide a baby-sitter and they couldn't afford their own. Wanting to help these parents, we instituted family nights at which single parents could network while their children watched a movie. We also set up single-parent support groups led by guidance counselors.

Another issue, the gender gap, surfaced when a father told us that he was often the only male at PTA meetings and that he felt invitations to be a class parent were made only to mothers. We encouraged principals citywide to attempt to lessen the achievement gap between boys and girls by promoting programs such as male mentoring, male-only parent dinners, and father-and-son reading clubs and by making teachers aware of how girls' and boys' learning interests and styles differ.

Successfully involving parents in their children's education remains a challenge, but it is crucial if we are to improve student achievement and support all members of the community. Public education is continually being redefined, but one constant that will never change is the need to communicate and engage parents fully in the educational mission. Schools that take this responsibility seriously will be the most successful in developing new, replicable practices. A better life for the next generation rests on the confidence and support of parents who believe that public education can and will succeed. Leaders who can instill this confidence in their communities will find strength in joining with parents to accomplish their goals.

—Carmen and Laura

Why Is Parent Leadership Crucial for School Success?

A strong home-school connection leads directly to improved student achievement, but too often communications from the school never make it out of the backpack. Predictable and sustainable procedures for communicating with parents ensure that the information they need reaches them in a timely fashion. Color-coding communications, establishing a public and predictable schedule for distributing important information, designating a place in the school where duplicates of communications can be retrieved, and appointing a liaison parent for each grade or department to answer questions all make your work easier and guarantee that parents will receive the information they are sent. Preparing and distributing a school-year calendar of events, rituals, traditions, and celebrations to which parents are invited ensures that they are able to participate fully in the life of the school. Many schools have their own websites that provide up-to-date information for parents; parents who don't have computers at home can view the sites at their local libraries.

Parental input and feedback regarding what happens in school produces a stronger commitment to the school's mission. Principals who understand the value parents bring to the school community and the power of keeping an open dialogue with them see to it that parents become full partners with them in setting the school agenda and supporting the school in the larger community. Students will be more successful academically and socially if many of the same strategies that work so well to build trust with teachers are used with parents: a variety of opportunities for written and oral communication, rituals and celebrations that unite the community, and traditions that are sustained over past, present, and future generations.

Rituals, traditions, and celebrations are opportunities for everyone in the school community—parents, students, and teachers—to share a sense of joy in and appreciation for their talents, history, and values. Some may be geared to a targeted audience—male caregivers, community merchants, faith-based organizations, or alumni, for example—with the hope that this audience will become more involved in school activities. Additional goals are to increase students' academic performance, improve their social skills, and provide positive public relations.

New principals need to understand existing school rituals, traditions, and celebrations, especially if several generations of community members have already enjoyed participating in them and expect to continue doing so. Think carefully before eliminating one of these valued rituals: It may serve a purpose beyond the event itself. For example, a dance festival in which students practice and perform ethnic dances may seem outdated and no longer of value, but for the community it may be a connecting thread through the generations that brings everyone together. If you create a new ritual, make sure it will interest all members of the school community or meet a common need.

Leaders who take the time to build trusting relationships with parents are more likely to have well-attended parent meetings and school events. Most important, parents' resulting confidence in educational decisions allows leaders to focus on instructional issues that lead to improved student achievement. Principals gain enormous benefits when parents are aware of all curriculum decisions, controversial issues, personnel decisions, and student activities. Principals who see communication with parents as an opportunity to think through their practices and make an effort to build a consensus find it easier to lead.

Parents with special expertise can form advisory committees to help meet a school's needs in these special areas. Prime examples are setting up before- and after-school programs for athletics, chess, drama, woodworking, science, technology, mathematics, and other areas of interest, because so many students need a safe and stimulating environment outside school hours, one not dominated by television. Inviting teachers, local artists, and community organizations to participate as well strengthens the bonds between the school and the community and enriches the learning of all involved. These committees can also raise funds to provide scholarships for students who may not be able to attend the programs otherwise.

At PS 6, three committees provided monumental service to the school and supported Carmen in accomplishing the school goals:

• The technology committee comprised computer-savvy parents who researched the school's current capabilities, surveyed the school community, researched best practices in other schools, interviewed outside consultants, and created a five-year plan. They then advocated for the implementation of this plan with politicians and grant providers and took responsibility for all implementation details, including overseeing the new wiring.

• The science committee reviewed the resources of nearby science institutions to see how they aligned with the school's science program grade by grade, then planned weekend family trips to these institutions so parents could participate in hands-on science learning. They also wrote grant applications to secure funding to expand the school's science program.

• A diversity committee was formed to acknowledge and celebrate the minority cultures represented in the school community, populations that were often ignored and misunderstood. The committee consisted of parents from different cultures, interested teachers, and outside experts. Together they planned and implemented a diversity week each year during which the school community immersed itself in a particular culture and acknowledged the members of that culture. The committee prepared a teaching packet—maps, a glossary of terms, a short history, background information, and current-events articles— that supported an entire week's lessons. Parents who were members of the culture were invited to talk to students about their lives and experiences. Seminars for upper-grade students and their parents provided in-depth information about relevant current issues. Evening performances, at which ethnic food was served, featured artistic expressions of the culture. (A ticket to one such performance is shown in Figure 9.1 on page 156.) Students from the culture wearing native costumes were hosts and answered questions from the audience. Parents received additional background information so they could continue the conversation at home. Parents who had never taken part in school events before found the experience transformational. Students did as well: see Figure 9.2 on page 156.

Schools must ensure that parents feel welcome, supported, and understood. To that end, New York City schools created the position of parent coordinator. A parent or school advocate who knows the community well is hired to reach out to parents, disseminate information (in a regular newsletter, among other

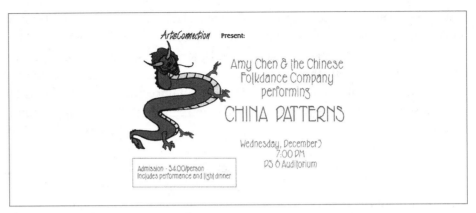

FIGURE 9.1 *Ticket to Diversity Week Event*

Dear, Mrs. Fariña

I am so glad you created an African week.

I had no idea that African Americans culture was intriguing and joyfull.

My favorite part diversity week was the dancers and drummers on thursday.

I was in the music group on monday with the dancers and drummers. The man with the gotee he's extremely funny.

The words stick in your mind like Super glue to paper.

My favorite song is Kei Kei Kei. I know it by heart.

I tried by best to get to "I Can Feel It In My Bones" but I couldn't make it and I was really disapointed that I didn't get to go.

I was trying to find a way to learn more more on this subject but I couldn't find anything on it till now.

After the lady from Essence came I bought an issue, it was simply marvelous.

Before, I had seen Essence in newstands but I never really stopped and looked.

Back then a magazine for African American most of ben a great success.

I would like to thank you again for having this Festivity at school. It was extremely fun.

I hope you arange this for next year as well or make it an annuall event.

Also I hope more of these type of week will be created over the years.

FIGURE 9.2 *Student Response to Diversity Week*

means), conduct monthly meetings, and schedule parent events. This person works especially closely with parents new to the school and parents of English language learners and special needs students.

Many parent coordinators are bilingual, helping meet the needs of non-English-speaking parents and at the same time promoting other cultures to the mainstream community. They can arrange for translators, English as a second language (ESL) classes, technology training, and general educational development (GED) certification. They also present new and potentially controversial curriculum initiatives at parent workshops. (In New York City, for example, a new HIV/AIDS education curriculum was first presented to parent coordinators so that they could answer parent questions and concerns.) The parent coordinator reports directly to the principal and in many cases is also a member of the executive council.

Many principals spend over half their time talking to individual parents, often the same ones again and again, usually in response to a crisis. Having a parent coordinator who can deal with parents in a caring and knowledgeable way defuses issues before they turn into crises, leaves the principal more time to focus on instructional issues, and demonstrates the principal's commitment to parents.

It is important to encourage not only the most active and outspoken parents but also the parents who understand that they must advocate for all children in the school community, not just their own children. Principals who reach out to all parents, not just a chosen few, understand that there are many roles parents can play. The PTA is not the only vehicle for parent leadership. Inviting a more diverse group of parents to participate in the life of the school creates natural advocates for the school mission and appropriate models for the students. It also forges stronger relationships with community-based organizations, health and recreation agencies, and faith-based organizations.

Current state and federal accountability measures are based only on test scores and fail to see the school in its entirety, to include parents' perceptions and the role they play in school progress. In a recent survey in New York City, parents expressed a high level of satisfaction with their local schools, while the impression of the general public was more negative. Clearly many principals are making a concerted effort to serve parent needs and can count on these parents as active supporters.

Finally, the school is many parents' political training ground. Principals who engage parents positively in school life engender their support, foster their talents, and ensure their long-term commitment to public education. Many of the best politicians get their start in local PTAs and on school boards, mentored by principals who think aloud as they model consensus-building strategies and collaborative decision making.

Getting Started: Step by Step

1. Create a brochure promoting the school, stating school offerings, and advertising what makes the school special. Include quotes from parents, teachers, and students and photographs of classes and events. The brochure can be used to recruit teachers, support students' applications to other schools, and accompany grant applications. School websites can also provide easily accessible information that is timely and greatly appreciated.

2. Send home a parent information folder on the first day of school. Include a welcoming letter (see Figure 9.3); a calendar of yearly events (vacations, parent-teacher conferences, test dates, special events, PTA meetings); the names of all teachers, the grades they teach, and their room numbers; other important names and phone numbers (grade liaisons, committee leaders, PTA executive board members); fund-raising information for the year; a letter from the PTA president stating the function of the PTA; a sign-up sheet for parents to volunteer for various committees and activities; and forms requesting essential information (emergency telephone numbers, health questionnaire, dismissal release; see Figure 9.4). Figure 9.5 is a letter from a superintendent reminding principals about the importance of making parents feel part of the school community.

Dear Parents,

"The grand essentials to happiness in this life are something to <u>do</u>, something to <u>love</u>, and something to <u>hope</u> for."

Joseph Addison

If the above quote is to be believed, then we must be ecstatic.

We all have something positive to <u>do</u>. This packet gives you a wonderful opportunity to use your strengths in areas where you can do the most good.

We all have something to <u>love</u>. For me it is always the children, the staff and even the parents. For you it is the wonderful opportunity to be in a safe, happy, intellectual environment that nurtures your child.

We all have something to <u>hope</u> for. For us this year is the year of science, TERC math, enrichment lunchtime, cycles, expanded arts programs and who knows what else a strong financial position might allow.

This packet will help you realize all the above in multiple ways; it also provides more information than you can possibly absorb at one time. Nonetheless it is an attempt of the administration and your PTA Executive Board to make you aware of all school-wide events as early as possible so that you can plan accordingly.

I urge you to read this entire folder carefully and to keep it handy for easy reference. Many of you have requested school calendars, areas of volunteering and updated information on school-wide projects. All this information is here in one convenient place, and I appreciate the effort it took to make it available to you.

I'm looking forward to the school year and seeing all of you at at least one major event!

Sincerely,

Carmen Farina

FIGURE 9.3 *Welcoming Letter*

DISMISSAL FORM

Dear_____

of Class_____

My Child _____

Has a playdate with_____

Will be picked up by_____

Message_____

_____

_____

_____

_____

FIGURE 9.4

Dear Colleagues:

As I reviewed the results of the Chancellor's "parent survey", it was heartwarming to see how many parents feel that their neighborhood schools are truly places where they and their children are received warmly and treated respectfully.

We need to make sure that all school personnel play a positive role in welcoming and assisting parent participation.

School secretaries, school aides and safety officers are often the first ones to greet new parents. Perhaps, setting up a parent-to-parent welcoming committee in the main lobby during the first week of school would help make for a smoother transition for new parents. Also, consider arranging for parents to provide translations so that everyone feels listened to and appreciated.

The book I have chosen to highlight is "Mama, If You Had a Wish." It focuses on the essence of what all parents wish for their children. I would hope teachers also have the same wishes for their students, especially in regard to making mistakes and looking different.

Wouldn't it be wonderful if all of us together could answer our student's questions, "If you could make one wish about me, what would it be?"

And all of us would answer, "I would wish for you to be yourself, because we love you just the way you are."

We all wish the same thing for our students – self-confidence, academic achievement and the best school year possible. Let's work with all our parents and encourage them to participate in whatever way they feel comfortable so that all our shared wishes can come true.

Have a wonderful beginning of the best school year ever.

Sincerely,

Carmen

Carmen Fariña
Community Superintendent

FIGURE 9.5 *Reminder to Principals About the Importance of Parent Involvement*

3. Prepare a parent handbook (in various languages, as necessary) outlining the school's mission, rules and regulations, curriculum, homework policy, discipline code, bus schedules, and important phone numbers. Be sure to include procedures parents may use to communicate their concerns and a specific time within which they will receive a response. List the names and numbers of people who can assist parents with specific problems (making clear that you are available as the final resource).

4. Have your teachers prepare a glossary of educational language to help parents understand terms like *balanced literacy*, *accountable talk*, and *guided reading*.

5. Have a committee of teachers and parents prepare answers to frequently asked questions (FAQs). Focus on areas where confusion is likely: *How will my child be taught spelling? How often will my child participate in physical activities? How will the teacher communicate with me if my child is having problems in school?*

6. Give a state-of-the-school address as early in the school year as possible, preferably in the first three weeks. This gathering sets the tone for the school year and is first and foremost a welcoming and inspirational event assuring parents that you have a clear vision for the school and that they have an important role. Share the successes of the previous year, provide current data, introduce new staff members, outline any new curriculum initiatives, and describe school traditions and celebrations. Include a question-and-answer period, but be sure you know your audience and anticipate controversial issues. You might ask parents to jot their questions on index cards, which gives you a little time to reflect before answering them. (Give another state-of-the-school address in June summing up how the year went.)

7. Schedule an orientation-to-curriculum night at the end of September to share specific grade-level or department goals. Each teacher can make a presentation in her classroom about the year's initiatives, standards the students must meet, short- and long-term projects, homework, and discipline. (See Figure 9.6.)

8. Hold grade-level or department meetings to address parents' questions and concerns. (Addressing groups of parents instead of individuals saves time and ensures that every parent is told the same thing.) Schedule these meeting in the early morning or in the evening so parents can more easily attend. Distribute minutes of these meetings to all parents with children in the respective grade or department whether they attended or not.

- At the first meeting, in October, address issues that have surfaced in a survey conducted by the parent coordinator or liaison. Explain policy decisions, specific curriculum initiatives, and academic goals.
- At a second meeting, in January, focus on curriculum initiatives. Have teachers demonstrate a typical lesson, especially if the curriculum is new.

September Parent Orientation Meeting

<u>At the beginning of the session:</u>
Tell parents that the purpose of this meeting is for you to give everyone information about the class. Since time is limited, specific concerns & questions can't be addressed now, but you can make an appointment if a parent wants to speak with you.

Some ideas...

1. Tell about yourself (prior work, student teaching, etc..)

2. Explain your room arrangement - discuss areas & reasons these are there

3. Describe a typical daily schedule (you can have this written ahead of time)

4. Describe special activities for your class (cluster periods, any special programs)

5. Discuss Currriculum Goals:
    ·Balanced Literacy Components
(Shared, Guided, Independent Reading, Word Study, Writing Workshop)
        ·TERC / CMP   (can show teacher's guide & some manipulatives)
        ·Social studies / science themes you plan to study

6. Discuss how you are assessing students (ECLAS, etc)

7. Discuss the importance of creating a classroom community and your exp[ectations: (working together, following rules, being kind to others)

8. Homework -- describe your expectations and types of assignments

9. Policy for parents who want to talk with you....ask them to leave a note or phone message in your mailbox

10. Tell parents that they will have an opportunity to visit the class during Open School Week in November and will also attend a parent-teacher conference in November

11. Emphasize the importance of coming to school regularly and coming on time!

12. Remind parents about completing and returning:
        ·an up-to-date emergency contact card
        ·a 2000-2001 lunch form
        ·a trip permission form
        ·other forms or notices you have sent home

FIGURE 9.6

◆ At a third meeting, in June, focus on next year's curriculum so parents can support their children during the summer with appropriate books or field trips. This is also a good time to introduce next year's new teachers.

9. Conduct parent-student-teacher conferences by appointment after the state-of-the-school address and the initial grade-level or department meeting. Setting up specific appointments of at least half an hour ensures privacy and allows enough time for a real conversation. Having the student present means that both parent and child will know exactly what was said. (At PS 6, divorced parents were urged to attend these meetings together so they each heard the same message as well.) Parents will already be familiar with curriculum mandates, so the conversations can focus on the needs of the child. Students should prepare for these meetings by talking with their teachers about their work so far, setting goals, and writing down their accomplishments and challenges. (As Figure 9.7 shows, even young students can asses their own learning and set their own goals.) A reflective self-evaluation like this empowers students and makes them accountable for their own progress. Secondary students can play a more active role in these meetings, discussing their goals and needs. These conferences are often difficult for new teachers, who may need to role-play challenging situations beforehand. Brief all teachers on appropriate and inappropriate language and remind them to bring examples of student work to back up their judgments. Using this precious time for a constructive conversation focused on the student's strengths will encourage a stronger relationship between parents and the school. Follow up with parents who do not attend; find out why and schedule an alternative time if necessary. (Allow extra time for conferences you know will be difficult; having additional school personnel, like the guidance counselor, attend may also be a good idea.)

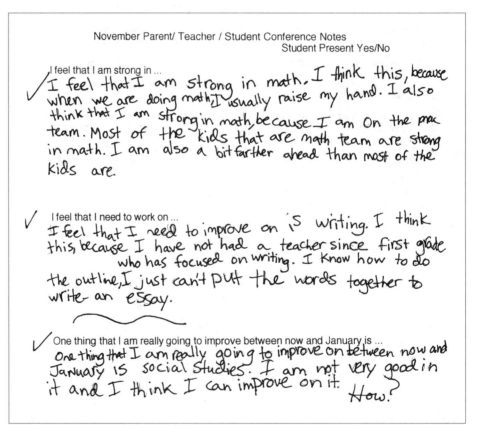

FIGURE 9.7 *A Student Self-Assessment*

10. Communicate school news in parent newsletters. These can be anything from a one-page list of monthly activities to literary magazines of student writing financed by ads from neighborhood merchants. (Figure 9.8 is the first page of an issue of *Connections*, PS 6's parent newsletter.)

```
CALENDAR UPDATES!

THURSDAY, APRIL 2              HALF DAY *******(EVERYONE!)
Thursday, April 9             Grandparents & Special Friends Day
April 10 - April 17           Spring Recess (including Friday)
Friday, May 15                Annual Square Dance

*****MARK YOUR CALENDARS - VERY IMPORTANT!!!


PROBLEM OF THE WEEK - (Answers will be printed next week)

K-2 - Bev, Nancy and Lynn each have 4 posters.  How many do they have altogether?

3-5 - Mary replaced 15 ceramic tiles in her workroom with new tiles.  Each new tile
measured 4 cm x 6 cm.  What area did the new tiles cover?

Last Week's answers: K-2 - (5 apples);   3-5 (33 bags).

SCHOOL AND COMMUNITY NEWS

THANK YOU - The family of the late                          wishes to
express its deep appreciation for the many expressions of sympathy.

DIVERSITY NIGHT - Many thanks to the members of the Diversity
Committee for all their hard work on the March 24 Diversity Night.

ANNENBERG MEETING - An important Annenberg Meeting will be held on April 6 at 3:00
pm.  Old members, potential new members and all others are welcome.


BOOK FAIR - The upcoming book fair is being planned.  Please save all of your good used
books for the Fair.  Only children's books will be accepted.  They may be sent, beginning
immediately, to the PTA office.

GLENNA FUND - Thank you to all third grade children and parents for their support and
delicious treats - our St. Patricks Day Glenna Fund bake sale was again a big success! Please
remember that our next, and last bake sale, is April 1.  Anyone can bake and everyone can
buy.  Everything is $.50.

YEAR BOOK - Students have been hard at work preparing for their yearbook!  In order to
do a high quality job and to supplement the budget, advertisements are being sought from
local merchants.  Business cards as ads will be accepted at a nominal charge of $35. which is
a tax deductible contribution.  All donations can be returned to the Yearbook Committee in
the PTA office.  Please include the name of the Merchant, their address and their donation.
```

FIGURE 9.8

11. Use a policy letter to provide especially important information (changes to existing practices, for example). Explain why the decisions were made and how the changes will be implemented. Immediately informing parents about safety and security issues, health concerns, school incidents, teacher reassignments, scheduling changes, and controversial neighborhood issues reduces parent anxiety and keeps things from escalating into crises. This is particularly true of issues that will be covered by the media.

12. Acknowledge benchmarks, both joyous and sad, in community-building letters. Congratulate students or teachers who have received an award; encourage parents to read with their children during a vacation or over the summer; invite them to join in reading the book of the month or participate in a public service project; announce the death of a member of the school community by highlighting his contributions and encouraging the community to grieve together and contribute to a memorial (see Figure 9.9).

Dear Parents:

Every once in a while a person comes along who deeply touches an entire community, each of us for different reasons. Jane was such a person.

To the teachers she was a supportive parent who always preferred to work behind the scenes and do the nitty gritty of class parent--phone calls, letter writing, book orders. She did not need the politics of committees. To other parents she was the person who always had extra room on half days, vacation days for those children whose parents needed the extra pair of hands. To the community at large she was an activist involved in many community affairs, specifically in sports programs that affected her children. However, it was as a mother that she excelled and it is in this role that we will remember her.

To honor her memory we are resurrecting the Samaritan Fund, which was begun by her. This fund will be renamed "Jane's Fund" and will be used for the purpose she intended- -to assist behind the scenes, students throughout the building who need a helping hand, and that the help is to be done totally anonymously.

In order to make this a true memorial, we are asking parents to bake with their children and use this shared time as a true testimonial to someone who felt that quality child/parent time was the highest priority. Also because of her love of holidays, the bake sale will be held in the following way:

- Thursday, February 12th - **Valentine's day**--only 4th graders to bake and 4th and 5th graders to purchase
- Tuesday, March 17th - **St. Patrick's Day**--only 3rd graders to bake and 1st, 2nd and 3rd graders to purchase
- Wednesday, April 1st - **April Fool's Day**--baking will be open to all who wish and purchasing will be held as long as there are baked goods.

FIGURE 9.9 *Community-Building Letter*

13. Have one-to-one conversations with parents about difficult situations or when communication has broken down and needs to be restored. Examples include helping a parent deal with a child's serious behavioral or academic problem; face a serious illness, divorce, custody battle, or loss of a loved one; negotiate a problem with a teacher; or resolve a conflict with another parent. At the end of the year, attempt to mend fences with any parent with whom a conflict remains unresolved or with whom communications have broken down; this way the new year can start with a clean slate.

14. Elect a school leadership team (comprising administrators, teachers, and parents) that meets regularly to develop a comprehensive plan of action and ensure that the school is conforming to state and federal mandates. Establish clear guidelines for and provide training in reaching agreement and resolving conflicts, so that controversial issues can be safely discussed and collaboratively decided. Subcommittees may be charged with writing the comprehensive school plan in specific areas. (The minutes in Figure 9.10 summarize a school leadership team meeting.)

15. Establish a good relationship with your PTA's executive board. These meetings can sometimes seem more an interrogation of the principal than a true sharing. Request that you be given time unrelated to a specific agenda item in which to update the board on current curriculum and educational concerns. Avoid sur-

Leadership Team Meeting
Minutes from Wednesday, May 10, 2:00pm

We discussed the School Mission/Vision Statement (see attached) that will be the focus of the CEP:

1. Parents returned few of the surveys; all concerns are being addressed.
2. Teacher committees are doing mission statements for each subject in their articulation teams. They produce a curriculum graph for the year.
3. In working to meet the needs of the children at the top percentile the staff is looking to come up with 2-5 ideas for new lunchtime clubs per grade. Staff or parents may teach these.
4. The science committee met to discuss how to enhance the classroom and came up with many good ideas. Renovation of the Science room in under discussion. 3rd Grade is interested in doing more with the Bronx Zoo. Expanding our astronomy program in collaboration with the new Rose Center at the Museum of Natural History is under discussion.
5. Extended math and current events are lined up for next year. 'Time For Kids' will be available to grades 3,4 & 5 partly thanks to a $500 donation from QSP resulting from the success of our magazine drive.
6. After school programs next year may be extended from 4:30 to 5:00.
7. Learning Specialists – support teams will be in place next year 10:30 – 4:30 doing extended day.   will work with grades 1,2,3.   will work with grades 4,5.   will with older children at risk.
8. Guidance Services should be enhanced next year due to a special grant, to help families deal with life crisis issues.
9. Discussion of possibility of a web site – could provide introduction to our school, calendar, and access to other sites such as NY Public Library. Would not have E-mail access to teachers.

10. Discussion of the possibility of adult education starting with a parent education workshop in computer literacy.
11. Discussion of fire safety after the incident on May 9th: Installing smoke detectors in closets is a possibility.
    PTA can pay for units if custodial staff installs and maintains them properly – including new batteries yearly.
12. May 24th – no school – all day staff development.

FIGURE 9.10

prises: at least forty-eight hours before the meeting, give the board a copy of your agenda, and ask to receive a copy of the board's agenda at that time as well. Discuss issues with the PTA president immediately before they turn into problems.

16. Greet parents and students at the beginning and end of each day. This demonstrates that you welcome informal conversation, models the power of social communication, and lets you gauge the mental health of the school. Shake students' hands, inquire about their day, and make mental notes about students who may need additional support. The atmosphere in the halls during arrival and dismissal is an indicator of the prevailing mood in the school; the more information you gather firsthand like this, the sooner and more effectively you can act.

17. Visit the cafeteria during the lunch hour, often the most difficult time of the day. Talk with students, observe their social interactions, and demonstrate your commitment to their health and well-being.

18. If you have the space, set up a room for parents, a welcoming space where they can find information on upcoming meetings and minutes of past meetings, opportunities to serve on committees, the comprehensive school plan, and professional development offerings. Provide extra copies of all school communications, a parent lending library, and computers they can use (or learn to use). A school volunteer should be in the room at all times, assisting parents and encouraging them to help out with whatever is needed that day (answering telephone calls about school events and school tours, for example). In secondary schools, the parent room can include information about college applications, scholarships, and other financial support; tutors; and extracurricular activities.

19. Form a beautification committee, overseeing such projects as building shelves in classrooms, painting the hallways, planting and maintaining gardens, maintaining the schoolyard, cleaning closets, inventorying supplies, or building benches for students in the library.

20. Set up a library committee. Committee members' jobs might include weeding out old books, reshelving books, conducting read-alouds before or after school, and helping parents understand their children's homework. This committee could also create a lending library for parents, ideally in a parent room, of books serving all languages and cultures in the community. These books might deal with parenting skills, health concerns, and career paths.

21. Establish a newcomers committee to welcome parents whose children are enrolling in the school for the first time. Members of this committee can translate materials for new parents, organize welcome breakfasts, match new parents with mentor parents who can fill them in on school history and help their children make friends, and help integrate new families into the life of the school.

22. As close as possible to the main entrance, set up a bulletin board with the dates and times of events in which parents can participate. (The board can be designed and maintained by parent volunteers.) The photographs in Figures 9.11a and b illustrate the power of welcoming parents to become fully engaged in the life of the school.

23. Have a book fair. (This has the added benefit of encouraging parents to read with their children.) Teachers can create book lists that include favorite authors and series for each grade and appropriate nonfiction titles integrated with science and social studies classes. Parents on the book fair committee can then arrange

FIGURE 9.11a *P.S. 199 Queens*

October 16, 2007
Kindergarten parents are invited to join our principal Mr. Inzerillo for a breakfast. At the breakfast we will be discussing how your children are adjusting to Kindergarten.
9:00 a.m.-9:45 a.m.
in the cafeteria.

Please Join us for

FAMILIES AS

READING

PARTNERS

Friday, October 5th
8:30 - 9:10 a.m.
Take this opportunity to read with a small group of children in your child's classroom.
Join us afterwards in the Outer Cafeteria from 9:10 - 9:30 a.m.
Refreshments sponsored by the PTA
PS 29's own Fair Trade Coffee
Healthy snacks provided by the PE/Wellness Committee
(a sub-committee of the SLT)
(Invitations going home via backpack.)

FIGURE 9.11b *P.S. 29 Brooklyn, Principal Melanie Woods*

for these books to be available for purchase during the fair. Parents can also assist students and other parents in choosing just the right book during the fair.

24. Get local merchants to donate a percentage of a day's profits to the school in exchange for some publicity. These places of business may also be a venue for celebrating student accomplishments: displays of writing and drawings, musical performances, poetry readings.

25. Offer multisession parent workshops led by teachers and specialists on topics like helping your child deal with divorce, surviving your child's adolescence, understanding the college application process, making the transition from elementary to middle school and from middle school to high school, and dealing with specific health issues like asthma and social issues like bullying, peer pressure, and gang membership. All these sessions should allow time for conversations and networking.

26. Offer sessions led by teachers on how to help your child deal with homework, plan a long-term project, or prepare for tests.

27. Offer sessions led by a school guidance counselor on helping children deal with the pressure of high-stakes testing, phobias, or eating disorders.

28. Arrange for parents with expertise in particular fields to lead workshops.

29. Start a First Fridays tradition to help parents of elementary school children become aware of their children's classroom activities and remain up-to-date on current practices and curriculum mandates. Invite parents to join their children in class for the first hour of the first Friday of every month. (During the hour, parents might read aloud to the class or talk about their careers.)

30. Invite the parents of secondary school students to spend a day in their children's shoes and attend condensed versions of their children's classes. (The "day" could take place in the evening to accommodate working parents.) Seeing their children's teachers in their classrooms providing instruction in their particular subjects gives parents a clear reference point for discussions about school, the curriculum, and teachers' styles and expectations.

31. Have alumni celebrations to tap into the most obvious base of community support. Reunions with former teachers and classmates are great networking opportunities for alumni and encourage them to become staunch school supporters. Alumni can contribute to an oral history of what the school was like when they attended, speak on career day or at graduation, mentor students who are interested in their line of work, or advise parents of current students about college and career choices. Alumni of schools that are experiencing difficult times can promote a positive image and a renewed sense of hope. They are also a likely source of cash and in-kind donations.

32. Lessen the gap between your school and the businesses in your community. One school district in New York City did this by creating First Tuesdays, an opportunity for parents and teachers to eat out while at the same time raising funds for the district's after-school sports program for middle school students. Participating restaurants in the neighborhood donated a portion of the dinner profits earned on the first Tuesday of each month, and members of the school community were encouraged to eat dinner at one of these restaurants that evening. Many of the participating restaurants continued their relationship with the district by sending their chefs to teach students how to cook, donating materials and services to school raffles, and mentoring students.

33. Create gender-specific initiatives to support male students, who don't often see male role models in school. Encourage men to participate in the life of the school by creating special events in which they demonstrate their success in academic activities as well as their social skills. In elementary school, have days when only male caregivers are invited to read aloud or listen to children read (Daddy Doughnut Day could begin with a doughnut breakfast; Daddy Pizza Day could include a pizza lunch, making the male presence visible in areas where it is too often missing). In middle schools, have male caregivers talk about their careers or the male heroes in their favorite adolescent novels. Special sports activities in which faculty and students compete against male caregivers generate great excitement and are a good way to recruit male volunteers. Members of faith-based and secular fraternal organizations often willingly volunteer to host panel discussions and initiate neighborhood awareness campaigns about the importance of positive male role models and to become these male mentors themselves.

34. Start reading clubs in which mothers and daughters or fathers and sons choose books to read together. This fosters a better understanding between generations and the challenges each faces and highlights reading as a rewarding context for sharing experiences and exchanging ideas. (You might want to have a parent coordinator, guidance counselor, or reading specialist work with these book clubs.)

35. Give school tours to advertise what makes your school special. Provide a map of the school on which the classrooms that will be visited are highlighted. Distribute the school brochure, parent newsletters, and information on upcoming fund-raising events and school celebrations. A school tour eases the transition parents of new students need to make and helps them prepare their children for the transition as well. Use the school tour to talk with prospective parents and members of the larger community about teaching and learning and the role the school plays. Parents who haven't considered sending their children to a public school may change their minds after a successful school tour, particularly when the tour is led by an articulate parent of a current student. Having parents as tour leaders also demonstrates your commitment to parent involvement and your trust in the ability of parents to communicate the school's vision. Establish a predictable school tour schedule (the first Wednesday of every month, for example) at the beginning of the school year and make sure it is well publicized. PTA leaders can sign people up and request the appropriate number of copies of the materials to be handed out. Greet your visitors personally when they arrive and join them again at the end of the tour to answer questions or concerns.

36. Don't neglect tours of secondary schools. They are particularly needed to alleviate the fears and concerns both students and parents have about this new level of education. Having a senior student and his or her parent speak about their own anxieties when the student was an entering freshman may help everyone have a nicer summer. This supportive big-brother or big-sister relationship can continue over the summer and into the new school year. Understanding the school's daily schedule, grading policy, electives and extracurricular activities, and rules and regulations before the year begins helps parents become true partners with their children at a time when parent involvement too often begins to wane.

37. Once a year, have a parent lead a school tour for members of the larger community, such as real estate agents, neighborhood merchants, local politicians, and school board members. These people are often key players in advancing the school's mission, providing extra resources and support, and creating a positive buzz. They are also excellent people to invite to join your school leadership team, because they will provide an outside perspective of how the school fits into the needs of the community.

38. Hold an orientation or welcome meeting for parents of secondary school students in June instead of August. Invite experts in adolescent development and other topics of special interest to parents of teenagers to speak. Outline expectations for parents, expected student behavior, and academic goals. Encourage parents to introduce themselves and exchange phone numbers so they can discuss questions and concerns when their adolescent children turn typically mum about what's going on in school.

39. Establish a grandparents and special friends day in your elementary school to recognize and celebrate the contribution of special people in students' lives. (You can introduce this special day in connection with a book of the month; see Figure 9.12.) Grandparents are often curious about their grandchildren's schooling, and this is an opportunity for them to see what it's like. (People in the school community such as cafeteria workers, school aides, and custodial workers often play grandparenting roles and can also be included.) Have students write an invitation to one grandparent or special friend. (Establish a way for invitees to RSVP to make sure you'll be able to accommodate everyone.) Begin with a light breakfast in the classroom; have students read books and share their current writing, and ask the visitors to tell what school was like when they were little. Have students entertain their visitors with songs, poems, and personal reflections. (Honor home languages; make these presentations multilingual.) Students may want to commemorate this day by making a booklet of their reflections and remembrances (the cover of one such booklet is shown in Figure 9.13).

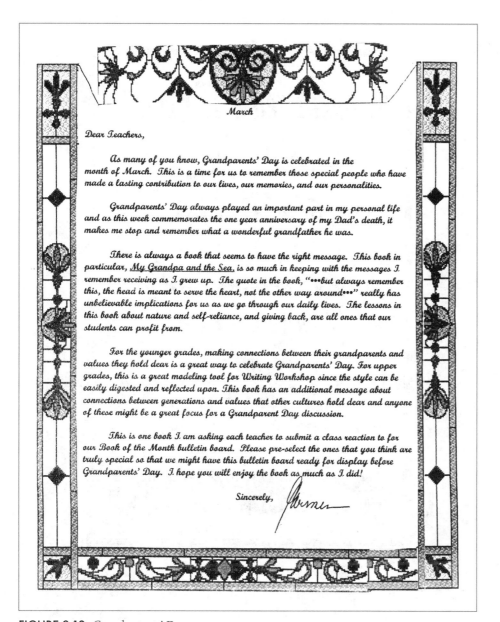

FIGURE 9.12 *Grandparents' Day*

40. Hold a thank-you assembly to honor and recognize people who contribute to the success of the school but tend to be overlooked. These people vary from school to school, but their common characteristic is having gone above and beyond to assist the community. Examples are the school crossing guard, local police precinct leaders, office and cafeteria workers, and community volunteers. If you keep a logbook during the year of volunteers and their specific responsibilities, nobody will be forgotten. The student entertainment at these assemblies should focus on saying thank you. You might also distribute thank-you letters written by students, certificates, and buttons saying, "I Make a Difference in the Life of a Child." Invite the local media!

FIGURE 9.13 *Cover of Grandparents' Day Booklet*

Avoiding Common Pitfalls

Make sure you understand the school's past parent-principal relationships before making any major changes. Talk to teachers, parents, and people in the wider community to get different perspectives on the role that parents play in the school. Observing parents interact when they drop off and pick up their children provides valuable information. One-to-one conversations with parent leaders can also yield important data. Don't rely on your predecessor's opinion about negative parents; make your own judgments.

On the other hand, knowing who the major naysayers in the school community are and what role they play can begin the process of building better relationships. There are many formal and informal parent power structures, and parents with no official title may play important roles. One ironclad rule: never badmouth a predecessor; simply begin to create a collaborative path that will allow you to fulfill your vision for school improvement.

It is common for a small group of parents (a power clique) to attempt to influence a principal's decisions to the benefit of a very narrow population. These groups do not speak for the majority. You need to be aware of these cliques and make a determined effort to solicit the participation of all parents, in all demographic groups. Be strategic. Appoint a committee chairman who shares your equalitarian views before the rest of the members are selected. And if you're a new principal, it may be easier to establish close relationships with parents who are also new to the school: they have no history there and will be eager to support your vision.

Collaborative decision making requires that you believe in parent empowerment and respect parents' perspective; you need to be flexible. Parents need to feel their opinions are being heard, that their agenda for their children is being met. If you simply assign a list of tasks for parents to accomplish, the opportunity for a true partnership is lost. Likewise, if you listen only to the parents who agree with you, you will miss many new and fresh ideas. Parents will fully participate in the school community when they see themselves as decision makers and agents of change.

Parents can and should be given leadership roles in collaboration with the principal with regard to curriculum, personnel, budget, and policy. Just be sure you provide clear guidelines regarding consensus and your ultimate responsibility for the success of the school. These guidelines need to be public, transparent, and understood and followed consistently by all members of the community. The liaisons you designate to deal with parent issues—the parent coordinator, an assistant principal, a guidance counselor, for example—need to update you continually, orally or in writing or both, so that you're not blindsided should an issue become the topic of a parent meeting, school gossip, or media attention.

You need these regular updates from every committee you establish so that you are aware of any and all decisions that affect the school. The chairperson is responsible for communicating regularly with you and preparing accurate and timely minutes of each meeting. In addition, whenever you create committees, make sure there is a public call for participation (include a list of committees in the parent folder) with clearly established criteria, stated responsibilities, and time commitments (list all meetings on the calendar of events).

All school committees should meet in easily accessible public places and have public agendas and minutes that are made available for all to read and review (these minutes are legal documents that can be consulted should issues arise later). Each committee should have stated goals, an action plan, and a clear time line for accomplishing the goals. Appointing an administrator or a teacher to a committee can help ensure that its work is articulated effectively and is aligned with the school's statement of purpose. In large schools many parents join committees because they want to interact with the principal personally, so you should attend at least one meeting (or part of a meeting) to thank members for their participation.

All committees generally have some financial component and therefore require careful oversight. When the main purpose of the committee is fund-raising, district oversight is a legal requirement. Financial mismanagement is a frequent reason for principal dismissal. Every principal should be aware of the legal ramifications of fund-raising:

- Funds raised must have a schoolwide purpose, and fund-raising events must be aligned with the school calendar and honor personnel and space constraints.
- If fund-raising events require an admission fee, complimentary admission might be offered to parents who cannot afford the fee.
- There must be consistent rules for who can attend fund-raising events and appropriate behavior at the events.
- Clearly stated financial accounting procedures must be followed.
- Proper security must be provided.
- Setup and cleanup responsibilities must be established.
- Additional liability insurance must be procured when outside vendors are involved.
- If their participation is required at the events, teachers should receive an invitation and their admission should be complimentary.

Parent rooms, helpful centers of parental involvement, can unfortunately also become havens for gossiping about teachers, watching TV, commandeering copy machines and telephones for personal use, and socializing inappropriately. Establish clear guidelines for how the room is to be used and make sure they are followed.

The community needs to see you as fair. Be cautious about appearing to favor those parents who are more involved in the life of the school. Things like classroom placement, access to special programs, participation in extracurricular activities, and grades and promotions need to be based on established criteria so that the community sees the rationale for your decisions.

Evaluating Success

To determine that parents are participating fully in the life of the school and that their participation is resulting in increased student achievement, look for evidence like this:

- Are there predictable, informative, and effective protocols for communicating with parents?
- Are parents better able to support their students because they understand and agree with the school mission? Do they eagerly attend workshops to support their children's academic needs? Do they follow the school's recommendations for their children because they trust you and their children's teachers?
- Do parents immediately feel welcome when they enter the school? Are there friendly signs, clearly stated procedures, and a prominently displayed directory of staff members' names and room numbers? Are these postings displayed in all languages represented in the student body? Is the safety officer or other wel-

coming person friendly and able to provide appropriate assistance?

- Is the feedback about the school's vision and mission that parents provide on surveys and in other local forums positive? Has parent attendance at school events, committee meetings, and celebrations increased? Are more cultures being represented? Are more fathers participating?

- Is the number of volunteers willing to support the school's mission increasing? Is every effort being made to include both English- and non-English-speaking parents and those who have not previously participated? Is care being taken to make them feel welcomed?

- Are conflict-resolution strategies in place so that parents, teachers, students, and leaders are able to resolve conflicts peacefully? Do these strategies diffuse controversial issues and encourage a give-and-take environment in which both sides come to understand the issues through deep and meaningful conversations? Do you look for every opportunity to mend fences and reestablish communication with difficult parents? Do you have one-to-one conversations in June with parents who have had a negative interaction with any member of the school staff, including you, in order to heal wounds, reestablish relationships, set guidelines for new behavior, and start fresh in the new school year?

- Are you benefiting from parental involvement by being able to spend more time visiting classrooms and meeting with the teachers? Are you no longer the only one parents turn to for assistance?

- Are you able to have meaningful conversations with parents about their children, the school initiatives, and the parents' interests and talents? Are there procedures for consistently acknowledging and thanking parents for their contributions? Are you celebrating both large and small indications of progress? Are these celebrations ongoing and varied?

- Do you discuss controversial issues with an executive board that includes parent members?

- Do parents receive sufficient information and support to become advocates for the school at the local, state, and federal levels? Do they positively influence funding and policy decisions?

A Final Word

Public education continues to be the subject of national debate, with everyone holding an opinion about how to improve student achievement. It seems every business leader, politician, or graduate with a masters in business administration feels he knows why so many students are still not ready to meet the demands of the global economy—and is quick to blame the insiders. Congress demands higher accountability, passes more mandates, and prescribes radical changes it believes will instantly lead to improved test scores. But those of us on the inside, who live with the realities of schools, understand the folly of swinging the pendulum from one extreme to another. We recognize that schools are imperfect, living organizations very different from businesses, because the products that schools generate are people. In education, children matter most, and the wisdom and experience of parents, principals, and teachers, along with their commitment to the complexities of educating our next generation, must be honored and respected when decisions about change are made.

We have been inspired by so many school leaders who selflessly invest their lives in their communities—certainly not for their own advancement or glory but to ensure that their mission to change the lives of the children they serve becomes reality. These leaders are very aware that there are no shortcuts in confronting the myriad problems—including poverty, inequitable opportunity, and low expectations—that so many of our children face each day. They understand that schools reflect the society in and for which they operate and that the only way to level the playing field is to focus on quality instruction in every classroom every day. In order to transform our schools, these leaders need to address what is not working (without making excuses) and then make the necessary changes. At this exciting time, with so many members of the community eager to get involved, the answers to the crisis of public education must come from many voices; everyone who wishes to contribute should be invited to do so. However, real, sustained change happens in the classroom, and decisions about what takes place there must include the voices of the people who do the work: the teachers, the parents who confidently support them, and the leaders who guide and inspire them.

We believe it is possible to reenergize public education by celebrating success, affirming excellence, and encouraging educators to share and borrow ideas, so that practical strategies can be replicated throughout a school and from school to school. Teachers change their beliefs and their behavior when they are surrounded by supportive colleagues; when they see effective strategies in action; and when they are encouraged to take risks, reflect on their beliefs, and revise their approach to teaching each day. They also need the necessary resources, generous amounts of time in which to study and reflect, and the respect of colleagues who believe in their ability. To prepare students for jobs that may not yet exist, we need schools that model critical thinking, collaborative problem solving, and shared decision making. Everyone needs to come to the table prepared for intellectual discourse. This is particularly challenging because often our own school experiences have not prepared us for this task and the overwhelming pressures of accountability often prevent the reflection necessary to prompt a leap of faith—to move beyond the model of the school as factory.

We wrote this book to share strategies we have used to build collaborative, reflective, energized communities that are fully invested in transforming schools. We believe that we learn best during conversations with one another in which we share our stories about how and why we make changes and that are supported by the visible evidence of seeing one another in action with real students in the classroom. These conversations and observations make our beliefs and theories concrete, extend our thinking, and encourage us to borrow and replicate effective practices.

In collaborative school communities, educators talk about what they do each day, observe one another in action, reflect on what is happening and why, and design curriculum together. Successes are celebrated and extended, reflective thinking becomes a way of life, expertise is built from within, and energy is sustained. The community owns its commitment to continual improvement.

Writing this book has given us the gift of time in which to reflect on our personal stories and talk in depth about our beliefs and hopes for public education. The common thread running through the strategies we have discussed is the power of conversation and collaboration to transform ideas into actions. Educators, now more than at any other time, need to be inspired, supported, and celebrated by leaders who understand the importance of personal connections. Recognizing and affirming what is working well, even small beginning steps, is often a better vehicle for improvement than mandates, sanctions, or labels ranking one school against another.

The promise of public education is worth fighting for because it is still the best place to demonstrate democracy in action: to level the playing field and give every child the opportunity to pursue the American dream. We hope this book will help you find the courage to raise your voice when confronted with policies that are not in the best interests of your students. Leaders who are able to harness the energy of their community and unite its members around a clear vision can reinvent the present and create a better future. Our children and grandchildren deserve no less.

Study Guide for
A School Leader's Guide to Excellence

We are delighted to hear from educators around the country who are using our book as a call to action to mobilize their communities in moving toward excellence. This study guide is intended to provide a framework for teams of educators to turn the strategies and big ideas in this book into reality in the daily life of schools. Since this work is all about collaboration, we suggest convening a study group to read the book, research best practices already in place, and create an action plan to extend and replicate strategies school-wide. And what better way to culminate the study than with a celebration to collect evidence, affirm progress, and cement the growing community of learners.

In this age of Twitter, FaceTime and Google, geographical boundaries to conversations no longer exist. Readers of this book can engage in study groups without having to travel to a common space to meet in person. The possibilities for collaboration are expanded by the technology available today and educators can join together in many ways—whether it is within one school community, throughout a district, across a city, from state to state, or globally.

Regardless of the context of the study group, members will have to make many important decisions including the roles and responsibilities of the members of the study group, the time frame of the study, the big questions to investigate and the tangible outcomes and intended goals. We suggest that you begin your study with the chapter that is most compelling for your community—because it is where the need is greatest, because it is where there is the most energy and interest, or because it is where with a little focus, consistency can be achieved. You will want to find a balance between talking about the big ideas and reflecting on the rationale for the strategies, and moving into action by researching and collecting evidence of best practices already in place and implementing them school-wide. Perhaps two sessions might be devoted to reading the chapter and reflecting on the meaning for your school community and two more sessions might be devoted to researching what's already in place and developing a plan of action to replicate and extend. For each chapter of the book, we designed the following sections: A Dear Reader letter to invite the reader into the conversation, a rationale to explain the purpose and intended outcomes for the strategies, a step-by-step guide full of artifacts to help you move into implementation, some common pitfalls to avoid, and some questions to help evaluate success. The study guide mirrors these sections to make it easier for you to promote conversation, share experiences, develop common understandings, and turn the big ideas into action.

Dear Reader is intended to share those personal experiences which helped us grow the big ideas and develop the strategies in the chapter. Our honest voice in relating our story is intended to share who we are as people and as leaders and to make visible our values, beliefs, and mission. We have discovered that as we share our stories in this open and inviting way, doors are opened and trust is built.

Activities

1. Members of the study group think about their reaction to the Dear Reader letter and the meaning it holds for them. They reflect on the essential beliefs that are communicated and the impact on their thinking about the issue.

2. Members think about and share their personal experiences with partners in formats like timelines, photo essays, and narrative accounts. In this work, participants naturally reflect on values, beliefs, and mission concerning the big ideas in the Dear Reader letter. Partners then present their artifacts and share their stories with the larger group.

3. Partners create an original Dear Reader letter inviting the larger community to the conversation or create lists that document points of agreement or disagreement with the big ideas in the chapter.

4. The study group uses sticky notes to document shared experiences, values, and beliefs to create a common mission.

Why Institute…is intended to explain the purpose, rationale, and intended outcomes of the strategies outlined in the chapter and present a compelling argument for how it will lead your school toward excellence. It connects the details of what to do with the big picture of why to do it and makes the link between who we are as human beings with the role we play as educators.

Activities

1. Members talk about their perception of where the school is with regard to these strategies and why the strategies are important to lift the level of achievement and improve the quality of life in the school.

2. Members generate a lists of school needs matched to anticipated benefits and tangible outcomes for the community.

3. Partners create a letter which explains the rationale for the strategies and a convincing argument for school-wide implementation to communicate with parents, teachers, students, and community members.

Getting Started: Step by Step is the heart of the book, explaining the actions to take and the artifacts that demonstrate successful implementation. It describes the process of making change transparent and the evidence that documents progress.

Activities

1. Members read all the steps and talk about the sequence of actions and any ideas that are new and interesting.

2. Decisions about which of the steps to implement, when to begin the work, and how to divide the tasks are the next step in the process.

3. Participants will want to think about where to begin and which of the steps to implement first. Before proceeding further, we suggest reading the **Avoiding Common Pitfalls** section now. The advice about avoiding missteps will help to make decisions about how to proceed.

4. If there is already some of the work in place in the school, begin the process of researching where these practices are happening and what kind of evidence can be found.

5. Members will then conduct a school search to collect evidence and find exemplars that can be used as models.

6. If choosing a new strategy, determine what task each member will work on and the timeline for completion.

7. Begin to plan ways to share and celebrate the work of the study group with the larger community.

8. Make the work visible and public to remind everyone of the learning and to encourage the continuation of the intellectual community.

Avoiding Common Pitfalls is intended to keep you safe from the missteps that could sabotage the successful implementation of the strategies. Hopefully, the reader can benefit from what we've learned as a result of the many mistakes made in our long careers.

Activities

1. Read and talk about the common pitfalls and make a list of those that might pertain.

2. Develop an action plan that outlines how the pitfalls will be avoided.

3. Role-play conversations and act out situations where potential conflict may occur. Coach each other.

4. Keep a journal of how pitfalls are avoided and what was learned as a result.

5. Document the challenges to implementation, the turning points, and the roadmap for overcoming obstacles with charts, a big book, video, or PowerPoint presentation.

6. Celebrate!

Evaluating Success is intended to help you measure the success of the implementation and reflect on the consistency and sustainability of the outcomes. The open-ended questions invite you to engage in deep conversation and compel you to research the evidence in your school. As you gather the evidence and search for consistency in implementation, you will be propelled into further action to continually improve your school.

Activities

1. Read each of the bulleted series of questions and talk about the meaning for your school community.

2. Decide which of the series of questions is most relevant for your school community and begin talking about collecting evidence and setting criteria for evaluating the work.

3. Plan a share fair to celebrate the findings of the evaluation.

4. Celebrate by having members of the study group share their learning. Create feedback stationery that documents and celebrates the exemplars from the share fair.

5. Make the artifacts public and visible.

Recommended Professional Reading

Principal Leadership

BARTH, R. 1994. *Improving Schools from Within: Principals, Teachers and Parents Can Make a Difference*. San Francisco: Jossey-Bass.

————. 2001. *Learning by Heart*. San Francisco: Jossey-Bass.

COLLINS, J. 2001. *From Good to Great: Why Some Companies Make the Leap . . . and Others Don't*. New York: HarperCollins.

FULLAN, M. 2003. *The Moral Imperative of School Leadership*. Thousand Oaks, CA: Corwin.

————. 2004. *Leading in a Culture of Change: A Personal Action Guide and Workbook*. San Francisco: Jossey-Bass.

FULLAN, M., and M. HARGREAVES. 1996. *What's Worth Fighting for in Your School*. New York: Teachers College Press.

GIBBONS, G. 1991. *Learning to Learn in a Second Language*. Portsmouth, NH: Heinemann.

GOLEMAN, D. 1997. *Emotional Intelligence: Why It Can Matter More Than IQ*. New York: Bantam Dell.

INTRATOR, S., and M. SCRIBNER, eds. 2003. *Teaching with Fire: Poetry That Sustains the Courage to Teach*. San Francisco: Jossey-Bass.

LANGER, J. 1994. *Getting to Excellence: How to Create Better Schools*. New York: Teachers College Press.

MARZANO, R., T. WATERS, and B. McNULTY. 2005. *School Leadership That Works*. Alexandria, VA: ASCD.

REEVES, D. 2006. *How to Focus School Improvement for Better Results*. Alexandria, VA: ASCD.

SERGIOVANNI, T. 1994. *Building Community in Schools*. San Francisco: Jossey-Bass.

————. 2004. *Moral Leadership: Getting to the Heart of School Improvement*. San Francisco: Jossey-Bass.

SIZER, T., and N. SIZER. 2004. *The Students Are Watching: Schools and the Moral Contract*. Boston: Beacon.

TICHY, N., and N. CARDWELL. 2004. *The Cycle of Leadership: How Great Leaders Teach Their Companies to Win*. New York: Harper Business.

Teacher Leadership

ACHINSTEIN, B., and S. ATHANOSES. 2006. *Mentors in the Making: Developing New Leaders for New Teachers*. New York: Teachers College Press.

DANIELSON, C. 2006. *Teacher Leadership That Strengthens Professional Practice*. Alexandria, VA: ASCD.

FRIED, R. 2001. *The Passionate Teacher: A Practical Guide*. Boston: Beacon.

GABRIEL, J. 2005. *How to Thrive as a Teacher Leader*. New York: ASCD.

LIEBERMAN, A., and L. MILLER. 2004. *Teacher Leadership*. San Francisco: Jossey-Bass.

MEYERS, E., and F. RUST. 2003. *Taking Action with Teacher Research*. Portsmouth, NH: Heinemann.

Teachers Network. www.teachersnetwork.org.

Curriculum Mapping

FISHER, D., and N. FREY. 2007. *Checking for Understanding: Formative Assessment Techniques for Your Classroom*. Alexandria, VA: ASCD.

JACOBS, H. H. 1997. *Mapping the Big Picture: Integrating Curriculum and Assessment K–12*. Alexandria, VA: ASCD.

———, ed. 2004. *Getting Results with Curriculum Mapping*. Alexandria, VA: ASCD.

WIGGINS, G., and J. MCTIGHE. 1998. *Understanding by Design*. Alexandria, VA: ASCD.

Best Practices

ALLINGTON, R., and P. CUNNINGHAM. 2006. *Schools That Work: Where All Children Read and Write*. New York: Pearson/Allyn and Bacon.

ANDERSON, C. 2003. *How's It Going? A Practical Guide to Conferring*. Portsmouth, NH: Heinemann.

———. 2005. *Assessing Writers*. Portsmouth, NH: Heinemann.

CALKINS, L. 1994. *The Art of Teaching Writing*. Portsmouth, NH: Heinemann.

———. 2001. *The Art of Teaching Reading*. Portsmouth, NH: Heinemann.

DANIELS, H., and S. ZEMELMAN. 2004. *Subjects Matter: Every Teacher's Guide to Content Area Reading*. Portsmouth, NH: Heinemann.

FLETCHER, R., and J. PORTALUPI. 2001. *Writing Workshop: The Essential Guide*. Portsmouth, NH: Heinemann.

HARVEY, S. and A. GOUDVIS. 2007. *Strategies That Work: Teaching Comprehension for Understanding and Engagement*. Portland, ME: Stenhouse.

ZEMELMAN, S., H. DANIELS, and A. HYDE. 2001. *Best Practices*. Portsmouth, NH: Heinemann.

A Short List of Picture Books for Leaders

Baylor, B. 1995. *I'm In Charge of Celebrations*. New York: Aladdin Paperback Books.

Bottner, B., and G. Kruglik. 2004. *Wallace's Lists*. New York: HarperCollins.

Byrd, R. 2003. *Leonardo: Beautiful Dreamer*. New York: Penguin.

Hills, J. 2002. *I Am Amazed*. Minneapolis, MN: Waldman House Press.

———. 2003. *Believe*. Minneapolis, MN: Waldman House Press.

Lewis, R. 2000. *I Love You Like Crazy Cakes*. New York: Little Brown and Company.

Muth, J. 2002. *The Three Questions*. New York: Scholastic.

Polacco, P. 1998. *Thank You, Mr. Falker*. New York: Philomel.

———. 2001. *Mr. Lincoln's Way*. New York: Philomel.

Waber, B. 2002. *Courage*. Boston: Houghton Mifflin.

Index

G

gender issues
  books addressing, 50
  fathers, 153, 169
  male students, 169
Gibbon, Pauline, 57
Giving Tree, The (Silverstein), 50
goals
  annual, 5
  communicating, 5, 107
  community focus on, 5–6
  as inquiry questions, 4–5
  interconnecting, 4–5
  professional development and, 103
  setting, 18
  for teacher leaders, 124
  vision and, 3, 4
Goodnight Moon (Brown), 41
grade/department leader meetings, 108–9, 143,
    144, 145
grade-level meetings, 160, 161–62
grandparents, 153, 170
group planning sessions, 140
Guess How Much I Love You (McBratney), 66
guest speakers, 118
guidance counselors, 112

H

Harvey, Stephanie, 143
Heard, Georgia, 49
Henkes, Kevin, 40, 49, 69
Hey World, Here I Am (Little), 49, 69
Hill, Kevin, 41
Hills, Jodi, 48, 49
HIV/AIDS education, 157
holiday celebrations, 59, 66
home-school connection, 153–54. *See also* par-
    ent involvement
honesty, 33
Hooray for Diffendoofer Day (Seuss), 49
Hooray for You! A Celebration of "You-ness" (Rich-
    mond), 69
Hooway for Wodney Wat (Lester), 43, 44
Horace and Delores (Howe), 50
Horn Book, 49
Howe, James, 50
How's It Going? (Anderson), 6
Hughes, Langston, 49
Huliska-Beith, Laura, 49

I

I Am Amazed (Hills), 48, 49
I Love You Like Crazy Cakes (Lewis), xix, 39
I'm in Charge of Celebrations (Baylor), 49, 58
immigrant students, 2. *See also* English language
    learners; non-English speaking parents
independent reading, 37
inquiry questions, 4–5
inspirational speeches, 12
inspirational texts, 105
institutes, 113
interactive learning. *See also* collaborative inquiry
  celebrating, 56, 57
  student-centered, xvii–xviii
intervisitations, 116–18
Intrator, Sam M., 105
introductory letters, for teacher portfolios, 93

issues. *See* concerns
It's Okay to Be Different (Parr), 50

J

Jacob, Heidi Hayes, 143
"janitors' class," 152
Julius, the Baby of the World (Henkes), 49, 69
June planning sessions, 140–41. *See also* school-
    wide planning
  agendas for, 143, 144, 145
  articulation teams and, 143, 148
  avoiding pitfalls, 149
  collaboration and, 142, 148
  community and, 141
  consistency and, 142, 149
  curriculum calendars, 145
  evaluating, 149–50
  grade/department leader meetings and, 143,
      144
  introducing, 142–43
  minutes, 145, 146
  new teachers and, 141
  parents and, 144, 145, 150
  publicizing dates and times of, 143
  purpose of, 140, 141–42
  schedule change requests, 147
  scheduling, 149
  steps, 142–48
  teachers and, 142–45, 150

K

"Kid's Poems" (Hill), 41
Kotch, Laura, vii–viii, xvi–xvii
Kroll, Kathleen, 50
Kruglik, Gerald, 50

L

Language Arts (National Council of Teachers of
    English), 49
leaders. *See also* teacher leaders
  appreciation expressed by, 44–45
  community and, 22–23
  conflicting messages from, 18
  feedback and, 19
  mentors and, 6
  moral messages and, 44
  parent leaders, 152–57
  personal conversations and, 22
  professional development and, 101
  risk-taking by, 56
  role of, 177
  sharing books with, 37–38
  vision and, 3–4
leadership
  challenges of, 2
  framework for, 7
  personal stories about, xv–xxi
  vision and, viii
Leading in a Culture of Change (Fullan), 6, 7
learning. *See also* collaborative inquiry; profes-
    sional development
  interactive, 56, 57
  materials for, 116
  ownership for, 120
  principals and, 100, 101
  professional development teams and, 106–7
  student-centered, xvii–xviii
  by teacher leaders, 123, 129–30